Math in Focus

Singapore Math®
by Marshall Cavendish

Student Edition

Program Consultant and Author
Dr. Fong Ho Kheong

Authors
Gan Kee Soon
Chelvi Ramakrishnan

Marshall Cavendish
Education

U.S. Distributor

Houghton Mifflin Harcourt.
The Learning Company™

Grade
4A

Contents

Chapter

1 Working with Whole Numbers

Multiplication and Division

Chapter Opener 89

How can you multiply by a 2-digit number?
How can you divide whole numbers?

RECALL PRIOR KNOWLEDGE 90

Multiplying as skip counting • Knowing multiplication facts of 2, 3, 4, 5, and 10 • Knowing multiplication facts of 6, 7, 8, 9, 11, and 12 • Multiplying two numbers to find a product • Multiplying using models • Multiplying without regrouping • Multiplying with regrouping • Dividing to share equally • Dividing to form equal groups • Dividing using related multiplication facts • Rounding and estimation • Solving two-step real-world problems

▶ Hands-on Activity

3 Fractions and Mixed Numbers

Chapter Opener — **221**

How can you represent fractions greater than 1?
How can you add and subtract fractions?
How can you multiply fractions and whole numbers?

RECALL PRIOR KNOWLEDGE — **222**

Understanding fractions and unit fractions • Making one whole with unit fractions • Expressing fractions in terms of unit fractions • Understanding like fractions • Representing fractions on a number line • Writing whole numbers as fractions • Understanding fractions as part of a set • Understanding equivalent fractions • Comparing and ordering fractions

▶ Hands-on Activity

Chapter

4 Decimals

▶ Hands-on Activity

Manipulative List

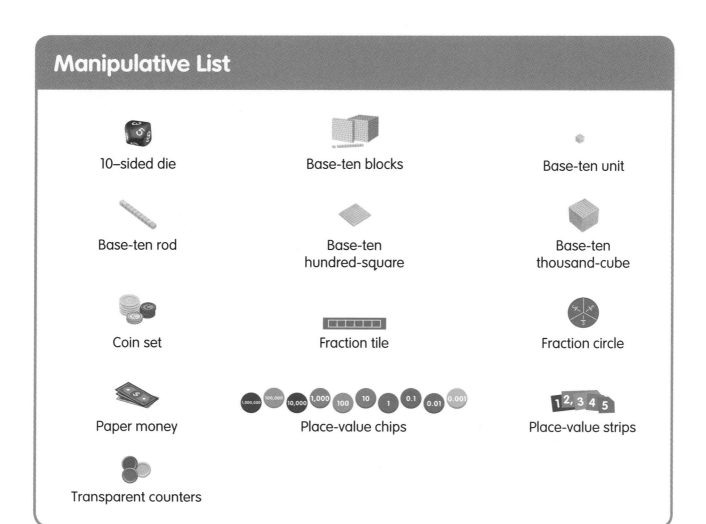

10–sided die

Base-ten blocks

Base-ten unit

Base-ten rod

Base-ten hundred-square

Base-ten thousand-cube

Coin set

Fraction tile

Fraction circle

Paper money

Place-value chips

Place-value strips

Transparent counters

Preface

Welcome!

Math in Focus® is a program that puts **you** at the center of an exciting learning experience! This experience is all about helping you to build skills and math ideas that make sense, sharing your thinking to deepen your understanding, and learning to become a strong and confident problem solver!

What's in your book?

Each chapter in this book begins with a real-world example of the math topic you are about to learn.

In each chapter, you will see the following features:

THINK introduces a problem for the whole section, to get you thinking creatively and critically. You may not be able to answer the problem right away but you can come back to it a few times as you work through the section.

ENGAGE introduces tasks that link what you already know with what you will be learning next. The tasks will have you exploring and discussing math concepts with your classmates.

LEARN introduces you to new math concepts through a Concrete-Pictorial-Abstract (C-P-A) approach, using examples and activities.

Hands-on Activity provides you with the experience of working very closely with your classmates. These Hands-On Activities allow you to become more confident in what you have learned and help you to uncover new concepts.

TRY provides you with the opportunity to practice what you are learning, with support and guidance.

INDEPENDENT PRACTICE allows you to work on different kinds of problems and apply the concepts and skills you have learned to solve these problems on your own.

Additional features include:

RECALL PRIOR KNOWLEDGE	Math Talk	MATH SHARING	GAME
Helps you recall related concepts you learned before, accompanied by practice questions	Invites you to explain your reasoning and communicate your ideas to your classmates and teachers	Encourages you to create strategies, discover methods, and share them with your classmates and teachers using mathematical language	Helps you to really master the concepts you learned, through fun partner games
LET'S EXPLORE	**MATH JOURNAL**	**PUT ON YOUR THINKING CAP!**	**CHAPTER WRAP-UP**
Extends your learning through investigation	Allows you to reflect on your learning when you write down your thoughts about the concepts learned	Challenges you to apply the concepts to solve problems in different ways	Summarizes your learning in a flow chart and helps you to make connections within the chapter
CHAPTER REVIEW	**Assessment Prep**	**PERFORMANCE TASK**	**STEAM**
Provides you with a lot of practice in the concepts learned	Prepares you for state tests with assessment-type problems	Assesses your learning through problems that allow you to demonstrate your understanding and knowledge	Promotes collaboration with your classmates through interesting projects that allow you to use math in creative ways

Let's begin your exciting learning journey with us! Are you ready?

Working with Whole Numbers

I wonder how many people this stadium can hold.

How many digits does each number have? How do I read each number?

Stadium	State	Seating Capacity
Rose Bowl	California	90,888
Ohio Stadium	Ohio	104,944
Sanford Stadium	Geogia	92,746
Kroger Field	Kentucky	61,000

What are three different ways that you can read and write whole numbers?

Name: _____ Date: _____

Reading and writing numbers

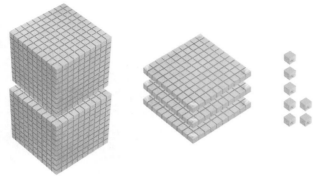

Expanded form: 2,000 + 300 + 7
Standard form: 2,307
Word form: two thousand, three hundred seven

▶ Quick Check

Use ▨ to count. Write the number in standard form and word form.

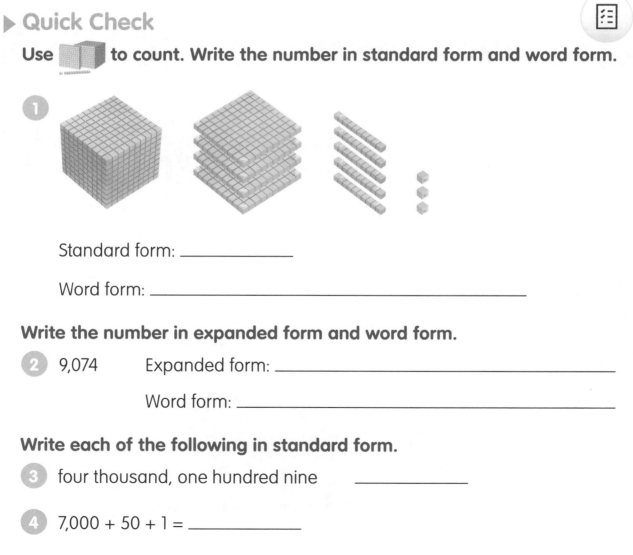

1

Standard form: _____

Word form: _____

Write the number in expanded form and word form.

2 9,074   Expanded form: _____

Word form: _____

Write each of the following in standard form.

3 four thousand, one hundred nine   _____

4 7,000 + 50 + 1 = _____

© 2020 Marshall Cavendish Education Pte Ltd

Counting on

Count on by ones: 5,101   5,102   5,103   5,104 …
Count on by tens: 2,001   2,011   2,021   2,031 …
Count on by hundreds: 4,200   4,300   4,400   4,500 …
Count on by thousands: 3,800   4,800   5,800   6,800 …

▶ Quick Check

Continue each number pattern. Count on by ones, tens, hundreds, or thousands.

5   5,400   5,500   5,600   5,700   _____

6   9,076   9,077   9,078   9,079   _____

7   4,320   5,320   6,320   7,320   _____

Identifying place value

In 4,728,

Thousands	Hundreds	Tens	Ones
4	7	2	8

stands for **4 thousands** 4,000   stands for **7 hundreds** 700   stands for **2 tens** 20   stands for **8 ones** 8

▶ Quick Check

Fill in each blank.

In 5,628,

8   the digit _____ is in the hundreds place.

9   the value of the digit 5 is _____.

10   the digit 2 stands for _____.

Write the value of each digit.

11

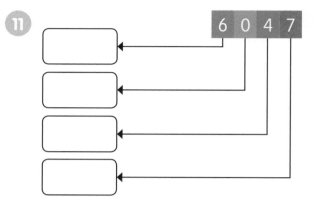

Comparing numbers

	Thousands	Hundreds	Tens	Ones
2,910	2	9	1	0
2,688	2	6	8	8

STEP 1 Compare the thousands. They are the same.

STEP 2 Compare the hundreds. 9 hundreds are greater than 6 hundreds.

So, 2,910 is greater than 2,688.

2,910 > 2,688

You can also say that 2,688 is less than 2,910.

2,688 < 2,910

▶ **Quick Check**

Compare each pair of numbers. Write <, >, or =.

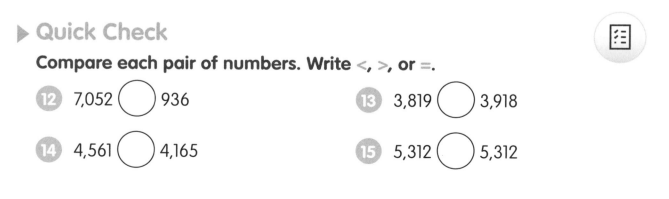

12 7,052 ◯ 936

13 3,819 ◯ 3,918

14 4,561 ◯ 4,165

15 5,312 ◯ 5,312

Ordering numbers

Order 4,319, 4,139, and 5,134 from least to greatest.

	Thousands	Hundreds	Tens	Ones
4,319	4	3	1	9
4,139	4	1	3	9
5,134	5	1	3	4

STEP 1 Compare the thousands. 5 thousands are greater than 4 thousands. So, 5,134 is the greatest.

STEP 2 The thousands in the other two numbers are the same. So, compare the hundreds. 1 hundred is less than 3 hundreds. So, 4,139 is the least.

From least to greatest, the numbers are:

4,139   4,319   5,134
least   greatest

▶ Quick Check

Order the numbers from greatest to least.

16   6,275   6,507   5,762   _____ _____ _____
                                  greatest   least

Finding missing numbers in a number pattern

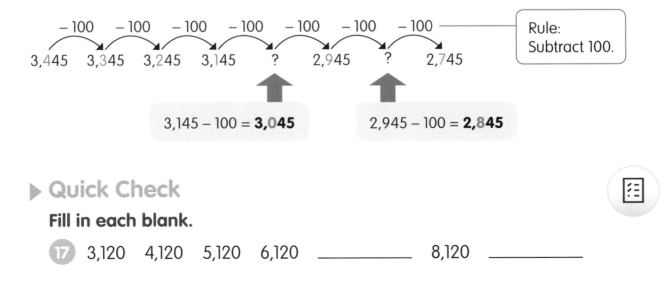

− 100   − 100   − 100   − 100   − 100   − 100   − 100

3,445   3,345   3,245   3,145   ?   2,945   ?   2,745

Rule: Subtract 100.

3,145 − 100 = **3,045**   2,945 − 100 = **2,845**

▶ Quick Check

Fill in each blank.

17   3,120   4,120   5,120   6,120   _____   8,120   _____

Rounding numbers to the nearest ten

If the digit in the ones place is 1, 2, 3, or 4, round the number to the lesser ten.

92 is between 90 and 100.
It is nearer to 90 than to 100.
92 is 90 when rounded to the nearest ten.

If the digit in the ones place is 5, 6, 7, 8, or 9, round the number to the greater ten.

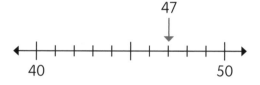

47 is between 40 and 50.
It is nearer to 50 than to 40.
47 is 50 when rounded to the nearest ten.

▶ Quick Check

Round each number to the nearest ten.

18 12

19 279

20 3,405

_____

Rounding numbers to the nearest hundred

If the digit in the tens place is 1, 2, 3, or 4, round the number to the lesser hundred.

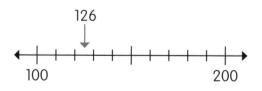

126 is between 100 and 200.
It is nearer to 100 than to 200.
126 is 100 when rounded to the nearest hundred.

If the digit in the tens place is 5, 6, 7, 8, or 9, round the number to the greater hundred.

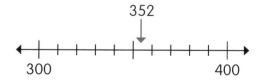

352 is between 300 and 400.
It is nearer to 400 than to 300.
352 is 400 when rounded to the nearest hundred.

▶ **Quick Check**

Round each number to the nearest hundred.

21 834

22 654

23 7,872

_____

_____

_____

Adding numbers

1,243 + 2,178 = ?

STEP 1 Add the ones.
Regroup the ones.

```
     1
  1, 2 4 3
+ 2, 1 7 8
_____
         1
```

3 ones + 8 ones
= 11 ones
= 1 ten 1 one

STEP 2 Add the tens.
Regroup the tens.

```
   1 1
  1, 2 4 3
+ 2, 1 7 8
_____
       2 1
```

1 ten + 4 tens + 7 tens
= 12 tens
= 1 hundred 2 tens

STEP 3 Add the hundreds.

```
   1 1
  1, 2 4 3
+ 2, 1 7 8
_____
     4 2 1
```

1 hundred + 2 hundreds
+ 1 hundred
= 4 hundreds

STEP 4 Add the thousands.

```
   1 1
  1, 2 4 3
+ 2, 1 7 8
_____
  3, 4 2 1
```

1 thousand + 2 thousands
= 3 thousands

▶ **Quick Check**

Add. Show your work.

24 8,198 + 207 = _____

25 2,475 + 5,736 = _____

Subtracting numbers

7,486 − 4,523 = ?

STEP 1 Subtract the ones.

```
  7, 4 8 6
− 4, 5 2 3
─────────
          3
```
6 ones − 3 ones
= 3 ones

STEP 2 Subtract the tens.

```
  7 4 8 6
− 4 5 2 3
─────────
      6 3
```
8 tens − 2 tens
= 6 tens

STEP 3 Regroup the thousands and hundreds.

```
  6  14
  7̶, 4̶ 8 6
− 4, 5 2 3
─────────
        6 3
```
7 thousands 4 hundreds
= 6 thousands 14 hundreds

STEP 4 Subtract the hundreds.

```
  6  14
  7̶, 4̶ 8 6
− 4, 5 2 3
─────────
      9 6 3
```
14 hundreds − 5 hundreds
= 9 hundreds

STEP 5 Subtract the thousands.

```
  6  14
  7̶, 4̶ 8 6
− 4, 5 2 3
─────────
  2, 9 6 3
```
6 thousands − 4 thousands
= 2 thousands

▶ **Quick Check**

Subtract. Show your work.

26 8,004 − 3,256 = _____

27 4,000 − 2,937 = _____

Solving real-world problems involving addition and subtraction

Samuel had 856 grams of flour. He bought another 450 grams of flour. He used 950 grams of flour to make some pies. How much flour did he have left?

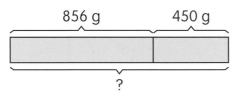

$856 + 450 = 1,306$

He had 1,306 grams of flour in all.

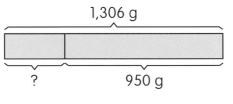

$1,306 - 950 = 356$

He had 356 grams of flour left.

▶ **Quick Check**

Solve. Draw a bar model to help you.

28 A baker baked 2,050 pretzels on Monday. He baked 580 fewer pretzels on Tuesday than on Monday. How many pretzels did he bake in all on Monday and Tuesday?

Name: _____ Date: _____

1 Numbers to 100,000

Learning Objectives:
- Read and write numbers to 100,000 in expanded form, standard form, and word form.
- State the place and value of each digit in a 5-digit number.

> **New Vocabulary**
> hundred thousand

THINK

Paige is thinking of a 5-digit number. Two pairs of digits in the number make 10 each. The sum of all the five digits is 25. What is the greatest possible 5-digit number Paige is thinking of?

ENGAGE

1. Use [cubes] to show 3,245. Write the number in expanded form and word form.

2. Ayden is thinking of a 4-digit number. Two pairs of digits in the number make 10 each. The digit 2 is in the hundreds place and the digit 1 is in the ones place. What is the least possible number Ayden is thinking of?

LEARN Read and write 5-digit numbers

1. Count in thousands.

(1,000) (1,000) (1,000) (1,000) (1,000) (1,000) (1,000) (1,000) (1,000) (1,000) → (10,000)

10 thousands = 1 ten thousand

Count on: 1,000   2,000   3,000   4,000   5,000
          6,000   7,000   8,000   9,000   10,000

2 Count in ten thousands.

10 ten thousands = 1 **hundred thousand**

Count on: 10,000   20,000   30,000   40,000   50,000
60,000   70,000   80,000   90,000   100,000

3 Use  to count.

a

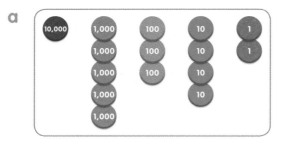

Standard form: 15,342
Word form: fifteen thousand, three hundred forty-two

b

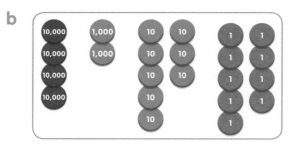

Standard form: 42,089
Word form: forty-two thousand, eighty-nine

4 Identify the value of each digit in 31,298.

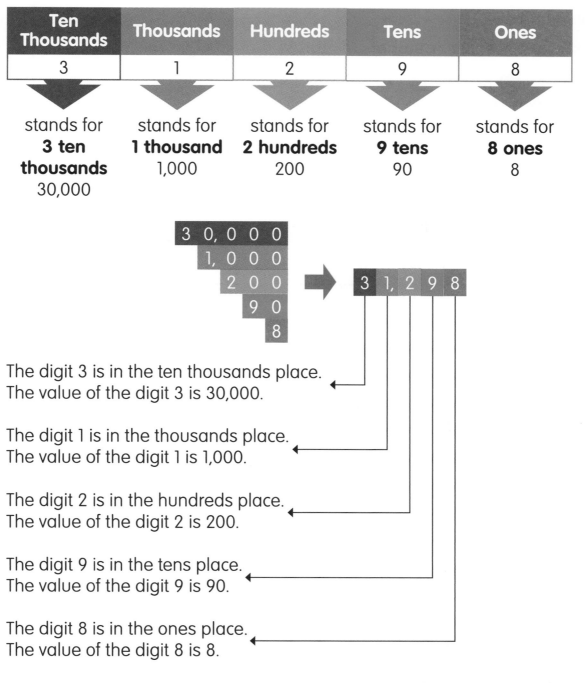

Ten Thousands	Thousands	Hundreds	Tens	Ones
3	1	2	9	8

stands for **3 ten thousands** 30,000

stands for **1 thousand** 1,000

stands for **2 hundreds** 200

stands for **9 tens** 90

stands for **8 ones** 8

The digit 3 is in the ten thousands place.
The value of the digit 3 is 30,000.

The digit 1 is in the thousands place.
The value of the digit 1 is 1,000.

The digit 2 is in the hundreds place.
The value of the digit 2 is 200.

The digit 9 is in the tens place.
The value of the digit 9 is 90.

The digit 8 is in the ones place.
The value of the digit 8 is 8.

31,298 = 3 ten thousands + 1 thousand + 2 hundreds + 9 tens + 8 ones

Expanded form: 30,000 + 1,000 + 200 + 90 + 8
Standard form: 31,298
Word form: thirty-one thousand, two hundred ninety-eight

Hands-on Activity

Work in pairs.

Activity 1   Writing numbers in standard form and word form

(1) Use 10,000 1,000 100 10 1 to show your partner a 5-digit number. Ask your partner to read the number.

(2) Write the number in standard form and word form.

Standard form: _41,211_

Word form: _forty-one, two-hundred eleven._

(3) Trade places. Repeat (1) and (2).

Standard form: _54,332_

Word form: _fifty-four, tousand- three hundred thirdy-two_

Activity 2   Saying the value of each digit

(1) Use 1 2 3 4 5 to show your partner a 5-digit number.

(2) Ask your partner to say the value of each digit in the number.

In 51,234,
The digit 5 stands for 50,000.
The digit 1 stands for 1,000.
The digit 2 stands for 200.
The digit 3 stands for 30.
The digit 4 stands for 4.

(3) Trade places. Repeat (1) and (2) three times.

TRY Practice reading and writing 5-digit numbers

Count. Write each number in standard form and word form.

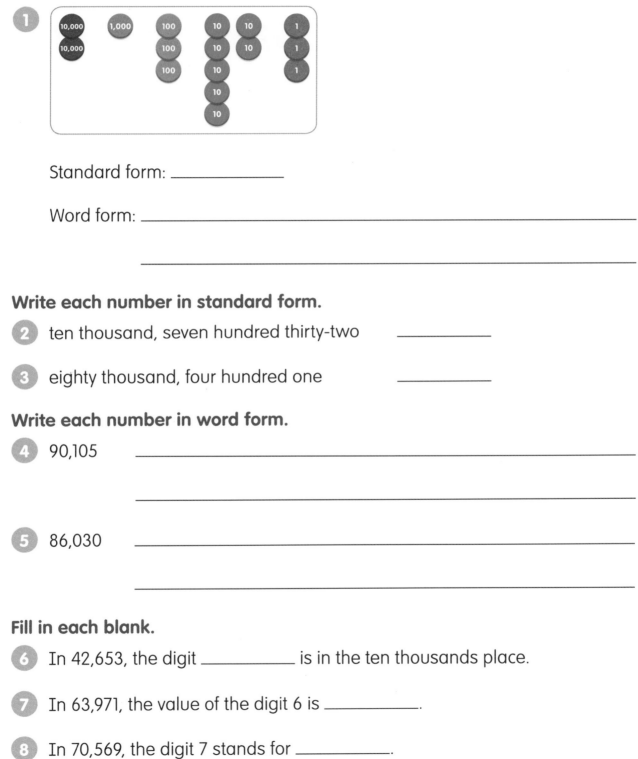

1

Standard form: _____

Word form: _____

_____

Write each number in standard form.

2   ten thousand, seven hundred thirty-two   _____

3   eighty thousand, four hundred one   _____

Write each number in word form.

4   90,105   _____

_____

5   86,030   _____

_____

Fill in each blank.

6   In 42,653, the digit _____ is in the ten thousands place.

7   In 63,971, the value of the digit 6 is _____.

8   In 70,569, the digit 7 stands for _____.

Write the value of the digit 5 in each number.

9 27,0**5**8

10 8**5**,027

11 **5**2,708

_____

_____

_____

Find each missing number.

12 32,508 = 3 ten thousands + _____ thousands + 5 hundreds + 8 ones

13 76,424 = 7 ten thousands + 6 thousands + _____ hundreds + 2 tens + 4 ones

14 65,061 = _____ ten thousands + 5 thousands + _____ tens + 1 one

15 1 ten thousand + _____ thousands + 2 hundreds + 9 tens + 4 ones = 18,294

Complete each expanded form.

16 50,328 = 50,000 + 300 + _____ + 8

17 _____ + 7,000 + _____ + 3 = 47,093

18 37,645 = 30,000 + 7,000 + _____ + 40 + _____

19 _____ + _____ + 800 + 1 = 69,801

20 70,030 = _____ + _____

MATH SHARING

Mathematical Habit 2 Use mathematical reasoning

How do you find the value of each digit in 76,842?
Tyler says he multiplies each digit by its place value.
Is he correct? Explain.

Discuss with your partner another way to find the value of each digit.

INDEPENDENT PRACTICE

Count. Write the number in standard form and word form.

1

Standard form: _____

Word form: _____

_____

Write each number in standard form.

2 thirty thousand, five hundred eleven   _____

3 forty-five thousand, eighty-nine   _____

4 sixteen thousand, nine   _____

Write each number in word form.

5 43,815   _____

_____

6 90,374   _____

_____

7 20,505   _____

_____

Fill in each blank.

8 In 20,675, the digit _____ is in the thousands place.

9 In 76,501, the digit in the hundreds place is _____.

10 In 39,472, the digit 3 stands for _____.

11 In 14,052, the value of the digit 5 is _____.

12 In 81,956, the digit 6 has a value of _____.

Write the value of the digit 4 in each number.

13 27,0**4**8   14 **4**2,708   15 8**4**,027

_____   _____   _____

Find each missing number.

16 54,904 = 5 ten thousands + _____ thousands + 9 hundreds + 4 ones

17 60,082 = _____ ten thousands + _____ tens + 2 ones

Find each missing number.

18 32,176 = _____ + 2,000 + _____ + 70 + 6

19 40,925 = _____ + _____ + 20 + 5

20 28,380 = _____ + 8,000 + _____ + 80

21 94,057 = 90,000 + _____ + _____ + _____

22 63,602 = _____ + _____ + _____ + _____

Numbers to 1,000,000

Learning Objectives:
- Read and write numbers to 1,000,000 in standard form, word form, and expanded form.
- State the place and value of each digit in a 6-digit number.

New Vocabulary
million
period

THINK

Sophie wrote down a 6-digit number. Two pairs of digits in the number make 10 each. The sum of the other two digits is 2. What is the greatest possible 6-digit number Sophie wrote down?

ENGAGE

Use 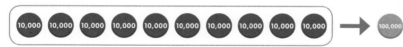 to show 99,999. What happens if you add one more? Write the number in expanded form. How can you read this new number that you have now?

LEARN Read and write 6-digit numbers

1. Count in ten thousands.

10 ten thousands = 1 hundred thousand

10,000	20,000	30,000
40,000	50,000	60,000
70,000	80,000	90,000
100,000		

1 ten thousand = 10 thousands
10 ten thousands = 100 thousands
So, 1 hundred thousand = 100 thousands.

2 Count in hundred thousands.

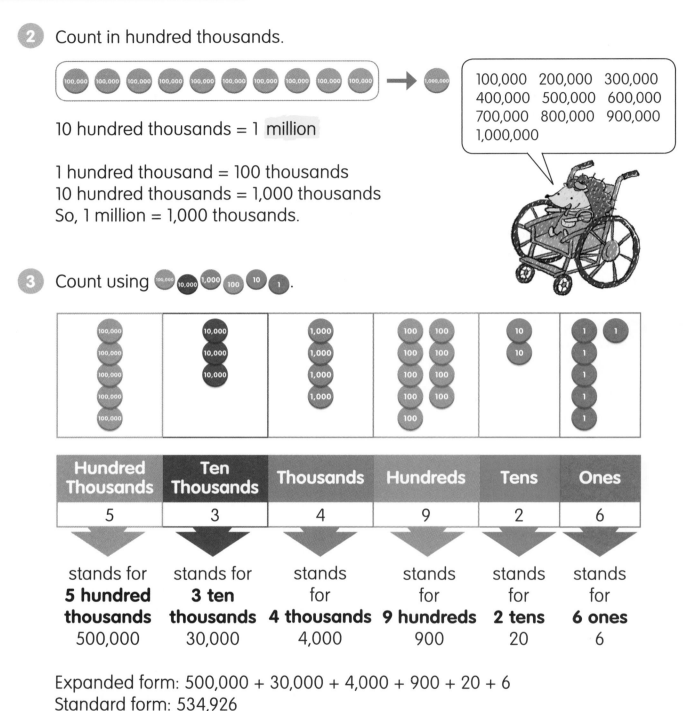

10 hundred thousands = 1 **million**

100,000 200,000 300,000
400,000 500,000 600,000
700,000 800,000 900,000
1,000,000

1 hundred thousand = 100 thousands
10 hundred thousands = 1,000 thousands
So, 1 million = 1,000 thousands.

3 Count using 🪙🪙🪙🪙🪙🪙.

Hundred Thousands	Ten Thousands	Thousands	Hundreds	Tens	Ones
5	3	4	9	2	6
stands for **5 hundred thousands** 500,000	stands for **3 ten thousands** 30,000	stands for **4 thousands** 4,000	stands for **9 hundreds** 900	stands for **2 tens** 20	stands for **6 ones** 6

Expanded form: 500,000 + 30,000 + 4,000 + 900 + 20 + 6
Standard form: 534,926
Word form: five hundred thirty-four thousand, nine hundred twenty-six

4 Groups of three places are called periods .
You can read numbers to 1,000,000 by grouping them into periods.

Hundred Thousands	Ten Thousands	Thousands	Hundreds	Tens	Ones
4	9	7	8	3	2

First, read the thousands period:
four hundred ninety-seven thousand

Then, read the remaining period:
eight hundred thirty-two

497,832 is read as four hundred ninety-seven thousand, eight hundred thirty-two.

Hands-on Activity Reading and writing 6-digit numbers

Work in pairs.

1 Use to show your partner a 6-digit number.
Ask your partner to read the number.

2 Write the number in standard form and word form.

Standard form: _____

Word form: _____

_____

3 Trade places. Repeat 1 and 2 .

Standard form: _____

Word form: _____

_____

TRY Practice reading and writing 6-digit numbers

Count. Write the number in standard form and word form.

1

100,000	10,000	10,000	1,000	100	100	10	1
100,000	10,000	10,000	1,000	100	100	10	
100,000	10,000		1,000	100	100		
100,000	10,000			100	100		
100,000	10,000			100			

Standard form: _____

Word form: _____

_____

Write each number in standard form.

2 six hundred seventy-three thousand, nine hundred eleven   _____

3 five hundred eighteen thousand, four   _____

4 two hundred thousand, one hundred six   _____

Write each number in word form.

5 320,176   _____

_____

6 438,830   _____

_____

7 906,095   _____

_____

Fill in each blank.

8 In 670,932, the value of the digit 6 is _____.

9 In 937,016, the digit _____ is in the hundreds place.

10 In 124,573, the digit in the hundred thousands place is _____.

11 In 971,465, the digit 6 is in the _____ place.

12 In 289,219, the digit 8 is in the _____ place.

13 In 504,932 the digit 5 stands for _____.

Write the value of the digit 2 in each number.

14 81**2**,679

15 **2**60,153

16 8**2**7,917

_____   _____   _____

Find each missing number.

17 104,087 = 1 hundred thousand + _____ thousands + 8 tens + 7 ones

18 650,002 = _____ hundred thousands + 5 ten thousands + 2 ones

Complete each expanded form.

19 761,902 = 700,000 + _____ + _____ + 900 + 2

20 124,003 = _____ + 20,000 + _____ + _____

21 800,000 + _____ + 600 + _____ + _____ = 840,625

22 900,000 + _____ + _____ + 6 = 900,356

23 204,080 = _____ + _____ + _____

FIND THE VALUE!

What you need:

Players: 3
Materials: 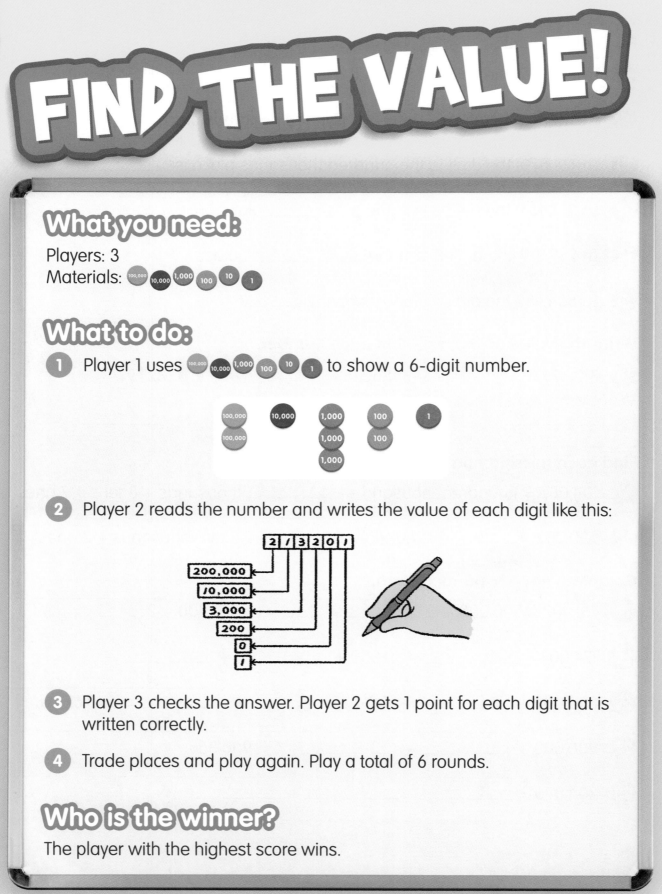 100,000 10,000 1,000 100 10 1

What to do:

1 Player 1 uses 100,000 10,000 1,000 100 10 1 to show a 6-digit number.

2 Player 2 reads the number and writes the value of each digit like this:

2 1 3 2 0 1

200,000
10,000
3,000
200
0
1

3 Player 3 checks the answer. Player 2 gets 1 point for each digit that is written correctly.

4 Trade places and play again. Play a total of 6 rounds.

Who is the winner?

The player with the highest score wins.

INDEPENDENT PRACTICE

Count. Write the number in standard form and word form.

1

| 100,000 | 10,000 | 1,000 | 100 | 100 | 1 |

Standard form: _____

Word form: _____

_____

Write each number in standard form.

2 two hundred thirty-five thousand, nine hundred forty-two _____

3 five hundred twenty thousand, three hundred eight _____

4 seven hundred thousand, four hundred ten _____

Write each number in word form.

5 612,835 _____

_____

6 806,115 _____

_____

7 300,049 _____

_____

Fill in each blank.

8 In 524,380, the digit _____ is in the ten thousands place.

9 In 405,816, the digit 4 is in the _____ place.

10 In 175,423, the digit 7 stands for _____.

11 In 658,027, the digit 6 has a value of _____.

12 In 206,005, the digit 6 has a value of _____.

Write the value of the digit 3 in each number.

13 214,**3**84   14 5**3**0,061   15 **3**00,004

_____   _____   _____

Find each missing number.

16 201,803 = _____ hundred thousands + 1 thousand + 8 hundreds + 3 ones

17 107,540 = 1 hundred thousand + 7 thousands + _____ hundreds

+ _____ tens

Complete each expanded form.

18 840,772 = 800,000 + _____ + _____ + _____ + 2

19 206,351 = _____ + 6,000 + _____ + 50 + _____

20 100,000 + _____ + 5,000 + _____ + 10 + 8 = 125,718

21 900,000 + _____ + 90 + _____ = 909,099

22 240,060 = _____ + _____ + _____

3 Comparing and Ordering Numbers

Learning Objectives:
- Compare and order numbers to 1,000,000.
- Identify how much more or less one number is than another.
- Find the rule to complete a number pattern.
- Create number patterns.

THINK

Think of different 6-digit numbers. Each number must have the digit 4 in the hundred thousands place and the digit 8 in the tens place. Write down the greatest and least possible numbers.

ENGAGE

1. Use 1,000 100 10 1 to show 4,517 and 4,537. Which is greater, 4,517 or 4,537?

2. Nicholas is thinking of two numbers. The first number is 3 ten thousands 4 thousands 58 ones. The second number is 2 ten thousands 14 thousands 85 ones. Which number is greater?

LEARN Compare and order numbers to 1,000,000

1. Which number is greater, 20,103 or 13,021?

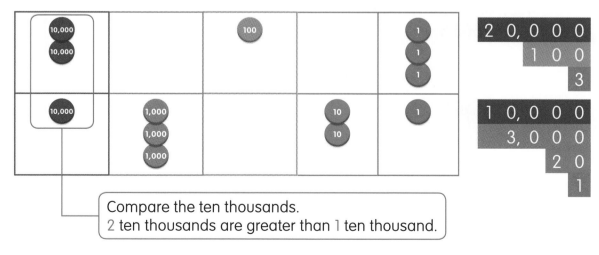

Compare the ten thousands.
2 ten thousands are greater than 1 ten thousand.

So, 20,103 is greater than 13,021.
20,103 > 13,021

2 Which number is less, 37,000 or 37,460?

Ten Thousands	Thousands	Hundreds	Tens	Ones
3	7	0	0	0
3	7	4	6	0

STEP 1 ▷ Compare the ten thousands. They are the same.

STEP 2 ▷ Compare the thousands. They are the same.

STEP 3 ▷ Compare the hundreds. 0 hundreds are less than 4 hundreds.

So, 37,000 is less than 37,460.
37,000 < 37,460

3 Which number is greater, 405,786 or 365,897?

Hundred Thousands	Ten Thousands	Thousands	Hundreds	Tens	Ones
4	0	5	7	8	6
3	6	5	8	9	7

Compare the hundred thousands.
4 hundred thousands are greater than
3 hundred thousands.

So, 405,786 is greater than 365,897.
405,786 > 365,897

4 Order 62,357, 29,638, and 28,986 from greatest to least.

Ten Thousands	Thousands	Hundreds	Tens	Ones
6	2	3	5	7
2	9	6	3	8
2	8	9	8	6

STEP 1 Compare the ten thousands. 6 ten thousands are greater than 2 ten thousands. So, 62,357 is the greatest.

STEP 2 The ten thousands in the two other numbers are the same. So, compare the thousands. 8 thousands are less than 9 thousands. So, 28,986 is the least.

From greatest to least, the numbers are:

62,357　　　29,638　　　28,986
greatest　　　　　　　　least

5 Order 641,246, 538,724, and 540,642 from least to greatest.

Hundred Thousands	Ten Thousands	Thousands	Hundreds	Tens	Ones
6	4	1	2	4	6
5	3	8	7	2	4
5	4	0	6	4	2

STEP 1 Compare the hundred thousands. 6 hundred thousands are greater than 5 hundred thousands. So, 641,246 is the greatest.

STEP 2 The hundred thousands in the two other numbers are the same. So, compare the ten thousands. 3 ten thousands are less than 4 ten thousands. So, 538,724 is the least.

From least to greatest, the numbers are:

538,724　　　540,642　　　641,246
least　　　　　　　　　　　greatest

Hands-on Activity

Activity 1   Comparing numbers to 1,000,000

Work in pairs.

(1) Use  to show 543,268. Ask your partner to show 533,987.

(2) Write the numbers in the place-value chart and compare them using "greater than" or "less than."

Hundred Thousands	Ten Thousands	Thousands	Hundreds	Tens	Ones

543,268 is _____ 533,987.

533,987 is _____ 543,268.

Activity 2   Ordering numbers to 1,000,000

Work in groups of four.

(1) Use four sets of number cards from 0 to 9. Shuffle the cards.

(2) Take turns drawing five or six cards and arranging them to form four 5-digit or 6-digit numbers.

(3) Compare the numbers and order them from least to greatest.

_____   _____   _____   _____

least   greatest

TRY Practice comparing and ordering numbers to 1,000,000

Compare the numbers and fill in each blank.

1

Ten Thousands	Thousands	Hundreds	Tens	Ones
	8	7	6	9
2	0	1	3	1

_____ is less than _____.

Compare each pair of numbers. Write < or >.

2 64,515 ◯ 65,500

3 16,735 ◯ 16,581

4 100,400 ◯ 99,900

5 143,820 ◯ 134,820

Circle the greatest number.

6 81,630   81,603   816,300   816,030

Circle the least number.

7 12,500   125,000   25,000   12,050

Order the numbers from least to greatest.

8 41,325   31,425   51,324   14,325

_____   _____   _____   _____
  least   greatest

Order the numbers from greatest to least.

9 645,321   654,987   645,231   654,978

_____   _____   _____   _____
  greatest   least

Write the number.

10 Use the digits 9, 2, 0, 4, and 7 to form the least possible 5-digit odd number.

_____

ENGAGE

1 Use 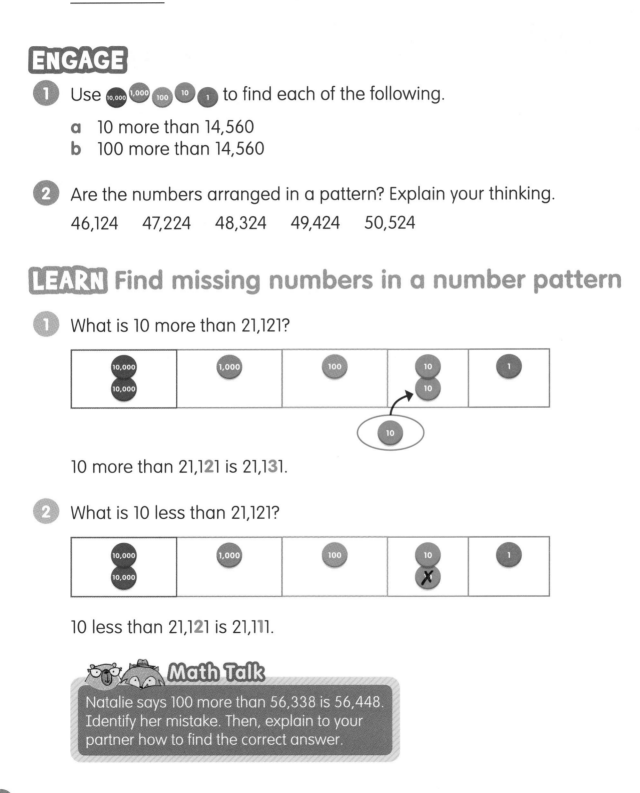 to find each of the following.

    a   10 more than 14,560

    b   100 more than 14,560

2 Are the numbers arranged in a pattern? Explain your thinking.

    46,124   47,224   48,324   49,424   50,524

LEARN Find missing numbers in a number pattern

1 What is 10 more than 21,121?

10 more than 21,1**2**1 is 21,1**3**1.

2 What is 10 less than 21,121?

10 less than 21,1**2**1 is 21,1**1**1.

Math Talk

Natalie says 100 more than 56,338 is 56,448.
Identify her mistake. Then, explain to your
partner how to find the correct answer.

3 Find the rule. Then, complete the number pattern.

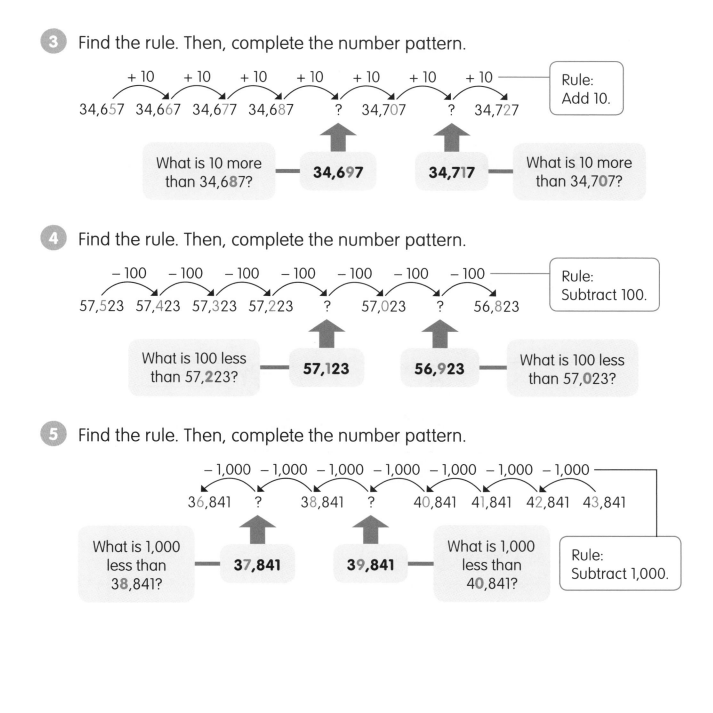

+10 +10 +10 +10 +10 +10 +10 ——— Rule: Add 10.

34,657 34,667 34,677 34,687 ? 34,707 ? 34,727

| What is 10 more than 34,6**8**7? | — | **34,697** | **34,717** | What is 10 more than 34,7**0**7? |

4 Find the rule. Then, complete the number pattern.

−100 −100 −100 −100 −100 −100 −100 ——— Rule: Subtract 100.

57,523 57,423 57,323 57,223 ? 57,023 ? 56,823

| What is 100 less than 57,**2**23? | — | **57,123** | **56,923** | What is 100 less than 57,**0**23? |

5 Find the rule. Then, complete the number pattern.

−1,000 −1,000 −1,000 −1,000 −1,000 −1,000 −1,000

36,841 ? 38,841 ? 40,841 41,841 42,841 43,841

| What is 1,000 less than 3**8**,841? | — | **37,841** | **39,841** | What is 1,000 less than 4**0**,841? | Rule: Subtract 1,000. |

Hands-on Activity Showing 10, 100, 1,000 more or less than a 5-digit number

Work in pairs.

① Roll 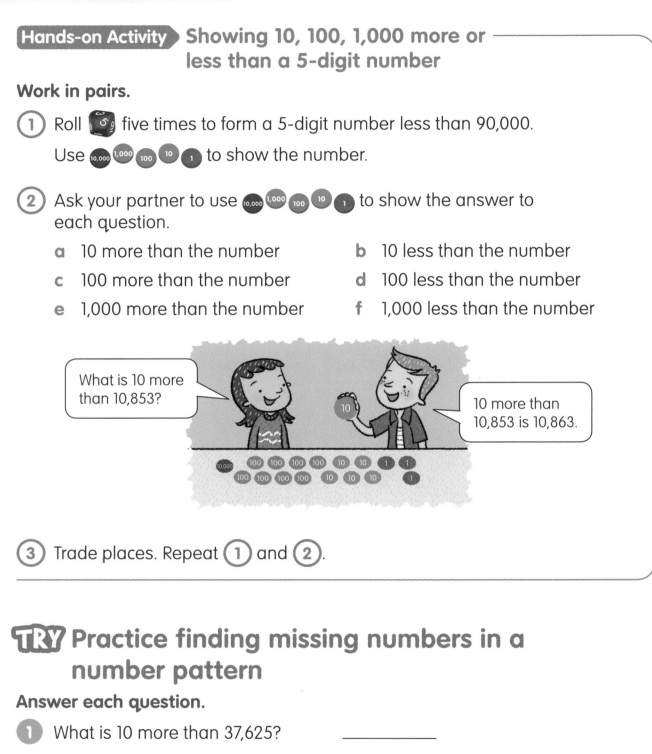 five times to form a 5-digit number less than 90,000. Use 🔵 🔵 🔵 🔵 🔵 to show the number.

② Ask your partner to use 🔵 🔵 🔵 🔵 🔵 to show the answer to each question.

    a 10 more than the number   **b** 10 less than the number

    c 100 more than the number   **d** 100 less than the number

    e 1,000 more than the number   **f** 1,000 less than the number

③ Trade places. Repeat ① and ②.

TRY Practice finding missing numbers in a number pattern

Answer each question.

① What is 10 more than 37,625? _____

② What is 100 more than 37,625? _____

③ What is 1,000 more than 37,625? _____

4 What is 10 less than 20,840? _____

5 What is 100 less than 20,840? _____

6 What is 1,000 less than 20,840? _____

Fill in each blank.

7 1,000 more than 19,503 is _____.

8 49,161 is 100 less than _____.

9 200 less than 86,932 is _____.

Complete each number pattern.

10 12,985   12,885   _____   12,685   12,585   12,485   12,385

11 66,935   67,935   68,935   69,935   _____   71,935

12 85,546   85,046   84,546   _____   83,546   83,046   _____

© 2020 Marshall Cavendish Education Pte Ltd

MATH SHARING

Mathematical Habit 7 Make use of structure

a Compare the numbers in the equation 34 + 52 = 31 + 55.
What do you notice?
Without adding, how can you tell if the equation is true?
Explain your strategy to your partner.
Hint: An equation is true if both sides of the equation are equal.

b Without subtracting, how can you find the missing number in the
following equation?
82 − 76 = 42 − ?

1 Brooke and Mateo each created a number pattern. Explain to your partner the rule of each pattern.
Brooke: 71, 69, 67, 65, 63
Mateo: 12, 15, 13, 16, 14, 17, 15

2 Create two different number patterns starting with 54. Ask your partner to explain the rule of each number pattern.

LEARN Create number patterns

1 William creates a number pattern. He starts from 1 and uses the rule "add 3." Find the next two numbers in the pattern.

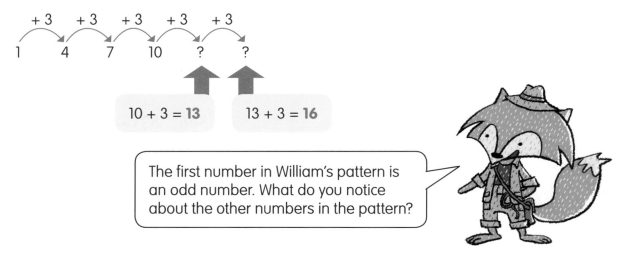

$$10 + 3 = \mathbf{13} \qquad 13 + 3 = \mathbf{16}$$

> The first number in William's pattern is an odd number. What do you notice about the other numbers in the pattern?

2 Carla creates a number pattern. She starts from 42 and uses the rule "subtract 8." Find the next two numbers in the pattern.

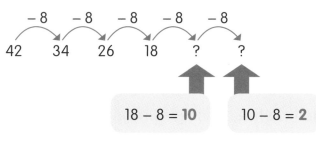

$$18 - 8 = \mathbf{10} \qquad 10 - 8 = \mathbf{2}$$

> The first number in Carla's pattern is an even number. What do you notice about the other numbers in the pattern?

3 Megan creates a number pattern. She starts from 4 and uses the rule "add 3, subtract 1." Find the next two numbers in the pattern.

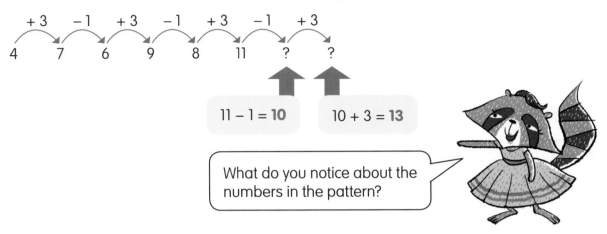

11 – 1 = **10**

10 + 3 = **13**

What do you notice about the numbers in the pattern?

Hands-on Activity Creating a number pattern

Work in pairs.

1 Roll a number cube. Use the number you rolled to make a rule for a number pattern, for example, "add 3."

2 Ask your partner to roll the number cube. Use the number he or she rolled to start the number pattern.

3 Write the first six numbers in the number pattern.

Rule: _____

_____ _____ _____ _____ _____ _____

4 **Mathematical Habit 8** Look for patterns
What do you notice about the numbers in the pattern?

TRY Practice creating number patterns

Complete each number pattern.

1 Diego's pattern starts from 1 and uses the rule "add 12."

1   13   25   _____   _____   _____   _____   _____

2 Taylor's pattern starts from 22 and uses the rule "add 16."

22   38   54   _____   _____   _____   _____   _____

Write the first eight numbers in each number pattern.

3 Start from 180 and use the rule "subtract 15."

_____   _____   _____   _____   _____   _____   _____   _____

4 Start from 30 and use the rule "add 5, subtract 4."

_____   _____   _____   _____   _____   _____   _____   _____

5 Start from 29 and use the rule "subtract 6, add 8."

_____   _____   _____   _____   _____   _____   _____   _____

INDEPENDENT PRACTICE

Compare each pair of numbers. Write the greater number.

1 90,847 or 69,948 _____

2 568,912 or 568,921 _____

Compare each pair of numbers. Write < or >.

3 24,630 $\bigcirc$ 26,403

4 42,100 $\bigcirc$ 41,002

5 285,359 $\bigcirc$ 283,395

6 345,932 $\bigcirc$ 435,990

Compare the numbers. Then, answer each question.

31,204   20,582   20,587   31,239

7 Which number is the greatest?   _____

8 Which number is the least?   _____

Order the numbers from least to greatest.

9 21,937   74,126   9,837

_____   _____   _____
    least   greatest

Order the numbers from greatest to least.

10 237,086   237,608   238,706   236,870

_____   _____   _____   _____
   greatest   least

Write the number.

11 Use the digits 9, 7, 2, 3, 4, and 8 to form the least possible 6-digit even number.

_____

Answer each question.

12 What is 10 more than 29,374? _____

13 What is 100 less than 17,002? _____

14 What is 1,000 less than 174,602? _____

Fill in each blank.

15 41,808 is _____ less than 41,818.

16 _____ is 100 more than 10,821.

17 16,235 is 600 less than _____.

Complete each number pattern.

18 38,825   38,725   38,625   _____   38,425   38,325

19 7,041   8,041   9,041   _____   11,041   12,041   13,041

Complete the number pattern.

20 Kaitlyn's pattern starts from 10 and uses the rule "add 4."

10   14   18   _____   _____   _____   _____   _____

Write the first eight numbers in each number pattern.

21 Start from 27 and use the rule "subtract 3."

_____   _____   _____   _____   _____   _____   _____   _____

22 Start from 8 and use the rule "add 2, add 5."

_____   _____   _____   _____   _____   _____   _____   _____

4 Adding and Subtracting Multi-Digit Numbers

Learning Objective:
• Add and subtract multi-digit numbers fluently.

THINK

Find the digits represented by each letter.

a   483,6A7 + B4,C6D = 57E,186

b   4W,20X − 9,Y48 = 37,5Z7

ENGAGE

a   Use 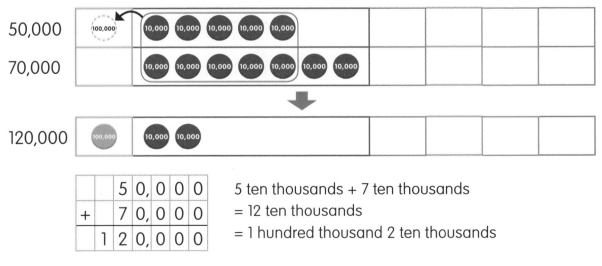 10,000 1,000 100 10 1 to show the 74,528. Then, fill in each blank.
74,528 = 6 ten thousands ____ thousands 5 hundreds ____ ones

b   Fill in each blank.
68,364 = ____ ten thousands 18 thousands ____ hundreds 26 tens 4 ones

LEARN Add multi-digit numbers

1 Company A earned $50,000 last month. Company B earned $70,000.
How much did the companies earn in all?

50,000 + 70,000 = ?

50,000	(100,000) 10,000 10,000 10,000 10,000 10,000
70,000	10,000 10,000 10,000 10,000 10,000 10,000 10,000

120,000	100,000 10,000 10,000

	5	0,	0	0	0
+	7	0,	0	0	0
1	2	0,	0	0	0

5 ten thousands + 7 ten thousands
= 12 ten thousands
= 1 hundred thousand 2 ten thousands

50,000 + 70,000 = 120,000

The companies earned $120,000 in all.

2 Add 374,528 and 42,965.

374,528 + 42,965 = ?

Step 1
Add the ones.
Regroup the ones.

					1	
	3	7	4,	5	2	8
+			4	2,	9	6	5
						3

8 ones + 5 ones
= 13 ones
= 1 ten 3 ones

Step 2
Add the tens.

				1		
	3	7	4,	5	2	8
+			4	2,	9	6	5
					9	3

1 ten + 2 tens + 6 tens
= 9 tens

Step 3
Add the hundreds.
Regroup the hundreds.

			1		1	
	3	7	4,	5	2	8
+			4	2,	9	6	5
				4	9	3

5 hundreds + 9 hundreds
= 14 hundreds
= 1 thousand 4 hundreds

Step 4
Add the thousands.

		1		1		
	3	7	4,	5	2	8
+			4	2,	9	6	5
			7,	4	9	3

1 thousand + 4 thousands
+ 2 thousands
= 7 thousands

Step 5
Add the ten thousands.
Regroup the ten thousands.

	1		1		1	
	3	7	4,	5	2	8
+			4	2,	9	6	5
		1	7,	4	9	3

7 ten thousands
+ 4 ten thousands
= 11 ten thousands
= 1 hundred thousand
  1 ten thousand

Step 6
Add the hundred
thousands.

	1		1		1	
	3	7	4,	5	2	8
+			4	2,	9	6	5
	4	1	7,	4	9	3

1 hundred thousand
+ 3 hundred thousands
= 4 hundred thousands

So, 374,528 + 42,965 = 417,493.

TRY Practice adding multi-digit numbers

Find each sum.

1.
```
    2 4, 3 7 5
  +    1, 0 2 3
```

2.
```
    5 6, 0 8 4
  + 3 7, 7 6 5
```

3.
```
    4 7, 3 9 2
  + 8 8, 4 9 9
```

4.
```
    4 7 8, 0 8 1
  +    5 6, 7 8 9
```

5.
```
    3 6 4, 7 6 3
  + 4 9 0, 8 7 8
```

6.
```
    5 8 3, 6 9 3
  + 3 2 5, 4 7 9
```

Solve. Show your work.

7. Find the sum of 417,809 and 562,376.

The sum of 417,809 and 562,376 is _____ .

ENGAGE

a Use to show and complete the following.

1,000 = _____ hundreds _____ tens _____ ones

b Then, find each missing digit.

```
  1 0, 0 0 0
−    7, 4 5 2
  ☐, 5 ☐ ☐
```

LEARN Subtract multi-digit numbers

1 A factory produced 100,000 bags last year. This year, 70,000 bags were produced. How many more bags did the factory produce last year?

100,000 − 70,000 = ?

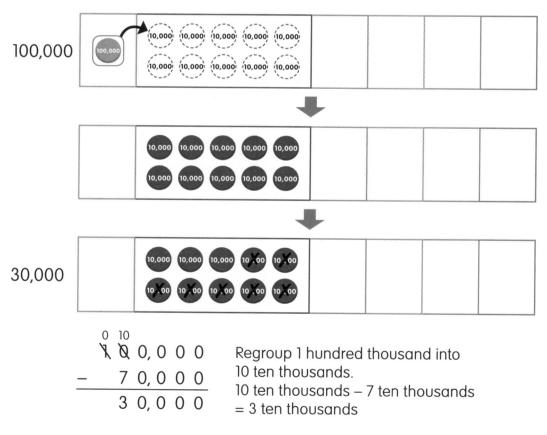

```
  0  10
  ⅟  ⅟  0, 0 0 0       Regroup 1 hundred thousand into
−     7 0, 0 0 0       10 ten thousands.
      3 0, 0 0 0       10 ten thousands − 7 ten thousands
                       = 3 ten thousands
```

100,000 − 70,000 = 30,000

The factory produced 30,000 more bags last year.

2 Subtract 179,361 from 358,792.

$358{,}792 - 179{,}361 = ?$

Step 1
Subtract the ones.

	3	5	8,	7	9	2
−	1	7	9,	3	6	1
						1

2 ones − 1 one = 1 one

Step 2
Subtract the tens.

	3	5	8,	7	9	2
−	1	7	9,	3	6	1
					3	1

9 tens − 6 tens = 3 tens

Step 3
Subtract the hundreds.

	3	5	8,	7	9	2
−	1	7	9,	3	6	1
				4	3	1

7 hundreds − 3 hundreds
= 4 hundreds

Step 4
Regroup the ten thousands.

4   18

	3	5̸	8̸,	7	9	2
−	1	7	9,	3	6	1
				4	3	1

5 ten thousands 8 thousands
= 4 ten thousands 18 thousands

Step 5
Subtract the thousands.

4   18

	3	5̸	8̸,	7	9	2
−	1	7	9,	3	6	1
			9,	4	3	1

18 thousands − 9 thousands
= 9 thousands

Step 6
Regroup the hundred thousands.

2   14   18

	3̸	5̸	8̸,	7	9	2
−	1	7	9,	3	6	1
			9,	4	3	1

3 hundred thousands
4 ten thousands
= 2 hundred thousands
14 ten thousands

Step 7
Subtract the ten thousands.

2   14   18

	3̸	5̸	8̸,	7	9	2
−	1	7	9,	3	6	1
		7	9,	4	3	1

14 ten thousands
− 7 ten thousands
= 7 ten thousands

Step 8
Subtract the
hundred thousands.

	2	14	18			
	3̶	5̶	8̶	7	9	2
−	1	7	9,	3	6	1
	1	7	9,	4	3	1

2 hundred thousands
− 1 hundred thousand
= 1 hundred thousand

So, 358,792 − 179,361 = 179,431.

TRY Practice subtracting multi-digit numbers

Subtract.

1
```
    5 4, 6 3 1
  − 2 3, 8 0 7
```

2
```
    7 0, 0 3 0
  − 4 2, 6 8 9
```

3
```
  1 3 7, 3 5 8
  −   5 7, 6 4 9
```

4
```
  6 8 4, 3 5 2
  − 3 9 6, 7 3 4
```

Solve. Show your work.

5 Subtract 20,619 from 100,008.

MATH SHARING

Mathematical Habit 2 Use mathematical reasoning

Hana subtracts 86,742 from 200,000 in the following way.

Explain to your partner how Hana regrouped 200,000.
Use Hana's method to subtract 256,482 from 400,000.
Explain how you did it.

1	9	9	9	9	10
2̶	0̶	0̶	0̶	0̶	0̶
−		8	6,	7	4	2
1	1	3,	2	5	8

INDEPENDENT PRACTICE

Add.

1
$$\begin{array}{r} 5\,4,6\,3\,1 \\ +\ \ 6,6\,3\,9 \\ \hline \end{array}$$

2
$$\begin{array}{r} 3\,7,3\,3\,7 \\ +1\,7,6\,7\,9 \\ \hline \end{array}$$

3
$$\begin{array}{r} 6\,2,0\,8\,5 \\ +2\,8,9\,4\,6 \\ \hline \end{array}$$

4
$$\begin{array}{r} 7\,5,8\,6\,8 \\ +9\,8,9\,2\,7 \\ \hline \end{array}$$

5
$$\begin{array}{r} 1\,5\,9,2\,3\,1 \\ +2\,7\,8,0\,6\,5 \\ \hline \end{array}$$

6
$$\begin{array}{r} 7\,2\,3,5\,0\,9 \\ +1\,5\,6,8\,5\,2 \\ \hline \end{array}$$

Solve. Show your work.

7 Add 21,574 and 183,261.

8 Add 408,396 and 237,825.

Subtract.

9
```
  6 2,4 8 5
−    7,8 3 8
```

10
```
  8 9,3 5 2
− 7 9,6 7 8
```

11
```
  5 3,4 0 4
− 3 6,1 8 9
```

12
```
  3 7 0,0 8 9
−    4 2,6 3 8
```

13
```
  6 0 0,0 0 9
− 2 1 5,3 2 8
```

14
```
  8 0 0,0 0 0
− 3 5 4,4 6 3
```

Solve. Show your work.

15 Subtract 164,387 from 562,480.

16 Subtract 281,852 from 707,613.

5 Rounding and Estimating

Learning Objectives:
- Round numbers to the nearest thousand.
- Estimate sums and differences.
- Decide whether an estimate or an exact answer is needed.

New Vocabulary
estimate

THINK

A desktop computer costs $1,835 and a laptop costs $948. Ms. Lee says she needs about $2,700 to buy both items. Mr. Turner says he needs about $3,000. How did they arrive at their estimates? Who has a better estimate? Why?

ENGAGE

Draw a number line with endpoints 1,000 and 2,000. How can you divide the number line to find 1,300? Explain your reasoning to your partner.
Is 1,300 nearer to 1,000 or 2,000? Explain.
What numbers are nearer to 1,000 than 2,000? Explain.

LEARN Round to the nearest thousand

① Round 7,300 to the nearest thousand.

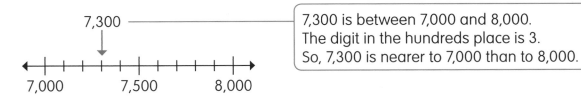

7,300 is between 7,000 and 8,000.
The digit in the hundreds place is 3.
So, 7,300 is nearer to 7,000 than to 8,000.

7,300 is 7,000 when rounded to the nearest thousand.

② Round 5,800 to the nearest thousand.

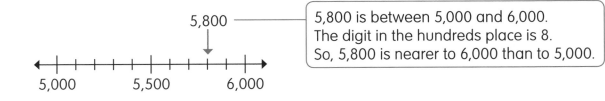

5,800 is between 5,000 and 6,000.
The digit in the hundreds place is 8.
So, 5,800 is nearer to 6,000 than to 5,000.

5,800 is 6,000 when rounded to the nearest thousand.

3 A store owner earned $102,500 in one month. Round the amount to the nearest thousand dollars.

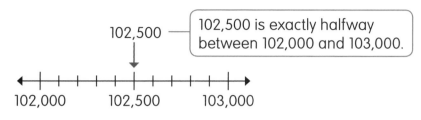

102,500 — 102,500 is exactly halfway between 102,000 and 103,000.

102,000   102,500   103,000

When the digit 5 is in the hundreds place, we round to the greater thousand.

102,500 is 103,000 when rounded to the nearest thousand dollars.

The store owner earned about $103,000 in one month.

Hands-on Activity **Rounding to the nearest thousand**

Work in pairs.

1 Roll a [die] five times to form a 5-digit number.

2 Use a number line to show the 5-digit number.

3 Ask your partner to round the number to the nearest thousand.

_____ is _____ when rounded to the nearest thousand.

TRY Practice rounding to the nearest thousand

Round the number to the nearest thousand.

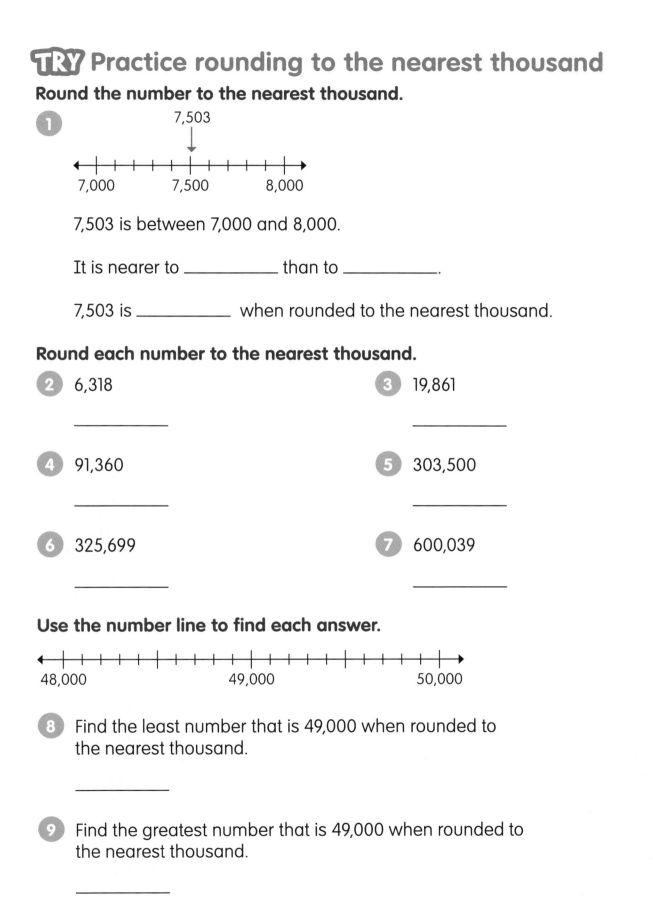

1

7,503

7,000   7,500   8,000

7,503 is between 7,000 and 8,000.

It is nearer to _____ than to _____.

7,503 is _____ when rounded to the nearest thousand.

Round each number to the nearest thousand.

2 6,318

_____

3 19,861

_____

4 91,360

_____

5 303,500

_____

6 325,699

_____

7 600,039

_____

Use the number line to find each answer.

48,000   49,000   50,000

8 Find the least number that is 49,000 when rounded to the nearest thousand.

_____

9 Find the greatest number that is 49,000 when rounded to the nearest thousand.

_____

ENGAGE

1 How can you use rounding to estimate the sum of 378 and 243?

2 Victoria rounded 675 to 670. Sebastian rounded 675 to 680. Who is right? Why?

LEARN Estimate sums and differences

1 A market sold 196 jars of grape jelly in September. In October, the market sold 389 jars. How many jars of grape jelly did the market sell over the two months?

196 + 389 = 585
The market sold 585 jars of grape jelly over the two months.

Estimate to check that the answer is reasonable. To estimate, we can round each number to the nearest hundred.

> To estimate is to find a value that is close to the actual answer.

Number	Rounded to the Nearest Hundred
196	200
389	400

Add: 200 + 400 = 600
The estimated sum is 600.

The answer 585 is close to 600. So, it is reasonable.

> Since both numbers are rounded to the greater hundred, the estimate is greater than the actual sum.

> We can use the same method to estimate differences and check that the answer is reasonable.

TRY Practice estimating sums and differences

Find the difference. Use rounding to check that your answer is reasonable.

1) There were 15,426 people at a baseball game. 9,563 of them were adults. How many children were at the baseball game?

15,426 − 9,563 = _____

There were _____ children at the baseball game.

Estimate to check that the answer is reasonable.
To estimate, we can round each number to the nearest thousand.

Number	Rounded to the Nearest Thousand
15,426	
9,563	

Subtract: _____ − _____ = _____

The estimated difference is _____.

Is your answer reasonable? Explain.

Find each sum or difference. Round each number to the nearest hundred to check that your answer is reasonable.

2 536 + 289 = _____

3 2,918 + 104 = _____

Estimate:

500 + 300 = _____

Estimate:

_____ + _____ = _____

4 681 − 203 = _____

5 1,842 − 436 = _____

Estimate:

_____ − _____ = _____

Estimate:

_____ − _____ = _____

Find each sum or difference. Round each number to the nearest thousand to check that your answer is reasonable.

6 7,192 + 1,642 = _____

7 16,290 + 25,500 = _____

Estimate:

7,000 + 2,000 = _____

Estimate:

_____ + _____ = _____

8 5,701 − 3,214 = _____

9 29,810 − 17,391 = _____

Estimate:

_____ − _____ = _____

Estimate:

_____ − _____ = _____

ENGAGE

a Carolina has 925 beads. She uses 375 beads to decorate a table. She needs 620 beads to decorate a lamp. Does she have enough beads left for the lamp? How do you know? Explain your thinking to your partner.

b Carolina wants to decorate 3 lamps. Beads are sold in bags of 500. How many more bags will she need? Explain your thinking to your partner.

LEARN Decide whether to find an estimate or an exact answer

1 A youth center raised $1,000. Is the amount raised enough to buy the following items? Decide if you need an exact answer or an estimate.

$599
Television

$705
Used piano

The question asks if the amount raised is **enough** to buy the items. So, we can use an estimate.

Estimate the total cost by rounding to the nearest hundred dollars.

$600 + $700 = $1,300

No, the amount raised is not enough to buy the items.

2 Mr. Baker wants to buy a dishwasher and a refrigerator for $1,720. He has saved $640. About how much more money does he need to buy both items?

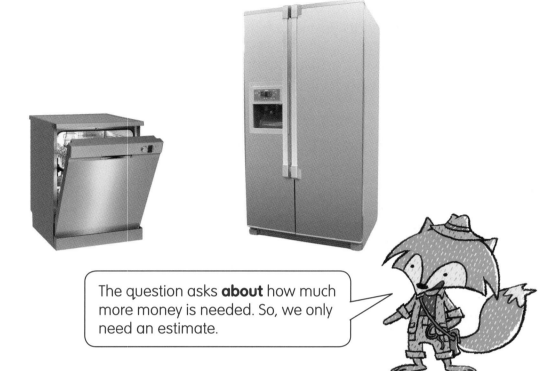

The question asks **about** how much more money is needed. So, we only need an estimate.

Estimate the difference by rounding to the nearest hundred dollars.

$1,700 – $600 = $1,100

He needs about $1,100 more to buy both items.

3 Ms. Smith bought a car that cost $33,542 before a discount of $1,200. How much did she pay for the car?

The question asks **how much** Ms. Smith paid. So, we need an exact answer.

$33,542 – $1,200 = $32,342

She paid $32,342 for the car.

TRY Practice deciding whether to find an estimate or an exact answer

Solve. Decide whether to find an estimate or an exact answer.

1) The table shows the number of cats that were adopted from shelters in one year.

Cats Adopted in a Year	Number
Male adults	12,760
Female adults	9,432
Kittens	20,979

How many cats were adopted in all that year?

2) Isaac has saved $250. He wants to spend $63 on a sweatshirt, $45 on running shoes, and $120 on a bicycle. Does he have enough money?

3 The Evans family saved $1,640 to buy some furniture. Last week, they bought a sofa and had $1,020 left. How much did they spend on the sofa?

4 A stadium has a seating capacity of 23,671. During a football game, there are 11,230 fans for Team A and 8,200 fans for Team B seated in the stadium. The rest of the seats are empty. About how many empty seats are there?

INDEPENDENT PRACTICE

Mark an ✗ on the number line to show 76,498. Then, round the number to the nearest thousand.

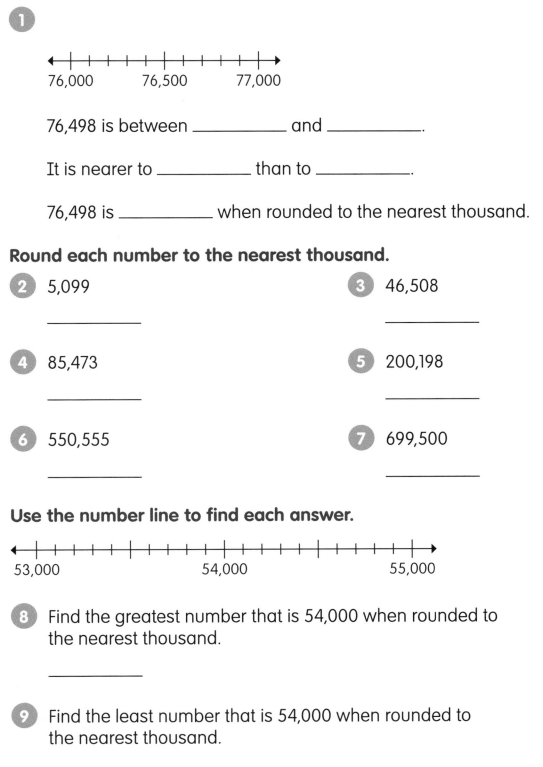

1

76,498 is between _____ and _____.

It is nearer to _____ than to _____.

76,498 is _____ when rounded to the nearest thousand.

Round each number to the nearest thousand.

2 5,099

_____

3 46,508

_____

4 85,473

_____

5 200,198

_____

6 550,555

_____

7 699,500

_____

Use the number line to find each answer.

53,000   54,000   55,000

8 Find the greatest number that is 54,000 when rounded to the nearest thousand.

_____

9 Find the least number that is 54,000 when rounded to the nearest thousand.

_____

Find each sum or difference. Estimate to check that your answer is reasonable.

10 7,271 + 438 = _____

Estimate:

_____ + _____ = _____

11 87,246 – 42,107 = _____

Estimate:

_____ – _____ = _____

Solve. Decide whether to find an estimate or an exact answer.

12 A restaurant made 428 sandwiches. It received three large orders.
Company A ordered 155 sandwiches. Company B ordered
120 sandwiches. Company C ordered 210 sandwiches.
Were there enough sandwiches to fill all three orders?

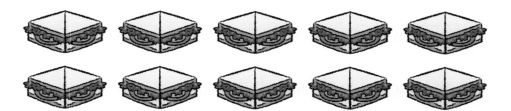

© 2020 Marshall Cavendish Education Pte Ltd

6 Real-World Problems: Addition and Subtraction

Learning Objective:
- Use bar models to solve real-world addition and subtraction problems.

THINK

Holly Elementary School and Melwood Elementary School raised a total of $27,200 for charity. Holly Elementary School raised $6,700 more than Melwood Elementary School. How much did Holly Elementary School raise?

ENGAGE

School X has 4,400 students enrolled. School Y has 250 more students enrolled than School X. School Z has 250 fewer students enrolled than School X. Draw a bar model to show the number of students in each school.

LEARN Solve real-world problems involving addition and subtraction

 A company has 12,568 workers. 4,678 of them work in offices. The rest work on the factory floor. How many more people work on the factory floor than in offices?

STEP 1 Understand the problem.

How many workers are there in all?
How many work in offices?
Are there more people working in offices than on the factory floor?
What do I need to find?

STEP 2 Think of a plan.
I can draw a bar model.

STEP 3 Carry out the plan.

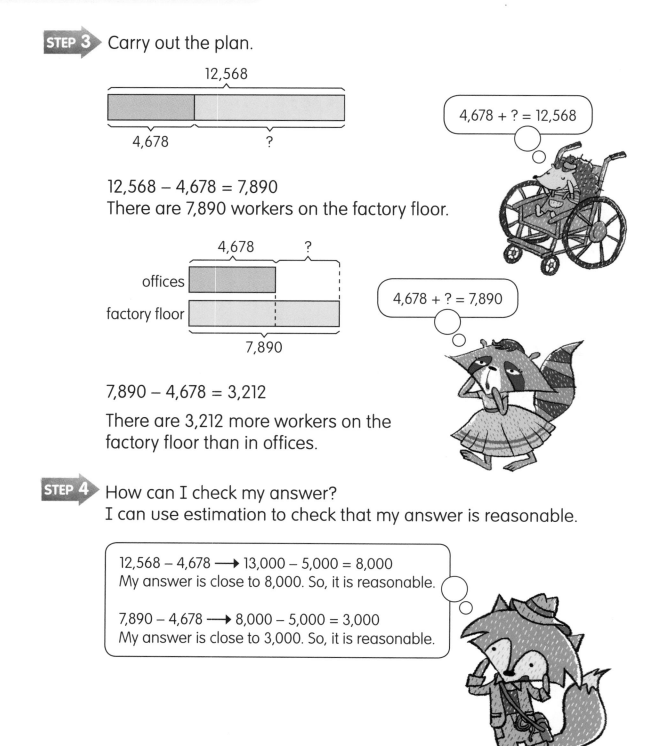

$12,568 - 4,678 = 7,890$
There are 7,890 workers on the factory floor.

4,678 + ? = 12,568

4,678 + ? = 7,890

$7,890 - 4,678 = 3,212$

There are 3,212 more workers on the factory floor than in offices.

STEP 4 How can I check my answer?
I can use estimation to check that my answer is reasonable.

$12,568 - 4,678 \longrightarrow 13,000 - 5,000 = 8,000$
My answer is close to 8,000. So, it is reasonable.

$7,890 - 4,678 \longrightarrow 8,000 - 5,000 = 3,000$
My answer is close to 3,000. So, it is reasonable.

2 Store A sold 16,245 baseball cards last year. Store A sold 5,648 more baseball cards than Store B. How many baseball cards did they sell in all?

16,245 − 5,648 = 10,597

Store B sold 10,597 baseball cards.

? + 5,648 = 16,245

16,245 + 10,597 = 26,842

They sold 26,842 baseball cards in all.

16,245 + 10,597 = ?

Use estimation to check that your answer is reasonable.

3 A museum had 101,723 visitors in June. There were 24,605 fewer visitors in July than in June. In August, there were 12,109 more visitors than the total number of visitors in June and July. How many visitors were there in August?

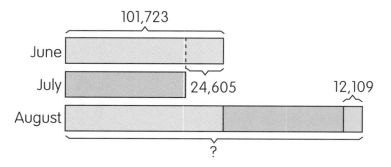

$101,723 - 24,605 = 77,118$

There were 77,118 visitors in July.

$101,723 + 77,118 = 178,841$

There were 178,841 visitors in June and July in all.

$178,841 + 12,109 = 190,950$

There were 190,950 visitors in August.

How can you check that your answer is reasonable?

4,150 (handwritten)

Hands-on Activity

Work in groups.

Activity 1   Completing stories

1) Complete each story. You may use the words and numbers in the box.

more	450	printer	700	less
computer	4,728	1,876	peaches	pears

(more, 450, printer, 700, computer crossed out)

a   Ms. Carter paid $1,150 for a computer and a printer.

The printer cost $ *450* (handwritten).

The _*computer*_ cost $ *700* *more* than the _*printer*_. (handwritten)

b   A factory produced 10,000 cans of fruit. _____ cans contained

pineapple. The rest contained peaches and pears.

There were _____ fewer cans of _____ than of pineapple.

The factory produced _____ cans of _____.

Activity 2   Creating real-world problems

1) Write a real-world problem involving addition and subtraction on the
next page. Use the words and numbers in the box below in your problem.

10,246	3,450	fewer	more	1,382
apples	oranges	rest	pieces of fruit	apricots

2) Ask another group to solve the real-world problem and explain how to
check the answers.

Real-world problem:

Solve. Draw a bar model to help you.

TRY Practice solving real-world problems involving addition and subtraction

Solve. Use the bar model to help you.

1 Mr. Nelson has $43,756 to buy furniture for his company.
He spends $2,199 on tables and $1,268 on chairs.
   a How much does Mr. Nelson spend in all?
   b How much does Mr. Nelson have left?

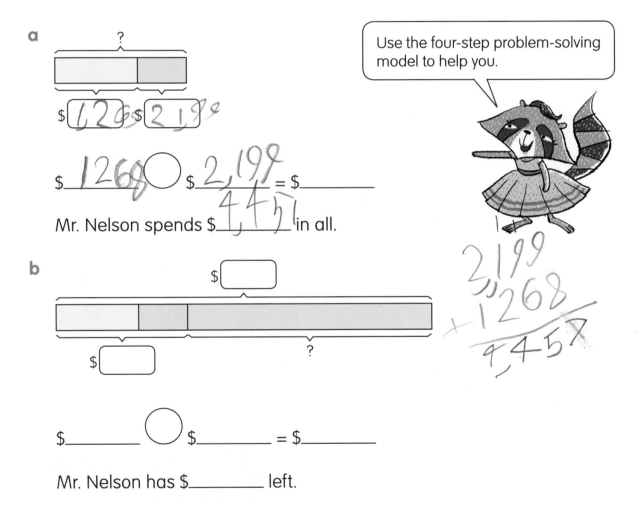

a

$ 1,268 $ 2,199

$ 1268 ◯ $ 2,199 = $_____

Mr. Nelson spends $ 4,451 in all.

Use the four-step problem-solving model to help you.

2,199
1,268
+ _____
4,457

b

$◯

$◯   ?

$_____ ◯ $_____ = $_____

Mr. Nelson has $_____ left.

2 Lily, Eli, and Matthew played a computer game. Lily scored 8,460 points and Eli scored 3,241 points. Their total score was 4,825 points more than Matthew's score. What was Matthew's score?

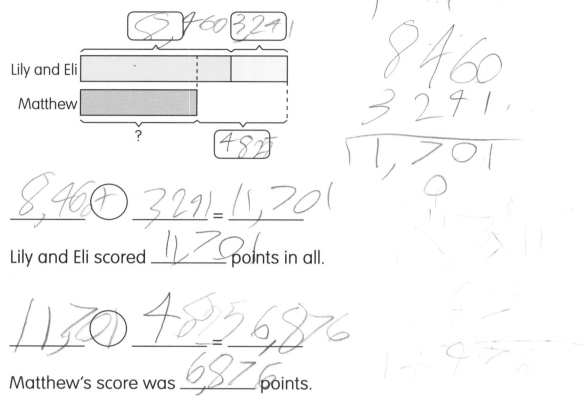

Lily and Eli

Matthew

?

$8,460 \bigoplus 3291 = 11,701$

Lily and Eli scored _____ 11,701 points in all.

$11,701 \bigcirc 4825 = 6,876$

Matthew's score was _____ 6,876 points.

3 A farm produced 3,245 kilograms of oranges and 10,550 kilograms of red and green apples. The mass of oranges was 1,034 kilograms more than the mass of red apples. What was the mass of green apples produced?

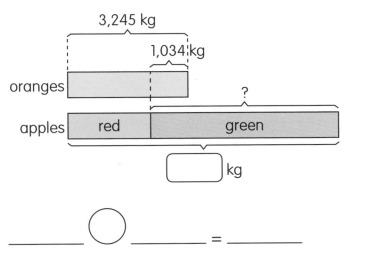

_____ ◯ _____ = _____

The farm produced _____ kilograms of red apples.

_____ ◯ _____ = _____

The mass of green apples produced was _____ kilograms.

4 Aubrey had 12,405 stamps. Ryan had 4,730 fewer stamps than Aubrey.
Aubrey gave Ryan some stamps and had 9,780 stamps left.
How many stamps did Ryan have in the end?

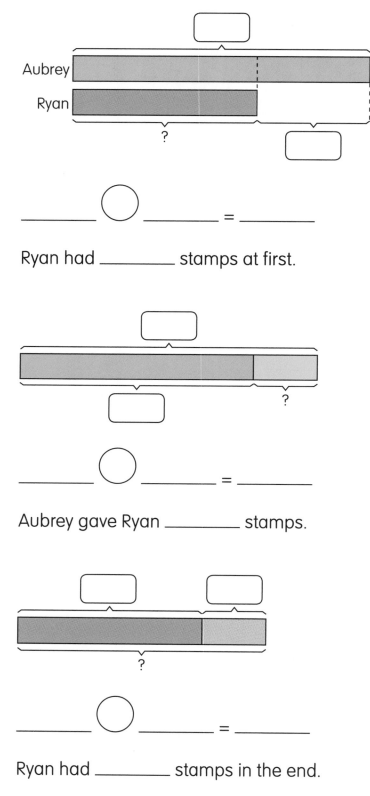

_____ ◯ _____ = _____

Ryan had _____ stamps at first.

_____ ◯ _____ = _____

Aubrey gave Ryan _____ stamps.

_____ ◯ _____ = _____

Ryan had _____ stamps in the end.

5 In a year, a store sold 102,375 pens, 43,509 more pencils than pens, and a number of rulers. The total number of pens, pencils, and rulers sold that year was 314,802. How many rulers were sold?

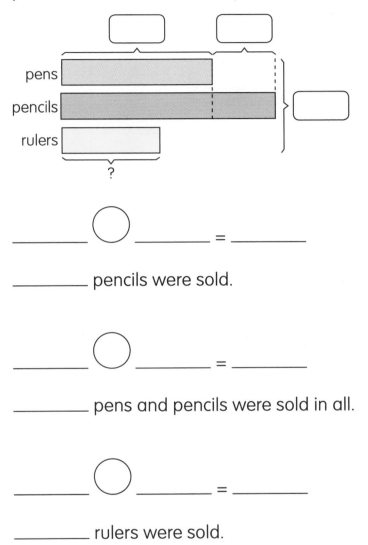

_____ ◯ _____ = _____

_____ pencils were sold.

_____ ◯ _____ = _____

_____ pens and pencils were sold in all.

_____ ◯ _____ = _____

_____ rulers were sold.

Look at the numbers in the table.

		40,432		
		30,432		
18,432	19,432	20,432	21,432	22,432
		10,432		
		432		

1 Read the numbers in the row that starts with 18,432.
   What do you notice?

2 Read the numbers in the column that starts with 40,432.
   What do you notice?

3 Read the numbers in the green boxes.
   Then, read the numbers in the yellow boxes.
   How are they alike?

4 Read the numbers in the purple boxes.
   Then, read the numbers in the blue boxes.
   How are they alike?

INDEPENDENT PRACTICE

Solve. Draw a bar model to help you.

1. A construction company needed 15,010 tiles to completely cover the lobby of a building. Some tiles were laid on the first week and 7,823 tiles were laid on the second week. At the end of the second week, 1,950 tiles were left. How many tiles were laid on the first week?

Ms. Martin and Mr. Jones saved $56,480 in all to open a coffee shop. Ms. Martin used some of her money to buy kitchen equipment and had $15,600 left. Mr. Jones spent $3,450 of his money on tables and chairs. In the end, they had $35,200 left in all.

    a How much did Ms. Martin spend on kitchen equipment?

    b How much did Ms. Martin have at first?

3 Last year, School A raised $24,950 for charity. School B raised $8,504 more than School A. School C raised $12,080 less than School B. How much did Schools B and C raise in all last year?

4. A machine produced 85,700 glass bottles on Friday. It produced 12,420 fewer bottles on Saturday than on Friday. Of the bottles produced on Saturday, 951 had cracks and were sent for recycling. The rest of the bottles from the two days were sold. How many bottles were sold in all?

Mathematical Habit 6 **Use precise mathematical language**

Look at the set of numbers.

Explain the steps you would take to order the numbers from least to greatest.

Explain how you know you are correct.

| 4,509 | 45 | 45,009 | 450 |

Problem Solving with Heuristics

1 **Mathematical Habit 8** Look for patterns

How many times does the digit 5 appear from 10,000 to 11,000?

You can use place value to find the answer.

2 **Mathematical Habit 1** Persevere in solving problems

Use the following clues to find the greatest 5-digit number.
- All five digits are different.
- None of the five digits are 1.
- The digit in the ten thousands place is greater than 7.
- The sum of all five digits is 18.
- The greatest digit is equal to the sum of the other four digits.

3 **Mathematical Habit 2** Use mathematical reasoning

Use the digits 0 to 9 to form two numbers that are 9,000 when rounded to the nearest thousand and have the greatest possible difference.
Use each digit only once.

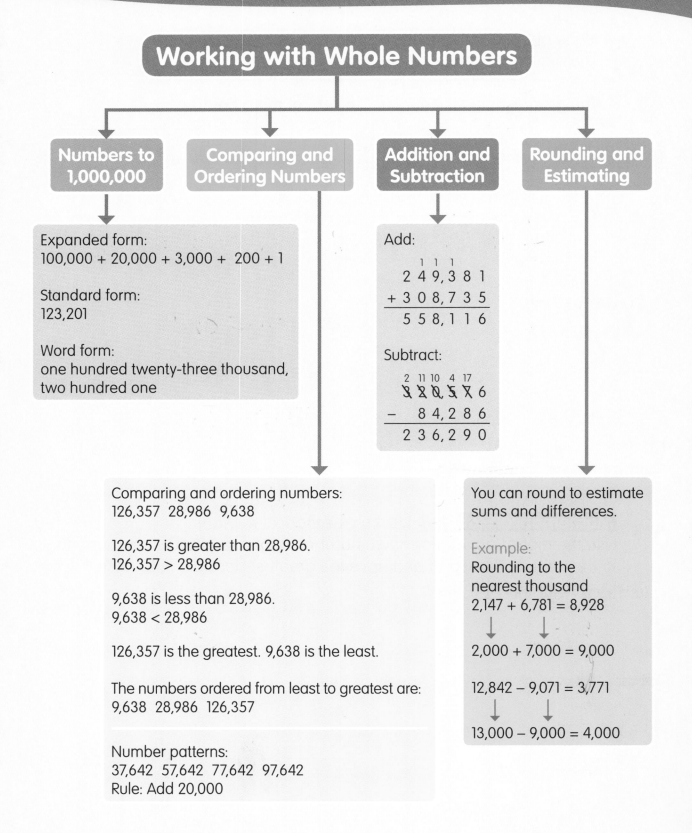

Working with Whole Numbers

Numbers to 1,000,000

Comparing and Ordering Numbers

Addition and Subtraction

Rounding and Estimating

Expanded form:
100,000 + 20,000 + 3,000 + 200 + 1

Standard form:
123,201

Word form:
one hundred twenty-three thousand, two hundred one

Add:

$$\begin{array}{r} \overset{1\ \ 1\ \ 1}{2\ 4\ 9{,}3\ 8\ 1} \\ +\ 3\ 0\ 8{,}7\ 3\ 5 \\ \hline 5\ 5\ 8{,}1\ 1\ 6 \end{array}$$

Subtract:

$$\begin{array}{r} \overset{2\ \ 11\ 10\ \ 4\ \ 17}{\cancel{3}\ \cancel{2}\ \cancel{0}{,}\cancel{5}\ \cancel{7}\ 6} \\ -\ \ \ \ 8\ 4{,}2\ 8\ 6 \\ \hline 2\ 3\ 6{,}2\ 9\ 0 \end{array}$$

Comparing and ordering numbers:
126,357 28,986 9,638

126,357 is greater than 28,986.
126,357 > 28,986

9,638 is less than 28,986.
9,638 < 28,986

126,357 is the greatest. 9,638 is the least.

The numbers ordered from least to greatest are:
9,638 28,986 126,357

Number patterns:
37,642 57,642 77,642 97,642
Rule: Add 20,000

You can round to estimate sums and differences.

Example:
Rounding to the nearest thousand
2,147 + 6,781 = 8,928
↓   ↓
2,000 + 7,000 = 9,000

12,842 − 9,071 = 3,771
↓   ↓
13,000 − 9,000 = 4,000

Name: _____ Date: _____

Write each number in standard form.

1 eighty thousand, five   _80,005_

2 two hundred thirty thousand, eight hundred ninety-one   _230,891_

Write each number in word form.

3 99,215   _Niney-niney thousand, two hundred fifteen_

4 317,990   _Three hundred seventeen thousand, nine hundred ninety_

Fill in each blank.

5 In 45,876, the value of the digit 5 is _5,000_.

6 In 634,871, the digit _6_ is in the hundred thousands place.

7 In 705,068, value of the digit 7 is _700,000_.

Complete each expanded form.

8 86,322 = 80,000 + _6,000_ + 300 + _20_ + 2

9 210,458 = _200,000_ + _10,900_ + 400 + 50 + 8

Compare each pair of numbers. Write < or >.

10 28,495 $<$ 29,854

11 210,999 $>$ 209,999

Order the numbers from greatest to least.

12 81,487   82,198   82,819   81,298

_82,819_   _82,198_   _81,487_   _81,298_
greatest   least

Find the missing number.

13 1,000 less than 67,549 is _66,549_.

Complete each number pattern.

14 24,907   23,907   22,907   21,907   20,907   _19,907_

15 42,005   42,405   42,805   43,205   _43,605_   44,005

Write the first eight numbers in a number pattern.

16 Start from 3 and use the rule "add 25."

3   28   53   78   103   128   153   178

Round each number to the nearest thousand.

17 3,516   _4,000_

18 19,472   _19,000_

Find each sum or difference. Estimate to check that your answer is reasonable.

19 7,159 + 446 = _7,605_

$$+ \begin{array}{r} 7{,}159 \\ 446 \end{array}$$

Estimate:

_7,000_ + _600_ = _____

$$\begin{array}{r} 7{,}605 \end{array} \quad 15$$

20 78,264 − 36,375 = _41,889_

$$\begin{array}{r} 78{,}264 \\ 36{,}375 \end{array}$$

Estimate:

78,264 − 36,3 = 41,889   41,889

21 68,354 + 30,879 = _99,233_ (handwritten: 99,233 64,354)

Estimate: _____ + _____ = _____

22 507,364 − 264,385 = _242,_ (handwritten: 48,233 242,979)

Estimate: _507 − 264 =_

(handwritten computations)

Solve. Draw a bar model to help you.

23 There were 23,980 toys in a large toy store. On Monday, 3,832 toys were sold. On Tuesday, 1,054 more toys were sold than on Monday. How many toys were left in the shop?

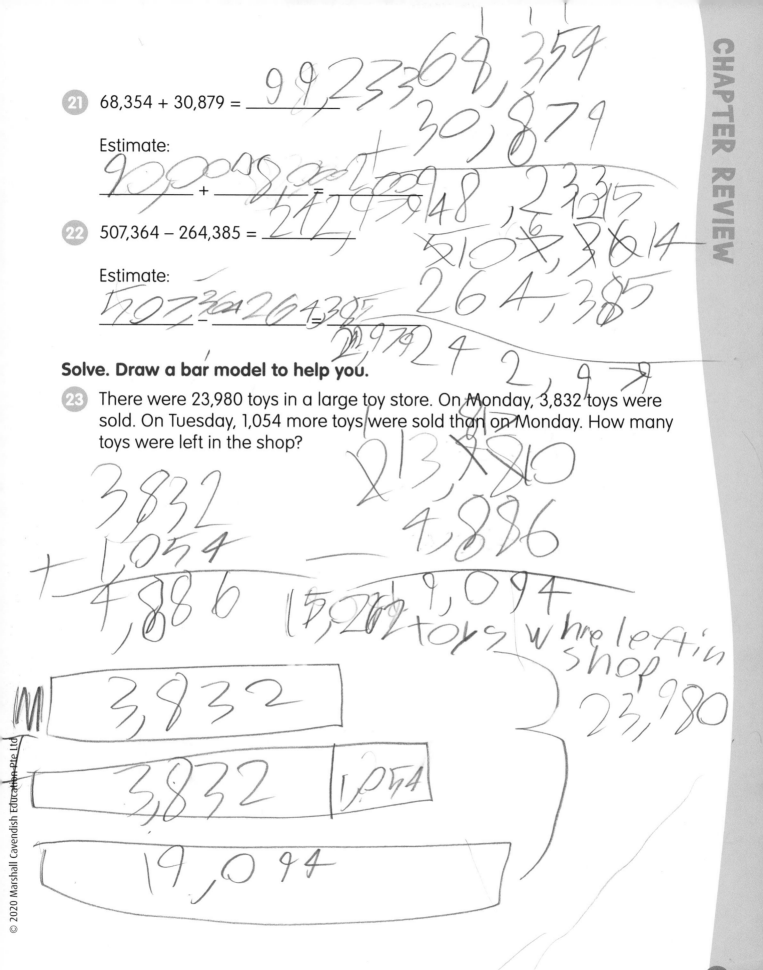

$$3832 + 1054 = 4886$$

$$4886 + 4886 = 4,094$$

15,269 toys whre left in shop

3,832

3,832 | 1,054

19,094

Assessment Prep

Answer each question.

24 Which two numbers make the comparison true?

$$\boxed{} > 64{,}891$$

(A) 54,891

(B) 64,918

(C) 64,779

(D) 63,981

(E) 65,012

25 In which number is the value of the digit 6 ten times the value of the digit 6 in 463,170?

(A) 65,127

(B) 147,610

(C) 609,180

(D) 826,459

26 Determine if the following equation is true or false.
684 − 567 = 284 − 267
Write your answer and explanation in the space below.

27 Jacob scored 18,140 points in the first round of a computer game. In the second round of the game, he scored 2,780 more points than in the first round. About how many points did he score in the second round of the game? Write your work and answer in the space below.

Game Scores

1 Evelyn bought a new sports video game on Monday. She kept a record of the number of points she scored during the week in a table. She scored 21,100 points on Monday. Help her complete the table.

Day	Score
Monday	21,100
Tuesday	
Wednesday	

a Evelyn scored sixteen thousand, ninety points on Tuesday. Write her score in the table.
Did she score fewer points on Monday or on Tuesday?
How many points fewer? Show your work.

b Evelyn scored nine hundred fewer points Wednesday than on Monday. How many points did Evelyn score on Wednesday? Write her score in the table. Use < or > to compare her scores for Tuesday and Wednesday.

c   Order Evelyn's scores for the three days from greatest to least.

_____ _____ _____
   greatest   least

2 In the game, Evelyn started as a Level 1 player. She then moved up one level for every 10,000 points she scored. At the end of the first week, her total score was 68,200 points.

a   Draw a number line to show the level Evelyn achieved at the end of the first week.

b   During the second week, Evelyn scored 45,850 points. What was her total score at the end of the second week? Show your work.

Rubric

Point(s)	Level	My Performance
7–8	4	• Most of my answers are correct. • I showed complete understanding of what I have learned. • I used the correct strategies to solve the problems. • I explained my answers and mathematical thinking clearly and completely.
5–6.5	3	• Some of my answers are correct. • I showed some understanding of what I have learned. • I used some correct strategies to solve the problems. • I explained my answers and mathematical thinking clearly.
3–4.5	2	• A few of my answers are correct. • I showed little understanding of what I have learned. • I used a few correct strategies to solve the problems. • I explained some of my answers and mathematical thinking clearly.
0–2.5	1	• A few of my answers are correct. • I showed little or no understanding of what I have learned. • I used a few strategies to solve the problems. • I did not explain my answers and mathematical thinking clearly.

Teacher's Comments

STEAM

Sports Stadiums

Is there a sports stadium near you? How many people can it hold? 1,000? 5,000? 10,000? More?

Some of the largest sports stadiums in the world are in the United States. The largest can hold more than 100,000 fans.

Task

Stadium Game

Work in pairs to design a stadium game.

1. Use library or internet resources to learn more about the largest sports stadiums in the United States. Make a "Top Ten" list. Next, organize the information you find in a table. Write the name of each stadium. Then, record its capacity, or the total number of people it can hold.

2. Together, use the information in your table to design a math game.

3. List the rules for your game and make or provide the materials players need. Illustrate your game to make it more interesting.

4. Exchange games and play. Afterward, discuss the game and ways to make it even more challenging.

How can you multiply by a 2-digit number?
How can you divide whole numbers?

Multiplying as skip counting

Skip count by 2.

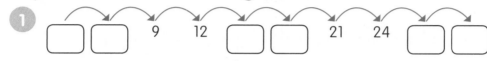

0 1 2 3 4 5 6 7 8
Start

$4 \times 2 = 8$

▶ **Quick Check**

Skip count. Find each missing number.

1 ☐ ☐ 9 12 ☐ ☐ 21 24 ☐ ☐

Knowing multiplication facts of 2, 3, 4, 5, and 10

$1 \times 2 = 2$	$1 \times 3 = 3$	$1 \times 4 = 4$	$1 \times 5 = 5$	$1 \times 10 = 10$
$2 \times 2 = 4$	$2 \times 3 = 6$	$2 \times 4 = 8$	$2 \times 5 = 10$	$2 \times 10 = 20$
$3 \times 2 = 6$	$3 \times 3 = 9$	$3 \times 4 = 12$	$3 \times 5 = 15$	$3 \times 10 = 30$
$4 \times 2 = 8$	$4 \times 3 = 12$	$4 \times 4 = 16$	$4 \times 5 = 20$	$4 \times 10 = 40$
$5 \times 2 = 10$	$5 \times 3 = 15$	$5 \times 4 = 20$	$5 \times 5 = 25$	$5 \times 10 = 50$
$6 \times 2 = 12$	$6 \times 3 = 18$	$6 \times 4 = 24$	$6 \times 5 = 30$	$6 \times 10 = 60$
$7 \times 2 = 14$	$7 \times 3 = 21$	$7 \times 4 = 28$	$7 \times 5 = 35$	$7 \times 10 = 70$
$8 \times 2 = 16$	$8 \times 3 = 24$	$8 \times 4 = 32$	$8 \times 5 = 40$	$8 \times 10 = 80$
$9 \times 2 = 18$	$9 \times 3 = 27$	$9 \times 4 = 36$	$9 \times 5 = 45$	$9 \times 10 = 90$
$10 \times 2 = 20$	$10 \times 3 = 30$	$10 \times 4 = 40$	$10 \times 5 = 50$	$10 \times 10 = 100$

▶ **Quick Check**

Multiply.

2 $3 \times 2 =$ _____

3 $4 \times 3 =$ _____

4 $8 \times 3 =$ _____

5 $7 \times 4 =$ _____

6 $9 \times 5 =$ _____

7 $5 \times 10 =$ _____

Knowing multiplication facts of 6, 7, 8, 9, 11, and 12

1 × 6 = 6	1 × 7 = 7	1 × 8 = 8	1 × 9 = 9	1 × 11 = 11	1 × 12 = 12
2 × 6 = 12	2 × 7 = 14	2 × 8 = 16	2 × 9 = 18	2 × 11 = 22	2 × 12 = 24
3 × 6 = 18	3 × 7 = 21	3 × 8 = 24	3 × 9 = 27	3 × 11 = 33	3 × 12 = 36
4 × 6 = 24	4 × 7 = 28	4 × 8 = 32	4 × 9 = 36	4 × 11 = 44	4 × 12 = 48
5 × 6 = 30	5 × 7 = 35	5 × 8 = 40	5 × 9 = 45	5 × 11 = 55	5 × 12 = 60
6 × 6 = 36	6 × 7 = 42	6 × 8 = 48	6 × 9 = 54	6 × 11 = 66	6 × 12 = 72
7 × 6 = 42	7 × 7 = 49	7 × 8 = 56	7 × 9 = 63	7 × 11 = 77	7 × 12 = 84
8 × 6 = 48	8 × 7 = 56	8 × 8 = 64	8 × 9 = 72	8 × 11 = 88	8 × 12 = 96
9 × 6 = 54	9 × 7 = 63	9 × 8 = 72	9 × 9 = 81	9 × 11 = 99	9 × 12 = 108
10 × 6 = 60	10 × 7 = 70	10 × 8 = 80	10 × 9 = 90	10 × 11 = 110	10 × 12 = 120

▶ **Quick Check**

Multiply.

8 3 × 7 = _____

9 4 × 8 = _____

10 6 × 9 = _____

11 3 × 9 = _____

12 4 × 11 = _____

13 5 × 12 = _____

Multiplying two numbers to find a product

3 × 4 = 12
12 is the product of 3 and 4.
The product 12 can be divided exactly by 3 and 4.

▶ **Quick Check**

Fill in each blank.

14 27 = _____ × 9

15 27 is the product of _____ and _____.

16 The product 27 can be divided exactly by 3 and _____.

Multiplying using models

Multiply 32 by 4.

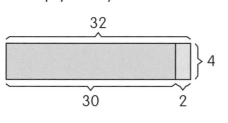

32×4
$= (30 \times 4) + (2 \times 4)$
$= 120 + 8$
$= 128$

Find 617×2.

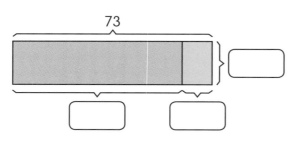

617×2
$= (600 \times 2) + (10 \times 2) + (7 \times 2)$
$= 1,200 + 20 + 14$
$= 1,234$

▶ Quick Check

Use the area model to find each product. Show your work.

17 $73 \times 5 = $ _____

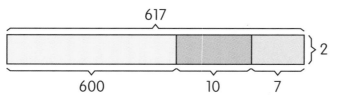

18 $408 \times 7 = $ _____

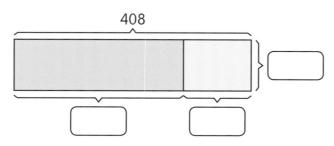

Multiplying without regrouping

Find 132 × 2.

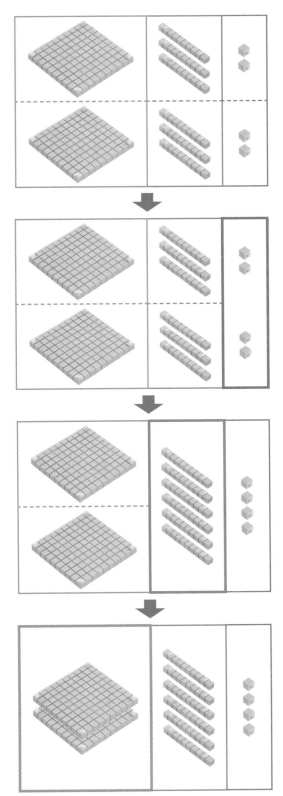

Step 1
Multiply the **ones** by 2.
2 ones × 2 = 4 ones

	1	3	2
×			2
			4

Step 2
Multiply the **tens** by 2.
3 tens × 2 = 6 tens

	1	3	2
×			2
		6	4

Step 3
Multiply the **hundreds** by 2.
1 hundred × 2 = 2 hundreds

	1	3	2
×			2
	2	6	4

So, 132 × 2 = 264.

▶ **Quick Check**

Multiply.

19 32 × 3 = _____

20 41 × 2 = _____

21 214 × 2 = _____

22 302 × 3 = _____

Multiplying with regrouping

Find the product of 235 and 7.

$235 \times 7 = ?$

Step 1
Multiply the **ones** by 7.
5 ones × 7 = 35 ones

Regroup the ones.
35 ones = 3 tens 5 ones

Step 2
Multiply the **tens** by 7.
3 tens × 7 = 21 tens

Add the tens.
21 tens + 3 tens = 24 tens

Regroup the tens.
24 tens = 2 hundreds 4 tens

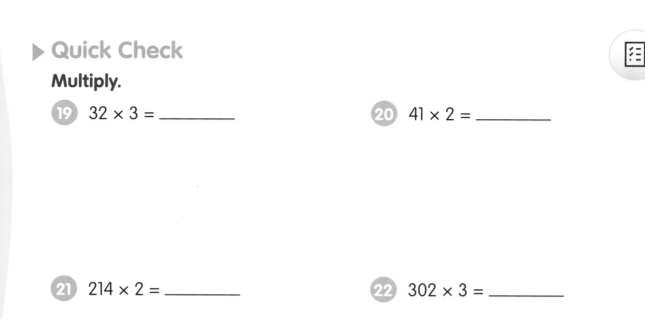

Step 3

Multiply the **hundreds** by 7.
2 hundreds × 7 = 14 hundreds

Add the hundreds.
14 hundreds + 2 hundreds = 16 hundreds

Regroup the hundreds.
16 hundreds = 1 thousand 6 hundreds

So, 235 × 7 = 1,645.

The product of 235 and 7 is 1,645.

▶ **Quick Check**

Multiply.

23 48 × 3 = _____

24 73 × 6 = _____

25 471 × 6 = _____

26 285 × 8 = _____

Dividing to share equally

Divide 20  into 5 equal groups.

How many does each group have?

$20 \div 5 = 4$

Each group has 4 .

▶ **Quick Check**

Solve.

27 Divide 21 stamps into 7 equal groups.
How many stamps does each group have?

Dividing to form equal groups

Divide 20 equally so that there are 5 in each group.
How many groups are there?

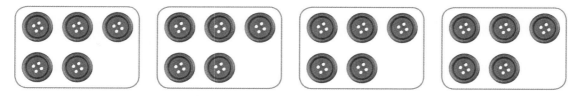

$20 \div 5 = 4$

There are 4 groups.

▶ Quick Check

Solve.

28 Paula has 18 books. She reads 2 books each week.
How many weeks will it take Paula to read all of the books?

Dividing using related multiplication facts

$63 \div 9 = ?$

Recall the multiplication facts of 9.
$7 \times 9 = 63$
So, $63 \div 9 = 7$.

▶ Quick Check

Fill in each missing number.

29 $36 \div 9 = ?$

_____ $\times 9 = 36$

So, $36 \div 9 =$ _____.

30 $49 \div 7 = ?$

$7 \times$ _____ $= 49$

So, $49 \div 7 =$ _____.

Rounding and estimation

You can check that your answers are reasonable by using rounding to estimate sums and differences.

a   Find the value of 15,780 + 8,316. Estimate to check that your answer is reasonable.

15,780 + 8,316 = 24,096
Estimate:
16,000 + 8,000 = 24,000
24,096 is close to 24,000. So, the answer is reasonable.

b   Find the value of 2,439 − 441. Estimate to check that your answer is reasonable.

2,439 − 441 = 1,998
Estimate:
2,400 − 400 = 2,000
1,998 is close to 2,000. So, the answer is reasonable.

▶ **Quick Check**

Find each sum or difference. Use rounding to check that each answer is reasonable.

31   197 + 1,826 = _____

Estimate:

_____ + _____ = _____

32   14,345 − 6,517 = _____

Estimate:

_____ − _____ = _____

Solving two-step real-world problems

There are 18 blue marbles and 24 red marbles in a bag. Avery buys 5 bags of these marbles. How many marbles does Avery have in all?

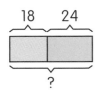

$18 + 24 = 42$

There are 42 marbles in each bag.

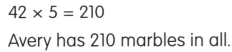

$42 \times 5 = 210$

Avery has 210 marbles in all.

▶ **Quick Check**

Solve. Draw a bar model to help you.

33 Alexander has 34 meters of cloth. He uses 6 meters to make a costume for a play. He cuts the remaining cloth into 7 equal pieces. What is the length of each piece of cloth?

Multiplying by a 1-Digit or 2-Digit Number

Learning Objectives:
- Multiply a 4-digit number by a 1-digit number.
- Multiply a 2-digit or 3-digit number by a 2-digit number.
- Estimate products.

THINK

Without multiplying, Orion says that 24 × 12 is equal to 240 × 2. Do you agree? Why? Write at least two other multiplication expressions that are equal to 24 × 12.

ENGAGE

Use 1,000 100 10 1 to model this problem.

Dara has 2 boxes of shells. Each box contains 2,153 shells. How many shells does he have in all? Show two ways to find your answer. Explain your thinking to your partner.

LEARN Multiply by a 1-digit number

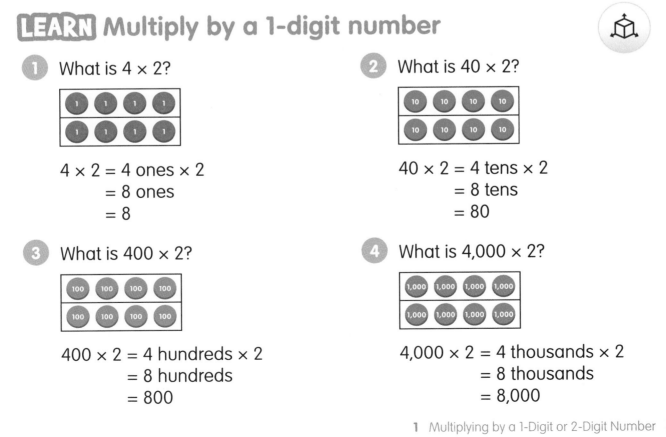

1 What is 4 × 2?

4 × 2 = 4 ones × 2
      = 8 ones
      = 8

2 What is 40 × 2?

40 × 2 = 4 tens × 2
       = 8 tens
       = 80

3 What is 400 × 2?

400 × 2 = 4 hundreds × 2
        = 8 hundreds
        = 800

4 What is 4,000 × 2?

4,000 × 2 = 4 thousands × 2
         = 8 thousands
         = 8,000

5 A store has 2 boxes of baseball cards. Each box has 1,403 cards. How many cards does the store have in all?

Multiply 1,403 by 2 to find out.

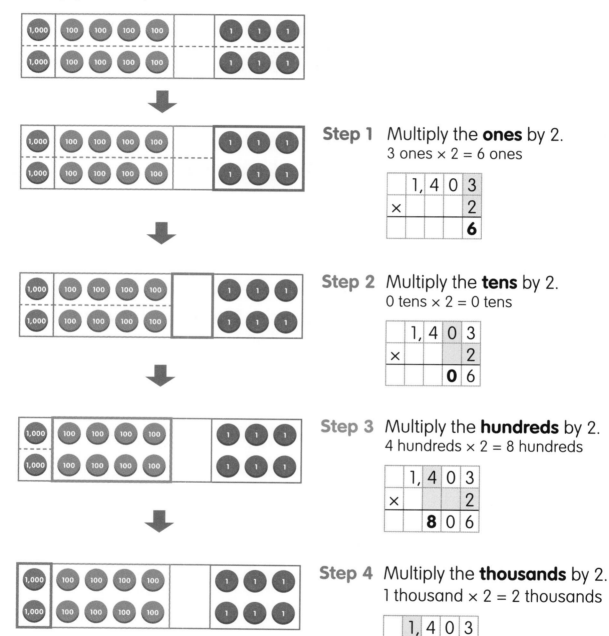

Step 1 Multiply the **ones** by 2.
3 ones × 2 = 6 ones

	1,	4	0	3
×				2
				6

Step 2 Multiply the **tens** by 2.
0 tens × 2 = 0 tens

	1,	4	0	3
×				2
			0	6

Step 3 Multiply the **hundreds** by 2.
4 hundreds × 2 = 8 hundreds

	1,	4	0	3
×				2
		8	0	6

Step 4 Multiply the **thousands** by 2.
1 thousand × 2 = 2 thousands

	1,	4	0	3
×				2
	2,	8	0	6

1,403 × 2 = 2,806

The store has 2,806 cards in all.

You can also use an area model to multiply.

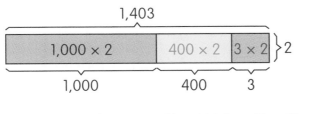

1,403

| 1,000 × 2 | 400 × 2 | 3 × 2 | } 2
| 1,000 | 400 | 3 |

Find the area of each rectangle. Then, add.

$1,403 \times 2 = (1,000 \times 2) + (400 \times 2) + (3 \times 2)$
$\qquad = 2,000 + 800 + 6$
$\qquad = 2,806$

6 Find the product of 3,341 and 3.

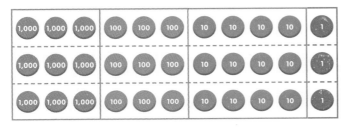

Step 1 Multiply the **ones** by 3.
1 one × 3 = 3 ones

	3,	3	4	1
×				3
				3

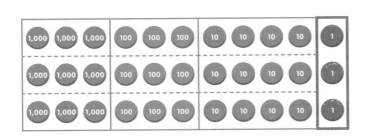

Step 2 Multiply the **tens** by 3.
4 tens × 3 = 12 tens

Regroup the tens.
12 tens = 1 hundred 2 tens

			1	
	3,	3	4	1
×				3
			2	3

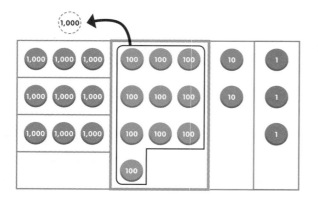

Step 3 Multiply the **hundreds** by 3.
3 hundreds × 3 = 9 hundreds

Add the hundreds.
9 hundreds + 1 hundred
= 10 hundreds

Regroup the hundreds.
10 hundreds = 1 thousand

	1	1		
	3,	3	4	1
×				3
		0	2	3

Step 4 Multiply the **thousands** by 3.
3 thousands × 3 = 9 thousands

Add the thousands.
9 thousands + 1 thousand
= 10 thousands

Regroup the thousands.
10 thousands = 1 ten thousand

	1	1		
	3,	3	4	1
×				3
1	**0,**	0	2	3

3,341 × 3 = 10,023

The product of 3,341 and 3 is 10,023.

How can you use an area model
to find the product of 3,341 and 3?

TRY Practice multiplying by a 1-digit number

Multiply.

1. $3 \times 2{,}000 =$ _____

2. $5 \times 1{,}000 =$ _____

3. $2{,}000 \times 2 =$ _____

4. $3{,}000 \times 3 =$ _____

Use the area model to find each product.

5.

2,340

$\}3$

[___] [___] [___]

$2{,}340 \times 3 = ($ _____ $\times$ ____$) + ($ _____ $\times$ ____$) + ($ _____ $\times$ ____$)$

$=$ _____ $+$ _____ $+$ _____

$=$ _____

6.

1,427

$\}4$

[___] [___] [___] [___]

$1{,}427 \times 4 = ($ ____ $\times$ ___$) + ($ ____ $\times$ ___$) + ($ ____ $\times$ ___$) + ($ ____ $\times$ ___$)$

$=$ _____ $+$ _____ $+$ _____ $+$ _____

$=$ _____

Multiply.

7　1,132 × 3 = _____

$$
\begin{array}{r}
1,132 \\
\times \qquad 3 \\
\hline
\end{array}
$$

8　2,014 × 2 = _____

$$
\begin{array}{r}
2,014 \\
\times \qquad 2 \\
\hline
\end{array}
$$

Multiply. Show your work.

9　3,524 × 3 = _____

10　4,576 × 8 = _____

11　3,568 × 9 = _____

12　8,125 × 4 = _____

MATH SHARING

Mathematical Habit　1　Persevere in solving problems

I multiplied 89 by 3 mentally in this way:
89 = 80 + 9
80 × 3 = 240
9 × 3 = 27
240 + 27 = 267

Use the same method to find 67 × 3 mentally.

ENGAGE

1 Axel arranges 30 rows of 156 red seats in a concert hall.
Madelyn arranges 3 rows of 156 blue seats and 10 rows of 156 red seats in another concert hall.

   a How many seats are arranged in each hall?

   b Are the number of seats in both halls the same?

Explain your reasons.

2 Find the number of seats in a concert hall that has 50 rows of 238 seats in each row.

LEARN Multiply by tens

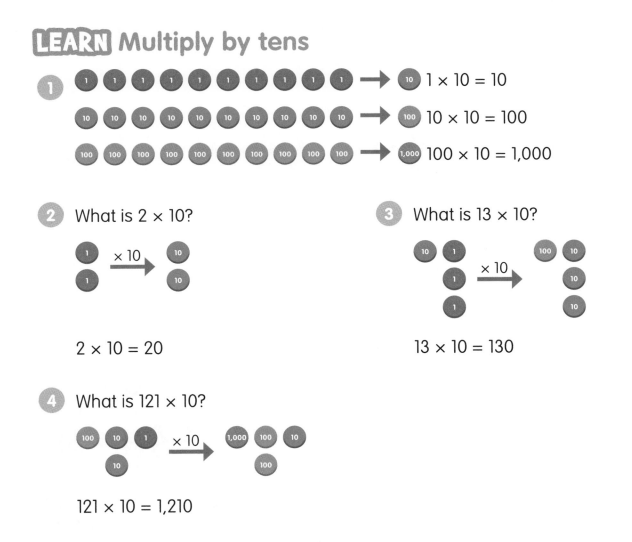

1

$1 \times 10 = 10$

$10 \times 10 = 100$

$100 \times 10 = 1,000$

2 What is 2×10?

$2 \times 10 = 20$

3 What is 13×10?

$13 \times 10 = 130$

4 What is 121×10?

$121 \times 10 = 1,210$

5 What is 32 × 20?

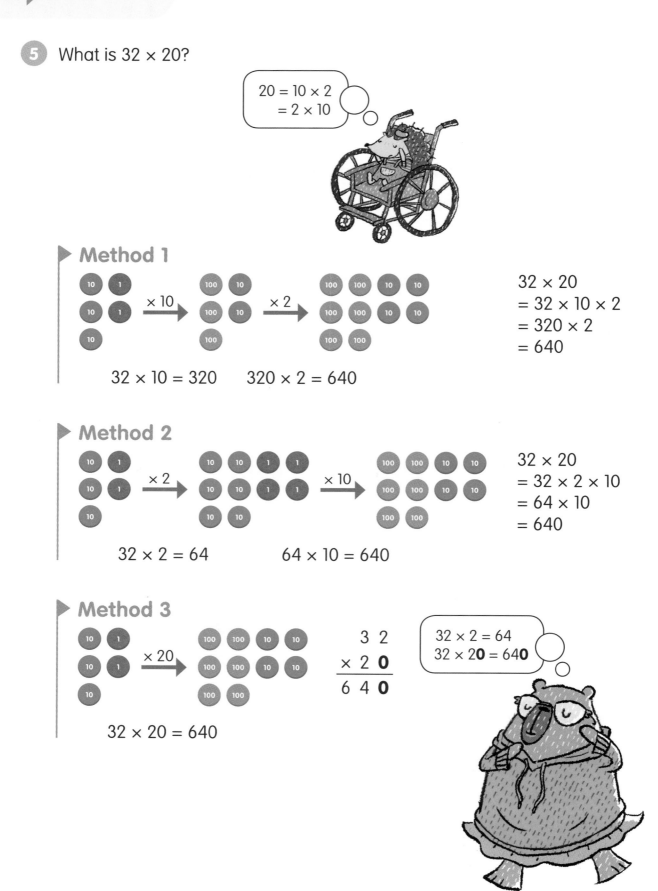

20 = 10 × 2
= 2 × 10

▶ **Method 1**

32 × 10 = 320   320 × 2 = 640

32 × 20
= 32 × 10 × 2
= 320 × 2
= 640

▶ **Method 2**

32 × 2 = 64   64 × 10 = 640

32 × 20
= 32 × 2 × 10
= 64 × 10
= 640

▶ **Method 3**

32 × 20 = 640

```
    3 2
×   2 0
───────
  6 4 0
```

32 × 2 = 64
32 × 2**0** = 64**0**

6 What is 102×30?

▶ **Method 1**

$$102 \times 30 = 102 \times 10 \times 3$$
$$= 1,020 \times 3$$
$$= 3,060$$

> $30 = 10 \times 3$
> $= 3 \times 10$

▶ **Method 2**

$$102 \times 30 = 102 \times 3 \times 10$$
$$= 306 \times 10$$
$$= 3,060$$

▶ **Method 3**

$$\begin{array}{r} 1\ 0\ 2 \\ \times\quad 3\ \mathbf{0} \\ \hline 3,0\ 6\ \mathbf{0} \end{array}$$

$$102 \times 30 = 3,060$$

> $102 \times 3 = 306$
> $102 \times 3\mathbf{0} = 3,06\mathbf{0}$

Hands-on Activity Explaining how to multiply by tens

Work in pairs.

① Use ⑩,⑩⑩⑩ ①,⑩⑩⑩ ⑩⑩ ⑩ ① to show and explain 3×10 to your partner.

② Ask your partner to use ⑩,⑩⑩⑩ ①,⑩⑩⑩ ⑩⑩ ⑩ ① to show and explain 3×20.

③ Trade places. Repeat ① and ② with each of the following.

a 7×10 and 7×30 b 18×10 and 18×40

c 23×10 and 23×50 d 105×10 and 105×20

e 80×10 and 80×20 f 600×10 and 600×30

TRY Practice multiplying by tens

Multiply.

1. $16 \times 10 = $ _____

2. $89 \times 10 = $ _____

3. $175 \times 10 = $ _____

Fill in each missing number.

4. $7 \times 40 = 7 \times$ ____ $\times 10$

   $= $ _____ $\times 10$

   $= $ _____

5. $5 \times 20 = 5 \times 10 \times 2$

   $= $ _____ $\times 2$

   $= $ _____

6. $70 \times 40 = $ _____ $\times$ ____ $\times 10$

   $= $ _____ $\times 10$

   $= $ _____

7. $50 \times 20 = 50 \times 10 \times$ ____

   $= $ _____ $\times$ ____

   $= $ _____

8. $700 \times 40 = $ _____ $\times$ ____ $\times 10$

   $= $ _____ $\times 10$

   $= $ _____

9. $500 \times 20 = 500 \times 10 \times$ ____

   $= $ _____ $\times$ ____

   $= $ _____

10. $78 \times 60 = 78 \times$ ____ $\times 10$

    $= $ _____ $\times 10$

    $= $ _____

11. $512 \times 80 = 512 \times 10 \times$ ____

    $= $ _____ $\times$ ____

    $= $ _____

Find the product of each pair of numbers. Show your work.

12. 47 and 50

13. 30 and 20

14. 315 and 60

15. 575 and 70

ENGAGE

a Use 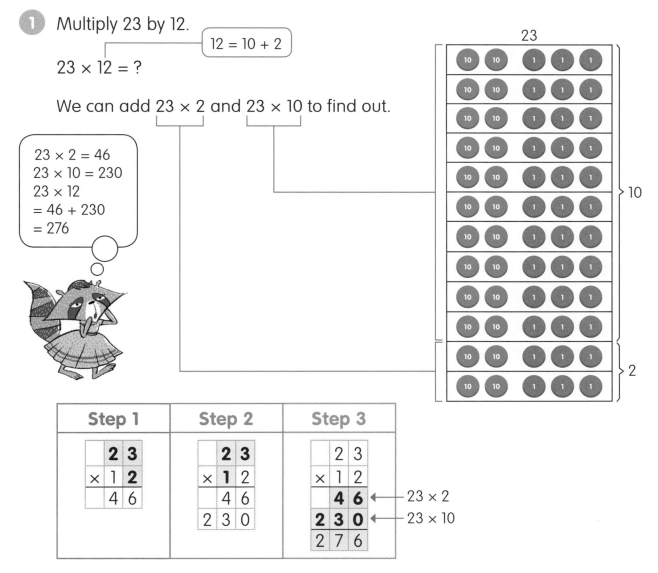 to model the problem:

John wrote the steps he took to find the value of 23 × 12.

STEP 1 23 × 10 = _____

STEP 2 23 × _____ = _____

So, 23 × 12 = _____

b Using the same way, write down the steps you take to find the value of 428 × 15.

LEARN Multiply by a 2-digit number

1 Multiply 23 by 12.

12 = 10 + 2

23 × 12 = ?

We can add 23 × 2 and 23 × 10 to find out.

23 × 2 = 46
23 × 10 = 230
23 × 12
= 46 + 230
= 276

23

10

2

Step 1	Step 2	Step 3
2 3 × 1 2 4 6	2 3 × 1 2 4 6 2 3 0	2 3 × 1 2 4 6 ← 23 × 2 2 3 0 ← 23 × 10 2 7 6

So, 23 × 12 = 276.

You can also use an area model to multiply 23 by 12.

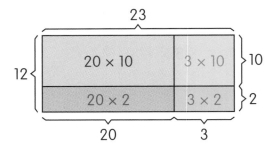

$23 \times 12 = (20 \times 10) + (3 \times 10) + (20 \times 2) + (3 \times 2)$
$= 200 + 30 + 40 + 6$
$= 276$

2 Multiply 359 by 24.

$24 = 20 + 4$

$359 \times 24 = ?$

You can add 359×4 and 359×20 to find out.

$359 \times 4 = 1,436$
$359 \times 20 = 7,180$
$359 \times 24 = 1,436 + 7,180$
$= 8,616$

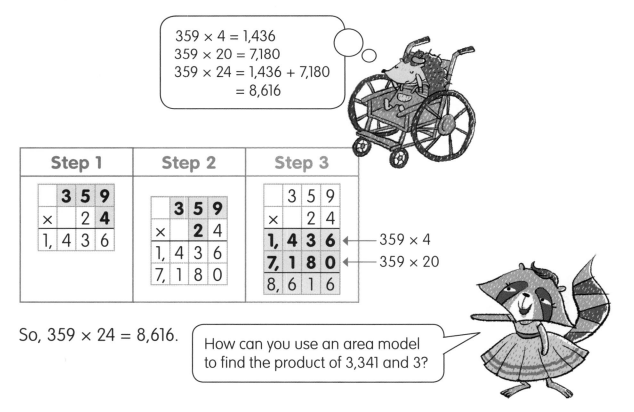

Step 1	Step 2	Step 3

So, $359 \times 24 = 8,616$.

How can you use an area model to find the product of 3,341 and 3?

TRY Practice multiplying by a 2-digit number

Use the area model to find each product.

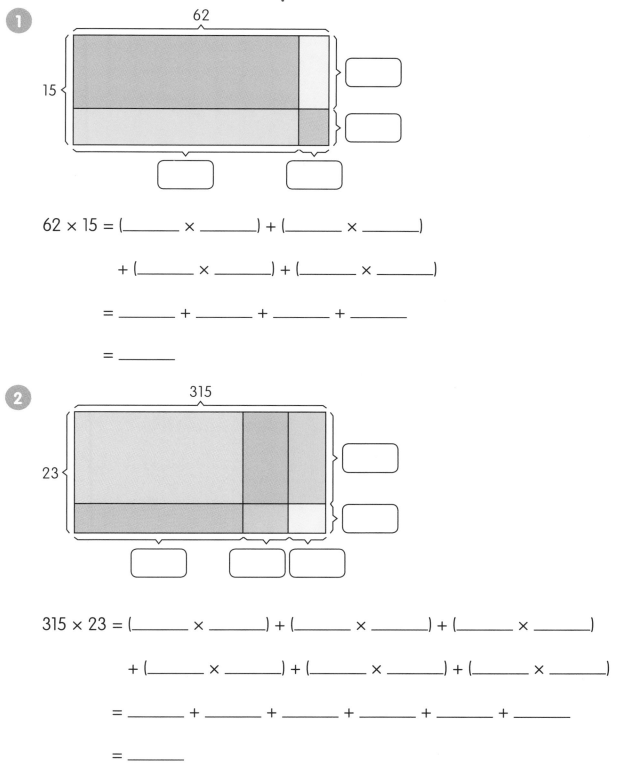

1

62

15

$62 \times 15 = ($ _____ $\times$ _____ $) + ($ _____ $\times$ _____ $)$

$+ ($ _____ $\times$ _____ $) + ($ _____ $\times$ _____ $)$

$=$ _____ $+$ _____ $+$ _____ $+$ _____

$=$ _____

2

315

23

$315 \times 23 = ($ _____ $\times$ _____ $) + ($ _____ $\times$ _____ $) + ($ _____ $\times$ _____ $)$

$+ ($ _____ $\times$ _____ $) + ($ _____ $\times$ _____ $) + ($ _____ $\times$ _____ $)$

$=$ _____ $+$ _____ $+$ _____ $+$ _____ $+$ _____ $+$ _____

$=$ _____

Multiply.

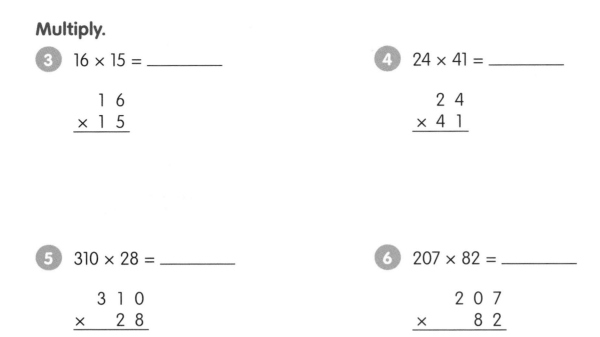

3 $16 \times 15 =$ _____

$$\begin{array}{r} 1\;6 \\ \times\;1\;5 \\ \hline \end{array}$$

4 $24 \times 41 =$ _____

$$\begin{array}{r} 2\;4 \\ \times\;4\;1 \\ \hline \end{array}$$

5 $310 \times 28 =$ _____

$$\begin{array}{r} 3\;1\;0 \\ \times\;\;\;2\;8 \\ \hline \end{array}$$

6 $207 \times 82 =$ _____

$$\begin{array}{r} 2\;0\;7 \\ \times\;\;\;8\;2 \\ \hline \end{array}$$

Multiply. Show your work.

7 $36 \times 49 =$ _____

8 $78 \times 42 =$ _____

9 $423 \times 19 =$ _____

10 $891 \times 74 =$ _____

ENGAGE

What are some possible estimates for 1,253 × 3? Create a story to represent the problem. What are two ways you can show that your estimate was reasonable?

LEARN Estimate products

1 A school bought 2 boxes of notebooks. Each box contained 326 notebooks. How many notebooks did the school buy?

326 × 2 = 652

The school bought 652 notebooks.

Estimate to check that the answer is reasonable.
You can round 326 to the nearest hundred and multiply by 2.

Number	Rounded to the Nearest Hundred
326	300

Multiply: 300 × 2 = 600
The estimated product is 600.

The answer 652 is close to 600.
So, it is reasonable.

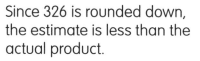

Since 326 is rounded down, the estimate is less than the actual product.

Hands-on Activity Estimating products

Work in pairs.

(1) Roll  four times to make a 4-digit number. Record the number in the table below.

(2) Ask your partner to roll the 🎲. If the number is 0 or 1, he or she should roll again. Record the number in the table.

(3) Fill in the table.

   a Estimate the product of the numbers in (1) and (2).

   b Multiply the numbers in (1) and (2).

(4) Trade places. Repeat (1) to (3) three more times.

(5) Compare each answer with the estimated value.
   Is each answer reasonable? Explain. Fill in the table.

4-digit Number	1-digit Number	Estimated Value	Answer	Check Reasonableness

TRY Practice estimating products

Find the product. Use rounding to check that your answer is reasonable.

1. Find 742 × 59.

742 × 59 = _____

The answer is _____.

Estimate to check that the answer is reasonable.
You can round each number to the greatest place value and then multiply.

Number	Rounded to the Greatest Place Value
742	
59	

Multiply: _____ × _____ = _____

The estimated product is _____.

Is your answer reasonable? Explain.

Math Talk

Emma uses a different method to estimate the product of 742 and 59. She rounds both numbers to the nearest hundred before multiplying them. What is her estimated product?

Which method gives a closer estimate? Why?

Find each product. Estimate to check that your answer is reasonable.

2 123 × 7 = _____

$$
\begin{array}{r}
1\ 2\ 3 \\
\times \qquad 7 \\
\hline
\end{array}
$$

Estimate:

_____ × 7 = _____

3 439 × 5 = _____

$$
\begin{array}{r}
4\ 3\ 9 \\
\times \qquad 5 \\
\hline
\end{array}
$$

Estimate:

_____ × 5 = _____

4 3,241 × 4 = _____

$$
\begin{array}{r}
3,2\ 4\ 1 \\
\times \qquad 4 \\
\hline
\end{array}
$$

Estimate:

_____ × 4 = _____

5 5,782 × 3 = _____

$$
\begin{array}{r}
5,7\ 8\ 2 \\
\times \qquad 3 \\
\hline
\end{array}
$$

Estimate:

_____ × 3 = _____

6 57 × 12 = _____

$$
\begin{array}{r}
5\ 7 \\
\times\ 1\ 2 \\
\hline
\end{array}
$$

Estimate:

_____ × _____ = _____

7 281 × 38 = _____

$$
\begin{array}{r}
2\ 8\ 1 \\
\times \qquad 3\ 8 \\
\hline
\end{array}
$$

Estimate:

_____ × _____ = _____

INDEPENDENT PRACTICE

Multiply. Show your work.

1. $27 \times 60 =$ _____

2. $54 \times 80 =$ _____

Draw an area model to find each product. Show your work.

3. $3,405 \times 8 = ?$

4. $52 \times 19 = ?$

Multiply. Show your work.
Estimate to check that each answer is reasonable.

5 3,094 × 4 = _____

6 4,173 × 6 = _____

Estimate:

_____ × _____ = _____

Estimate:

_____ × _____ = _____

7 38 × 17 = _____

8 32 × 65 = _____

Estimate:

_____ × _____ = _____

Estimate:

_____ × _____ = _____

9 124 × 56 = _____

10 603 × 76 = _____

Estimate:

_____ × _____ = _____

Estimate:

_____ × _____ = _____

2 Quotient and Remainder

Learning Objective:
• Find the quotient and remainder in a division problem.

> **New Vocabulary**
> remainder

THINK

There are some apples in a basket. If I pack the apples into bags of 5, there will be 1 apple remaining. If I pack the apples into bags of 7, there will be no apples remaining. How many apples are there in the basket?

ENGAGE

1 Share 11 ⬤ equally with your partner. How did you do it? Draw a sketch to explain your thinking.

2 You and your partner shared some 🔵 equally. Each of you received 14 🔵 and there is a remainder of 1 🔵. How many counters did both of you share?

LEARN Find the quotient and remainder

1 Michael has 9 pens. He placed the pens equally into 4 containers.

a How many pens are there in each container?

$9 \div 4 = ?$

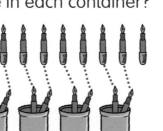

$$
\begin{array}{r}
2 \quad \longleftarrow \text{Quotient} \\
4\overline{)9} \\
\underline{8} \quad \longleftarrow 2 \times 4 = 8 \\
1 \quad \longleftarrow \text{Remainder}
\end{array}
$$

$9 \div 4 = 2$ in each group with a remainder of 1
  $= 2 \text{ R } 1$

"R" stands for remainder.

> When 9 is divided by 4, the quotient is 2 and the remainder is 1.

There are 2 pens in each container.

b How many pens are left?
There is 1 pen left.

Hands-on Activity Finding the quotient and remainder

Work in pairs.

① Take turns using 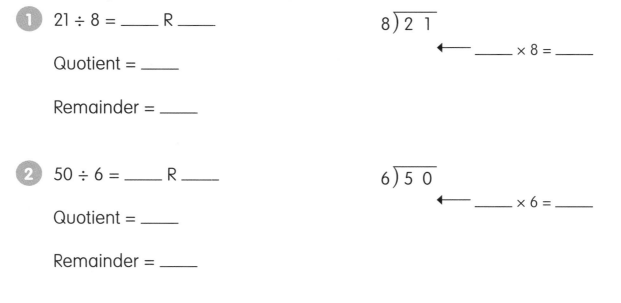 to show each division.

② Write each division equation, quotient, and remainder.

a Divide 11 by 2.

_____ ÷ _____ = _____ R _____

Quotient: _____

Remainder: _____

b Divide 12 by 6.

_____ ÷ _____ = _____ R _____

Quotient: _____

Remainder: _____

c Divide 13 by 4.

_____ ÷ _____ = _____ R _____

Quotient: _____

Remainder: _____

d Divide 17 by 5.

_____ ÷ _____ = _____ R _____

Quotient: _____

Remainder: _____

TRY Practice finding the quotient and remainder

Find each quotient and remainder.

① $21 \div 8 =$ _____ R _____

Quotient = _____

Remainder = _____

$8\overline{)2\ 1}$

⟵ _____ × 8 = _____

② $50 \div 6 =$ _____ R _____

Quotient = _____

Remainder = _____

$6\overline{)5\ 0}$

⟵ _____ × 6 = _____

Name: _____ Date: _____

INDEPENDENT PRACTICE

Solve.

1 Divide 18 keychains equally among 7 children. How many keychains are left?

$18 \div 7 = ?$

$$7\overline{)\,1\ 8}$$

Quotient = ____

Remainder = ____

So, $18 \div 7 =$ ____ R ____

Each child receives ____ keychains.

There are ____ keychains left.

Find each quotient and remainder.

2 15 ÷ 6 = _____ R _____   6)15

Quotient = _____

Remainder = _____

3 25 ÷ 3 = _____ R _____   3)25

Quotient = _____

Remainder = _____

4 23 ÷ 7 = _____ R _____   7)23

Quotient = _____

Remainder = _____

5 40 ÷ 9 = _____ R _____   9)40

Quotient = _____

Remainder = _____

6 59 ÷ 8 = _____ R _____   8)59

Quotient = _____

Remainder = _____

3 Dividing by a 1-Digit Number

Learning Objectives:
- Divide a 2-digit, 3-digit, or 4-digit number by a 1-digit number with or without regrouping.
- Estimate quotients.

THINK

Find each missing digit: 6 ? 9 ÷ 3 = ? 1 ?

ENGAGE

Use 🔵1,000 🔵100 🔵10 🔵1 to model the problem:

Vanessa bought 60 potatoes and 900 apples for her store. She placed the potatoes equally in 3 crates. She also placed the apples equally in the same 3 crates. How many potatoes and apples are there in each crate?

LEARN Divide by a 1-digit number without regrouping and no remainder

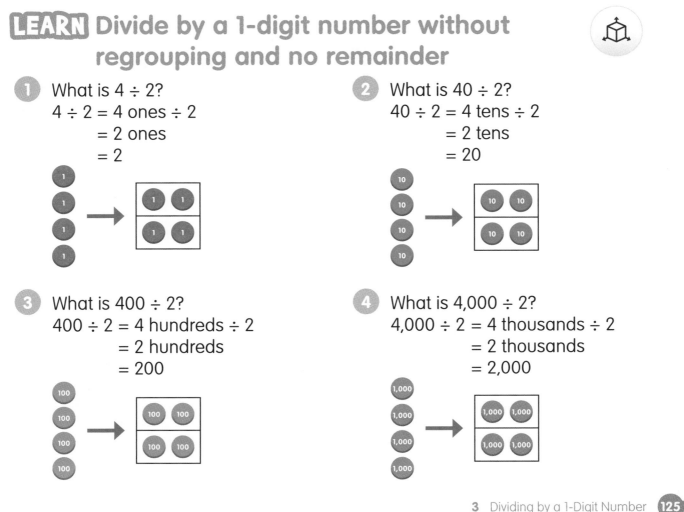

1. What is 4 ÷ 2?
    4 ÷ 2 = 4 ones ÷ 2
    = 2 ones
    = 2

2. What is 40 ÷ 2?
    40 ÷ 2 = 4 tens ÷ 2
    = 2 tens
    = 20

3. What is 400 ÷ 2?
    400 ÷ 2 = 4 hundreds ÷ 2
    = 2 hundreds
    = 200

4. What is 4,000 ÷ 2?
    4,000 ÷ 2 = 4 thousands ÷ 2
    = 2 thousands
    = 2,000

5 A gardener has 63 potted plants. He puts an equal number of potted plants on 3 benches. How many potted plants are there on each bench?

Divide 63 by 3 to find out.
63 ÷ 3 = ?

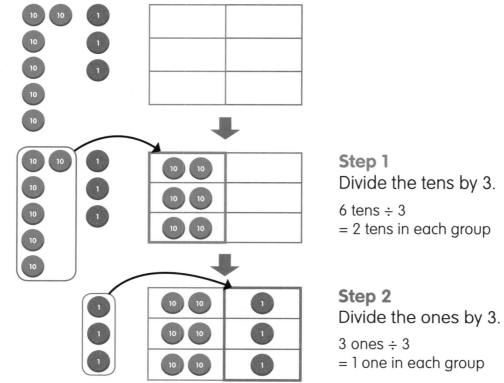

Step 1
Divide the tens by 3.

6 tens ÷ 3
= 2 tens in each group

Step 2
Divide the ones by 3.

3 ones ÷ 3
= 1 one in each group

63 ÷ 3 = 21

There are 21 potted plants on each bench.

Let's Recap!

Step 1	Step 2

2
3)6 3
  6
	2 1
	3)6 3
	  6
	    3
	    3
	    0

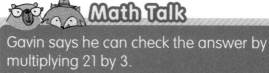

Math Talk

Gavin says he can check the answer by multiplying 21 by 3.
Is he correct? Explain.

What other ways can he check the answer?

6 What is 303 ÷ 3?

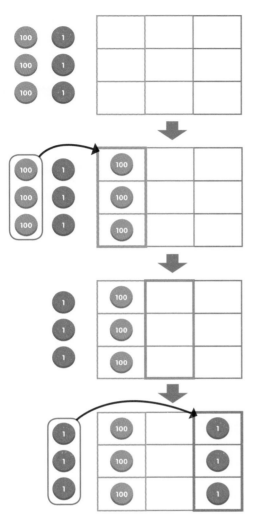

Step 1
Divide the hundreds by 3.

3 hundreds ÷ 3
= 1 hundred in each group

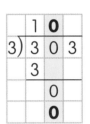

Step 2
Divide the tens by 3.

0 tens ÷ 3
= 0 tens in each group

Step 3
Divide the ones by 3.

3 ones ÷ 3
= 1 one in each group

303 ÷ 3 = 101

Let's Recap!

Step 1	Step 2	Step 3
1 3)3 0 3 3	1 0 3)3 0 3 3 0 0	1 0 1 3)3 0 3 3 0 0 3 3 0

TRY Practice dividing by a 1-digit number without regrouping and no remainder

Fill in each missing number.

1 $600 \div 2 = $ _____ hundreds $\div 2$

            $= $ _____ hundreds

            $= $ _____

2 $6{,}000 \div 6 = $ _____ thousands $\div 6$

            $= $ _____ thousand

            $= $ _____

Divide.

3 $84 \div 4 = $ _____

$4\overline{)8\ 4}$

4 $930 \div 3 = $ _____

$3\overline{)9\ 3\ 0}$

5 $6{,}084 \div 2 = $ _____

$2\overline{)6{,}0\ 8\ 4}$

6 $3{,}960 \div 3 = $ _____

$3\overline{)3{,}9\ 6\ 0}$

ENGAGE

Use to divide 150 into two equal groups. Describe the steps you followed to your partner.

LEARN Divide by a 1-digit number with regrouping and no remainder

1. A farmer sells his crops to 2 restaurants. He divides 212 heads of lettuce equally among the 2 restaurants. How many heads of lettuce does each restaurant receive?

$212 \div 2 = ?$

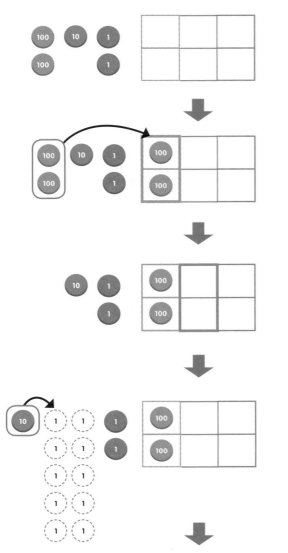

Step 1
Divide the hundreds by 2.

2 hundreds ÷ 2
= 1 hundred in each group

```
    1
2)2 1 2
  2
```

Step 2
Divide the tens by 2.

1 ten ÷ 2
= 0 tens in each group
  with remainder 1 ten

```
    1 0
2)2 1 2
  2
      1
```

Regroup the 1 ten.

1 ten = 10 ones

Add the ones.

10 ones + 2 ones = 12 ones

```
    1 0
2)2 1 2
  2
      1 2
```

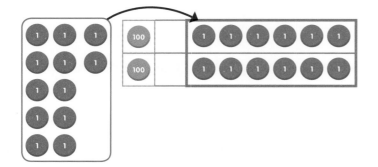

Step 3

Divide the ones by 2.

12 ones ÷ 2
= 6 ones in
each group

$212 \div 2 = 106$

Let's Recap!

Step 1	Step 2	Step 3

$\begin{array}{r} 1 \\ 3\overline{)2\,1\,2} \\ 2 \end{array}$

$\begin{array}{r} 1\,0 \\ 2\overline{)2\,1\,2} \\ 2 \\ \hline 1 \end{array}$

$\begin{array}{r} 1\,0\,6 \\ 2\overline{)2\,1\,2} \\ 2 \\ \hline 1\,2 \\ 1\,2 \\ \hline 0 \end{array}$

2. Rebeca and Joshua each used an area model to divide 212 by 2.

Rebeca's method:

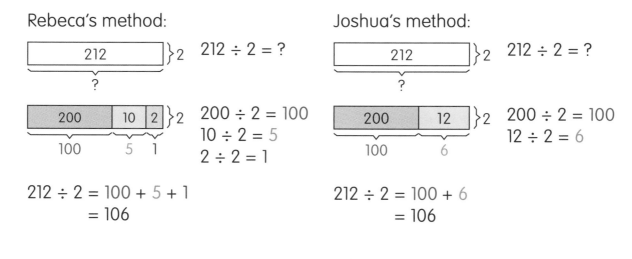

$212 \div 2 = ?$

$200 \div 2 = 100$
$10 \div 2 = 5$
$2 \div 2 = 1$

$212 \div 2 = 100 + 5 + 1$
$ = 106$

Joshua's method:

$212 \div 2 = ?$

$200 \div 2 = 100$
$12 \div 2 = 6$

$212 \div 2 = 100 + 6$
$ = 106$

Math Talk

Explain to your partner at least one other way of decomposing 212 to find the quotient.

3 Divide 1,547 by 7.

$1{,}547 \div 7 = ?$

Regroup.
1 thousand = 10 hundreds

Add the hundreds.
10 hundreds + 5 hundreds = 15 hundreds

Step 1
Divide the hundreds by 7.
15 hundreds ÷ 7
= 2 hundreds in each group with remainder 1 hundred

```
        2
7) 1, 5  4  7
   1 4
      1
```

Regroup.
1 hundred = 10 tens

Add the tens.
10 tens + 4 tens = 14 tens

```
       2
7) 1, 5  4  7
   1 4
      1  4
```

Step 2
Divide the tens by 7.
14 tens ÷ 7
= 2 tens in each group

```
       2  2
7) 1, 5  4  7
   1 4
      1  4
      1  4
```

Step 3
Divide the ones by 7.
7 ones ÷ 7
= 1 one in each group

```
       2  2  1
7) 1, 5  4  7
   1 4
      1  4
      1  4
            7
            7
            0
```

$1{,}547 \div 7 = 221$

Let's Recap!

Step 1	Step 2	Step 3

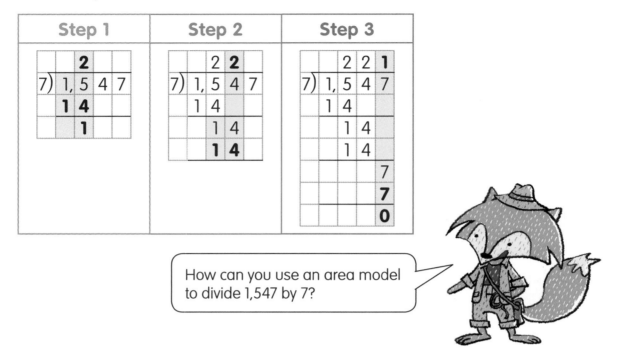

How can you use an area model to divide 1,547 by 7?

TRY Practice dividing by a 1-digit number with regrouping and no remainder

Use the area model to find the quotient. Show your work.

1 2,548 ÷ 4 = _____

2,548

} 4

Divide.

2 54 ÷ 3 = _____

$$3\overline{)5\;4}$$

3 578 ÷ 2 = _____

$$2\overline{)5\;7\;8}$$

4 345 ÷ 5 = _____

$$5\overline{)3\;4\;5}$$

5 8,790 ÷ 6 = _____

$$6\overline{)8,\;7\;9\;0}$$

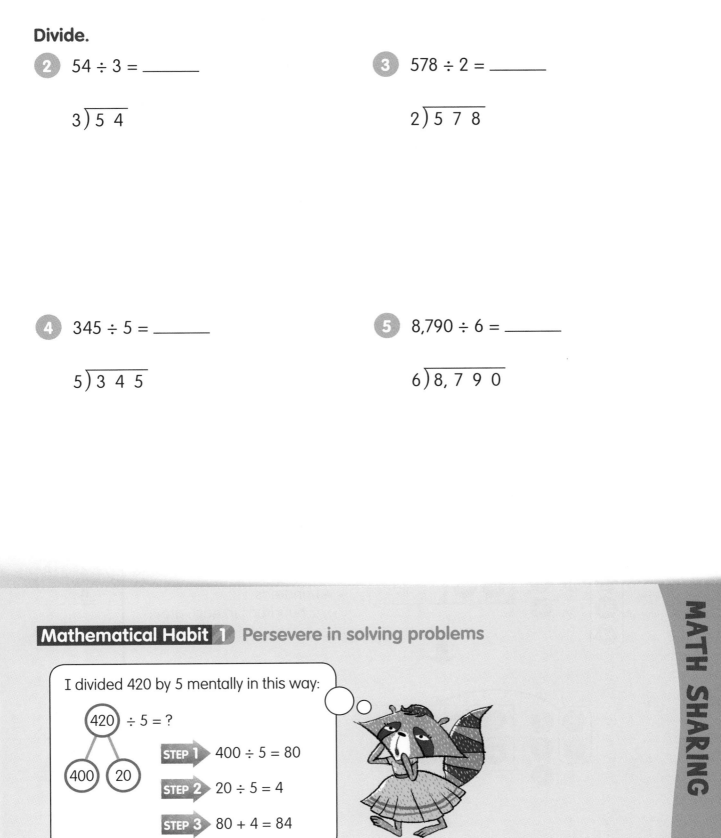

Mathematical Habit 1 Persevere in solving problems

I divided 420 by 5 mentally in this way:

420 ÷ 5 = ?

420
/   \
400   20

STEP 1 400 ÷ 5 = 80

STEP 2 20 ÷ 5 = 4

STEP 3 80 + 4 = 84

Share how you can find 220 ÷ 4 in the same way.

ENGAGE

Use 10 1 to model this problem.
There are 65 students in the fourth grade. Mr. Morris wants to divide the students into 3 classes equally. What problem does Mr. Morris meet? Can you tell him what to do?

LEARN Divide by a 1-digit number without regrouping with remainder

1   Mr. Wilson puts 423 oranges equally into 2 cartons.
How many oranges are there in each carton?
How many oranges are left over?

$423 \div 2 = ?$

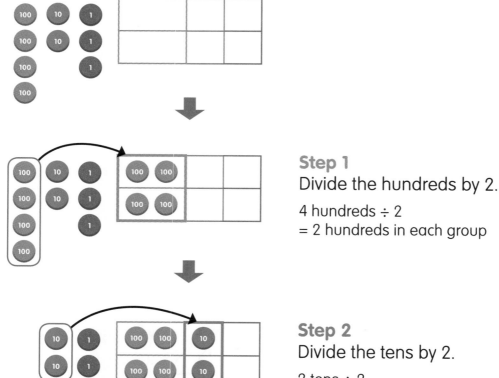

Step 1
Divide the hundreds by 2.

4 hundreds ÷ 2
= 2 hundreds in each group

```
      2
2) 4  2  3
   4
```

Step 2
Divide the tens by 2.

2 tens ÷ 2
= 1 ten in each group

```
      2  1
2) 4  2  3
   4
      2
      2
```

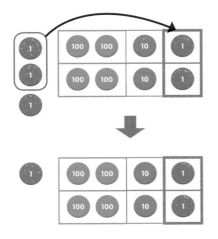

Step 3

Divide the ones by 2.

3 ones ÷ 2
= 1 one in each group with
a remainder of 1

423 ÷ 2 = 211 R 1

There are 211 oranges in each carton. There is 1 orange left over.

Let's Recap!

Step 1	Step 2	Step 3

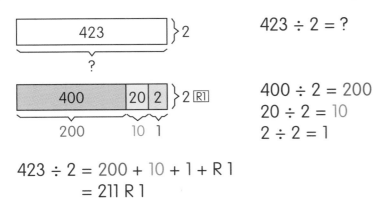

2   You can use an area model to divide 423 by 2.

423 ÷ 2 = ?

400 ÷ 2 = 200
20 ÷ 2 = 10
2 ÷ 2 = 1

423 ÷ 2 = 200 + 10 + 1 + R 1
= 211 R 1

3 Divide 6,932 by 3.

Step 1
Divide the thousands by 3.
6 thousands ÷ 3
= 2 thousands in each group

```
      2,
  3) 6, 9 3 2
      6
```

Step 2
Divide the hundreds by 3.
9 hundreds ÷ 3
= 3 hundreds in each group

```
      2, 3
  3) 6, 9 3 2
      6
         9
         9
```

Step 3
Divide the tens by 3.
3 tens ÷ 3
= 1 ten in each group

```
      2, 3 1
  3) 6, 9 3 2
      6
         9
         9
            3
            3
```

Step 4
Divide the ones by 3.
2 ones ÷ 3
= 0 ones in each group with a remainder of 2 ones

```
      2, 3 1 0
  3) 6, 9 3 2
      6
         9
         9
            3
            3
              2
```

6,932 ÷ 3 = 2,310 R 2

Let's Recap!

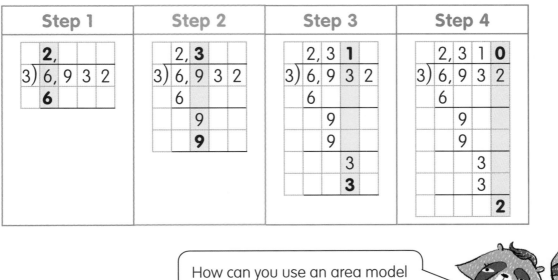

Step 1	Step 2	Step 3	Step 4
2, 3)6,9 3 2 6	2,3 3)6,9 3 2 6 9 9	2,3 1 3)6,9 3 2 6 9 9 3 3	2,3 1 0 3)6,9 3 2 6 9 9 3 3 2

How can you use an area model to divide 6,932 by 3?

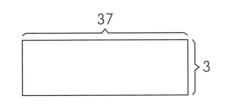

TRY **Practice dividing by a 1-digit number without regrouping with remainder**

Use the area model to find the quotient. Show your work.

1 37 ÷ 3 = _____

```
        37
 ┌─────────────────┐
 │                 │ ┐
 │                 │ ├ 3
 │                 │ ┘
 └─────────────────┘
```

Divide.

2 97 ÷ 3 = _____

   3)97

3 483 ÷ 4 = _____

   4)483

4 708 ÷ 7 = _____

   7)708

5 8,269 ÷ 2 = _____

   2)8,269

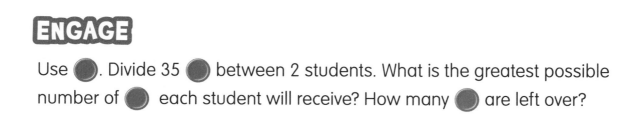

ENGAGE

Use ⬤. Divide 35 ⬤ between 2 students. What is the greatest possible number of ⬤ each student will receive? How many ⬤ are left over?

LEARN Divide by a 1-digit number with regrouping with remainder

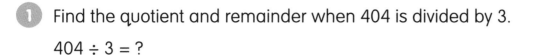

1. Find the quotient and remainder when 404 is divided by 3.

   404 ÷ 3 = ?

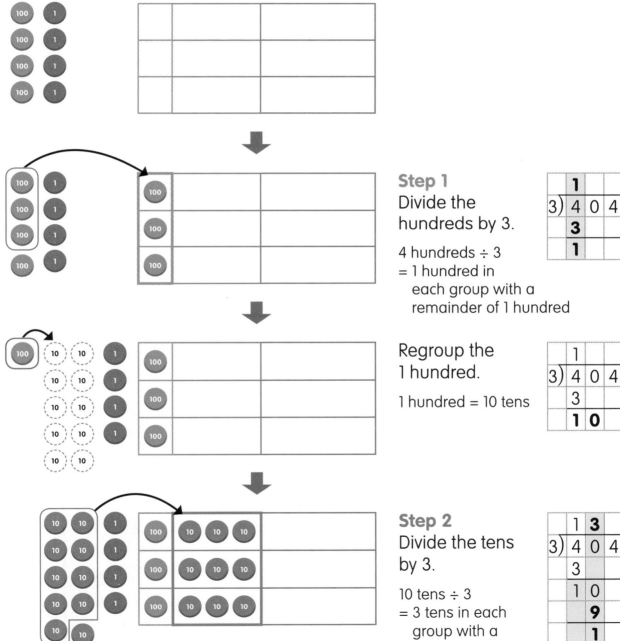

Step 1
Divide the hundreds by 3.

4 hundreds ÷ 3
= 1 hundred in each group with a remainder of 1 hundred

Regroup the 1 hundred.

1 hundred = 10 tens

Step 2
Divide the tens by 3.

10 tens ÷ 3
= 3 tens in each group with a remainder of 1 ten

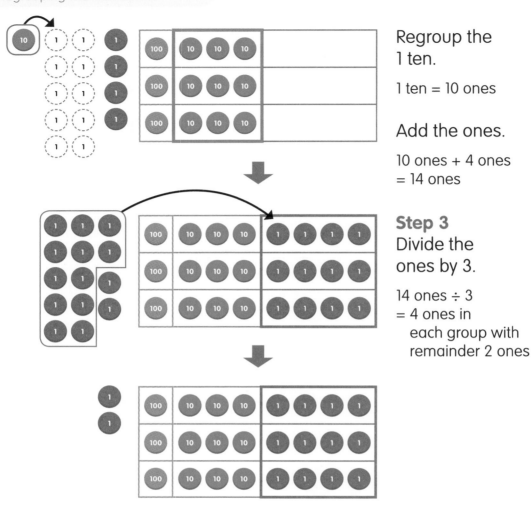

Regroup the 1 ten.

1 ten = 10 ones

Add the ones.

10 ones + 4 ones = 14 ones

Step 3
Divide the ones by 3.

14 ones ÷ 3
= 4 ones in
each group with
remainder 2 ones

404 ÷ 3 = 134 R 2
The quotient is 134. The remainder is 2.

Let's Recap!

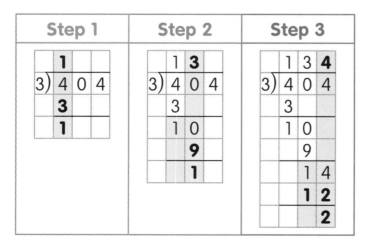

How can you use an area model to divide 404 by 3?

2 Divide 2,413 by 6.

$2{,}413 \div 6 = \, ?$

Regroup.

2 thousands = 20 hundreds

Add the hundreds.

20 hundreds + 4 hundreds = 24 hundreds

Step 1

Divide the hundreds by 6.

24 hundreds ÷ 6

= 4 hundreds in each group

```
        4
6) 2, 4  1  3
   2 4
```

Step 2

Divide the tens by 6.

1 ten ÷ 6

= 0 tens in each group with a remainder of 1 ten

```
        4  0
6) 2, 4  1  3
   2 4
         1
         0
         1
```

Regroup.

1 ten = 10 ones

Add the ones.

10 ones + 3 ones = 13 ones

```
        4  0
6) 2, 4  1  3
   2 4
         1
         0
         1  3
```

Step 3

Divide the ones by 6.

13 ones ÷ 6

= 2 ones in each group with a remainder of 1 one

```
        4  0  2
6) 2, 4  1  3
   2 4
         1
         0
         1  3
         1  2
            1
```

$2{,}413 \div 6 = 402 \text{ R } 1$

Let's Recap!

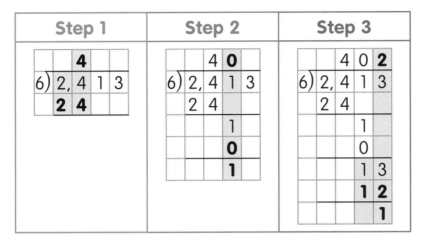

Step 1	Step 2	Step 3

Step 1:
```
        4
6) 2,4 1 3
   2 4
```

Step 2:
```
      4 0
6) 2,4 1 3
   2 4
        1
        0
        1
```

Step 3:
```
      4 0 2
6) 2,4 1 3
   2 4
        1
        0
        1 3
        1 2
          1
```

How can you use an area model to divide 2,413 by 6?

Math Talk

Ava also divided 2,413 by 6 and arrived at the answer 402 R 1.
She checked her answer in this way:

$402 \times 6 = 2,412$
$2,412 + 1$ (the remainder) $= 2,413$
So, the answer is correct.

Divide 724 by 6.
Explain to your partner how you would use Ava's method to check your answer.

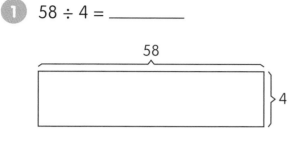 **Practice dividing by a 1-digit number with regrouping with remainder**

Use the area model to find the quotient. Show your work.

1 58 ÷ 4 = _____

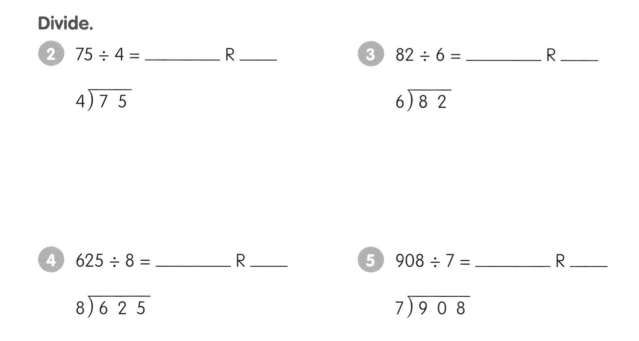

Divide.

2 75 ÷ 4 = _____ R _____

4)7 5

3 82 ÷ 6 = _____ R _____

6)8 2

4 625 ÷ 8 = _____ R _____

8)6 2 5

5 908 ÷ 7 = _____ R _____

7)9 0 8

6 $5{,}227 \div 3 =$ _____ R ____

$3\overline{)5,2\ 2\ 7}$

7 $8{,}075 \div 6 =$ _____ R ____

$6\overline{)8,0\ 7\ 5}$

8 $2{,}838 \div 7 =$ _____ R ____

$7\overline{)2,8\ 3\ 8}$

9 $6{,}100 \div 8 =$ _____ R ____

$8\overline{)6,1\ 0\ 0}$

In the classroom library, there are 74 books. Ms. Anderson wants to put them equally onto shelves but each shelf cannot hold more than 20 books. Estimate how many shelves she will need and how many books will be on each shelf. Explain your thinking to your partner.

LEARN Estimate quotients

① Brian had a box of 72 building blocks. He divided the blocks equally among his 3 friends. How many blocks did each of them receive?

$72 \div 3 = 24$

Each of them received 24 blocks.

Since division is the opposite of multiplication, use related multiplication facts to check that your answer is reasonable.

$3 \times 2 = 6$ $3 \times 20 = 60$
$3 \times 3 = 9$ $3 \times 30 = 90$

72 is nearer to 60 than to 90.
So, $72 \div 3$ is about $60 \div 3$.

Divide: $60 \div 3 = 20$
The estimated quotient is 20.

The answer 24 is close to 20.
So, it is reasonable.

Think of the multiplication facts of 3. Then, find a product that is near to 72.

Hands-on Activity Estimating quotients

Work in pairs.

① Roll  four times to make a 4-digit number. Record the number in the table below.

② Ask your partner to roll the 🎲. If the number is 0 or 1, he or she should roll again. Record the number in the table.

③ Fill in the table.

    a Estimate the quotient of the numbers in ① and ②.

    b Divide the numbers in ① and ②.

④ Trade places. Repeat ① to ③ three more times.

⑤ Compare each answer with the estimated value.
Is each answer reasonable? Explain. Fill in the table.

4-digit Number	1-digit Number	Estimated Value	Answer	Check Reasonableness

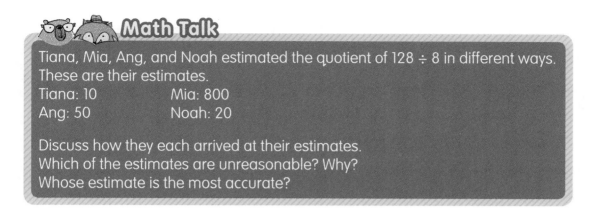

Math Talk

Tiana, Mia, Ang, and Noah estimated the quotient of 128 ÷ 8 in different ways.
These are their estimates.

Tiana: 10   Mia: 800
Ang: 50   Noah: 20

Discuss how they each arrived at their estimates.
Which of the estimates are unreasonable? Why?
Whose estimate is the most accurate?

TRY Practice estimating quotients

Find the quotient. Estimate to check that your answer is reasonable.

1. Find 176 ÷ 4.

    176 ÷ 4 = _____

    The answer is _____.

    Use related multiplication facts to check that your answer is reasonable.

    4 × 4 = _____   4 × 40 = _____

    4 × 5 = _____   4 × 50 = _____

    Divide: _____ ÷ 4 = _____

    The estimated quotient is _____.

    Is your answer reasonable? Explain.

Think of the multiplication facts of 4. Then, find a product that is close to 176.

Divide. Estimate to check that each answer is reasonable.

2 57 ÷ 3 = _____

3$\overline{)57}$

3 96 ÷ 4 = _____

4$\overline{)96}$

Estimate:

_____ ÷ 3 = _____

Estimate:

_____ ÷ 4 = _____

Divide. Show your work. Estimate to check that each answer is reasonable.

4 165 ÷ 5 = _____

Think of the multiplication facts of 5. Then, find a product close to 160.
5 × ? = 15
5 × ? = 150

Estimate:

_____ ÷ 5 = _____

5 5,346 ÷ 6 = _____

Estimate:

_____ ÷ 6 = _____

Math Talk

Share with your partner one other way to estimate each of the quotients of 165 ÷ 5 and 5,346 ÷ 6.

Name: _____ Date: _____

INDEPENDENT PRACTICE

Divide.

1 500 ÷ 5 = _____

2 9,000 ÷ 3 = _____

3 240 ÷ 8 = _____

4 3,600 ÷ 9 = _____

Use the area model to find each quotient. Show your work.

5 52 ÷ 2 = _____

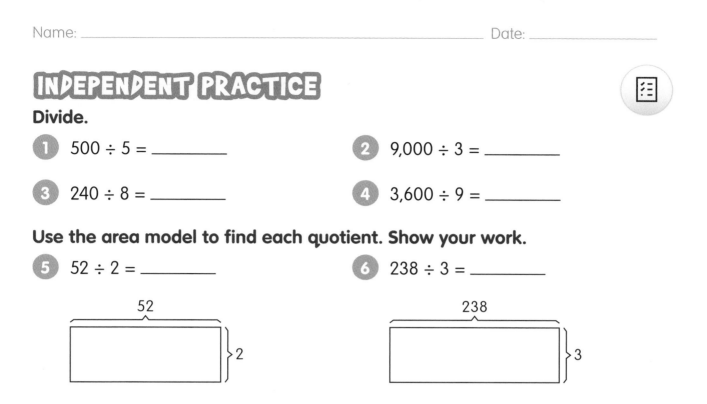

52

2

6 238 ÷ 3 = _____

238

3

Divide. Show your work. Estimate to check that each answer is reasonable.

7 64 ÷ 2 = _____

8 9,006 ÷ 3 = _____

Estimate:

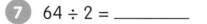

_____ ÷ _____ = _____

Estimate:

_____ ÷ _____ = _____

9 411 ÷ 3 = _____

10 2,364 ÷ 3 = _____

Estimate:

_____ ÷ _____ = _____

Estimate:

_____ ÷ _____ = _____

11 5,670 ÷ 6 = _____

12 8,323 ÷ 7 = _____

Estimate:

_____ ÷ _____ = _____

Estimate:

_____ ÷ _____ = _____

13 $35 \div 3 = \underline{\hspace{2cm}}$

14 $775 \div 7 = \underline{\hspace{2cm}}$

Estimate:

$\underline{\hspace{2cm}} \div \underline{\hspace{2cm}} = \underline{\hspace{2cm}}$

Estimate:

$\underline{\hspace{2cm}} \div \underline{\hspace{2cm}} = \underline{\hspace{2cm}}$

15 $795 \div 6 = \underline{\hspace{2cm}}$

16 $858 \div 9 = \underline{\hspace{2cm}}$

Estimate:

$\underline{\hspace{2cm}} \div \underline{\hspace{2cm}} = \underline{\hspace{2cm}}$

Estimate:

$\underline{\hspace{2cm}} \div \underline{\hspace{2cm}} = \underline{\hspace{2cm}}$

17 $961 \div 4 =$ _____

18 $6,492 \div 8 =$ _____

Estimate:

_____ ÷ _____ = _____

Estimate:

_____ ÷ _____ = _____

19 $8,074 \div 3 =$ _____

20 $9,264 \div 9 =$ _____

Estimate:

_____ ÷ _____ = _____

Estimate:

_____ ÷ _____ = _____

4 Real-World Problems: Multiplication and Division

Learning Objectives:
- Use bar models to solve real-world multiplication problems.
- Use bar models to solve real-world division problems.

THINK

James multiplies a number by 9. When he divides the product by 7, the quotient is 172 and the remainder is 2. What is the number?

ENGAGE

June and Zachary sold funfair tickets on two days. They sold fewer than 5,000 tickets on both days. On the first day, they sold a total of 1,200 tickets. June sold twice as many tickets as Zachary on the second day. What was the greatest number of tickets June sold on the second day?

LEARN Solve real-world problems involving multiplication

1. A gas station sold 1,235 gallons of gas on Thursday. On Friday, the gas station sold 3 times the amount of gas it sold on Thursday. How many gallons of gas did the gas station sell on Friday?

 STEP 1 Understand the problem.

How many gallons of gas were sold on Thursday? On which day was more gas sold? What do I need to find?

STEP 2 Think of a plan.
I can draw a bar model.

STEP 3 Carry out the plan.

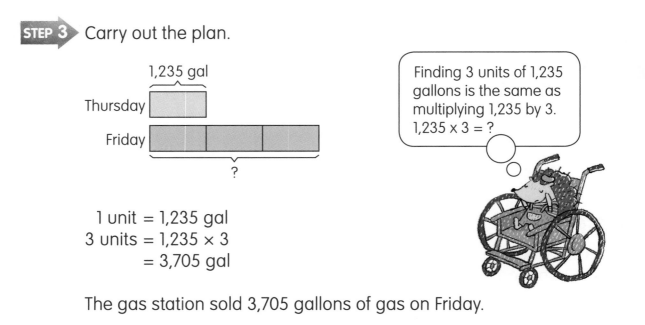

Finding 3 units of 1,235 gallons is the same as multiplying 1,235 by 3. 1,235 × 3 = ?

1 unit = 1,235 gal
3 units = 1,235 × 3
= 3,705 gal

The gas station sold 3,705 gallons of gas on Friday.

STEP 4 Check the answer.
I can use estimation to check that my answer is reasonable.

1,235 × 3
↓
1,000 × 3 = 3,000
My answer is close to 3,000.
So, it is reasonable.

What other ways can you check your answer?

2 Ms. Castillo saved $148 a month. What was the total amount she saved in one year?

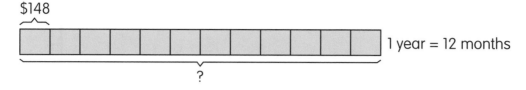

$148 × 12 = $1,776

The total amount she saved in one year was $1,776.

3 The floor of a supermarket is covered with tiles of the same size. There are 28 rows of tiles and 35 tiles in each row. How many tiles are there in all?

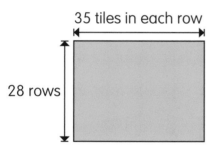

28 × 35 = 980

There are 980 tiles in all.

Hands-on Activity Writing a real-world problem involving multiplication

Work in pairs.

1 Write a real-world problem on the next page for the bar model below.

2 Ask your partner to solve the problem and explain how they check their answers.

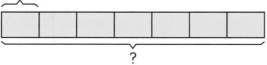

Real-world problem:

Solve. Show your work.

TRY Practice solving real-world problems involving multiplication

Solve. Use the bar model to help you.

1. An office worker earns $2,025 a month. How much does he earn in 6 months?

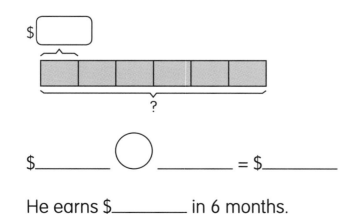

$_____ ◯ _____ = $_____

He earns $_____ in 6 months.

Use the four-step problem-solving model to help you.

2 A store has 2,356 cans of paint. Each can contains 5 liters of paint. How many liters of paint are there in all?

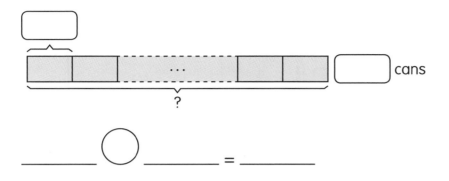

_____ ◯ _____ = _____

There are _____ liters of paint in all.

3 Anthony makes a necklace with 27 beads. He uses 15 times as many beads to make a bag. How many beads does he use to make the bag?

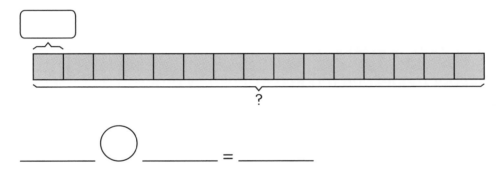

_____ ◯ _____ = _____

He uses _____ beads to make the bag.

4 A bookstore has 11 shelves of books. Each shelf has 48 books. How many books are there in all?

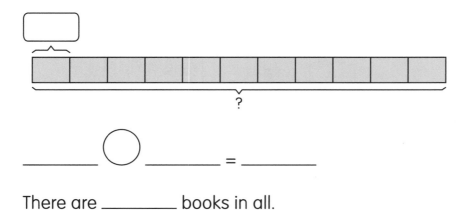

_____ ◯ _____ = _____

There are _____ books in all.

ENGAGE

A grocer packed 600 strawberries equally into 6 boxes.

a Draw a bar model to find the number of strawberries in each box. Share your bar model with your partner.

b Ivanna drew a bar model and made a mistake by drawing a unit less. Without calculating, explain if there will be more or fewer strawberries for each box now.

LEARN Solve real-world problems involving division

1 1,000 paper clips are packed equally into 8 boxes. How many paper clips are there in each box?

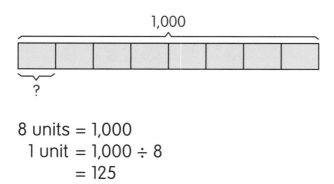

$8 \times ? = 1,000$

8 units = 1,000
1 unit = 1,000 ÷ 8
= 125

There are 125 paper clips in each box.

2 A store owner packs 1,278 kilograms of rice into 5-kilogram bags.

   a How many bags of rice are there in all?

   b How many kilograms of rice are left over?

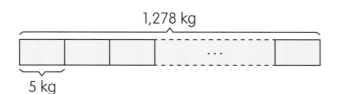

1,278 kg

5 kg

   a $1,278 \div 5 = 255$ R 3

      There are 255 bags of rice in all.

   b 3 kilograms of rice are left over.

3 Samantha and Andrew have 96 marbles in all. Samantha has 5 times as many marbles as Andrew. How many marbles does Andrew have?

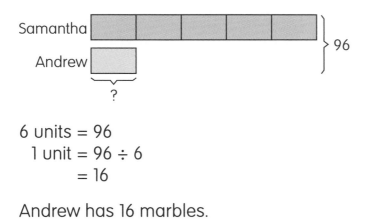

Samantha

Andrew

96

?

6 units = 96

  1 unit = $96 \div 6$

       = 16

Andrew has 16 marbles.

Hands-on Activity Writing a real-world problem involving division

Work in pairs.

(1) Write a real-world problem for the bar model below.

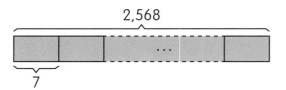

(2) Ask your partner to solve the problem and explain how they check their answers.

Real-world problem:

Solve. Show your work.

TRY Practice solving real-world problems involving division

Solve. Use the bar model to help you.

1. Alonso and Kayla have 819 magnets in all. Alonso has twice as many magnets as Kayla. How many magnets does Kayla have?

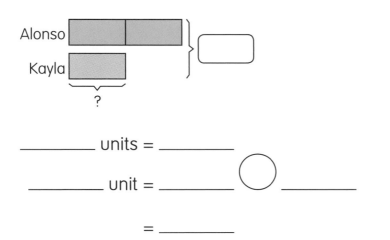

_____ units = _____

_____ unit = _____ ◯ _____

= _____

Kayla has _____ magnets.

2. Mr. Ortiz paid $2,120 for 4 suits. Each suit was the same price. What was the price of each suit?

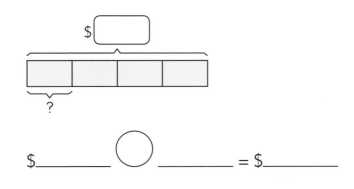

$_____ ◯ _____ = $_____

The price of each suit was $_____.

3 A grocer buys 1,462 peaches. He packs them into bags of 6 peaches each.

   a How many bags of peaches does he have?

   b How many peaches are left over?

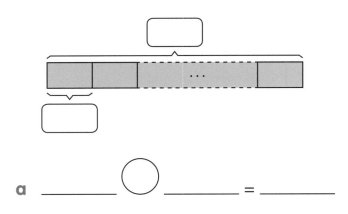

a _____ ◯ _____ = _____

   He has _____ bags of peaches.

b There are _____ peaches left over.

4 There were 576 more adults than children at a fair. If 4 times as many adults as children attended the fair, how many children attended?

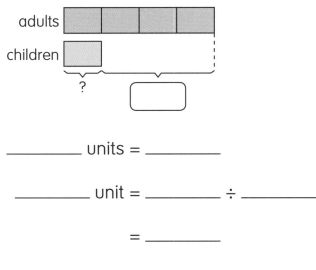

_____ units = _____

_____ unit = _____ ÷ _____

= _____

_____ children attended the fair.

INDEPENDENT PRACTICE

Solve. Draw a bar model to help you.

1) A company ordered 9 boxes of printing paper. Each box contained 2,008 sheets of paper. How many sheets of paper did the company order in all?

2) A factory produces 9,236 computers and 4 times as many keyboards. How many keyboards does the factory produce?

3 A factory produced 438 chairs in 3 days. How many chairs did the factory produce each day?

4 A store sells 5-liter cans of paints. Last month, the store sold a total of 2,480 liters of paint. How many cans of paint did the store sell last month?

5 María and Xavier collected game cards. María has 34 cards in her collection. Xavier has 13 times as many cards as María. How many game cards does Xavier have?

6 A florist uses 9 roses to make one bouquet. The florist has 1,086 roses in all.

　a How many bouquets can the florist make?

　b How many roses will be left over?

7 Ms. Cooper walks 850 feet every morning. What is the total distance she walks in 25 days?

8 A dance club had 3 times as many members as an art club. The art club had 3,598 fewer members than the dance club. How many members did the art club have?

5 Factors

Learning Objectives:
- Find the factors of a whole number.
- Find the common factors of two whole numbers.
- Identify prime and composite numbers.

THINK

Isaiah and Angelina met each other on Tuesday at a library. Isaiah visits the library once every 3 days while Angelina visits the same library once every 5 days. On which day of the week will they meet again?

ENGAGE

1 Use ⬤⬤. What are all the ways you can share 10 evenly?

2 What are the factors of 4 and 6? Which factors are the same?

LEARN Find the factors of a whole number

1 Express 12 as a product of two whole numbers.

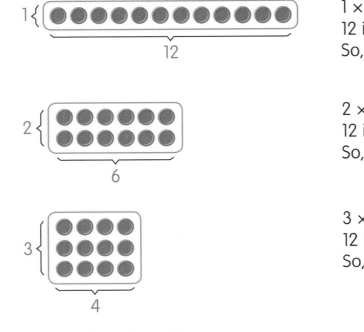

$1 \times 12 = 12$
12 is the product of 1 and 12.
So, 1 and 12 are factors of 12.

a factor pair of 12

$2 \times 6 = 12$
12 is the product of 2 and 6.
So, 2 and 6 are factors of 12.

$3 \times 4 = 12$
12 is the product of 3 and 4.
So, 3 and 4 are factors of 12.

So, 1, 2, 3, 4, 6, and 12 are factors of 12.

2 Are 2 and 3 factors of 14?

You can use division to find the factors of a number.

a

$$2\overline{)14}$$
$$\underline{14}$$
$$0$$
(quotient 7)

> The remainder is 0.
> So, 7 is also a factor of 14.

14 can be divided exactly by 2.
So, 2 is a factor of 14.

b

$$3\overline{)14}$$
$$\underline{12}$$
$$2$$
(quotient 4)

> There is a remainder.
> Is 4 a factor of 14?

14 cannot be divided exactly by 3.
So, 3 is not a factor of 14.

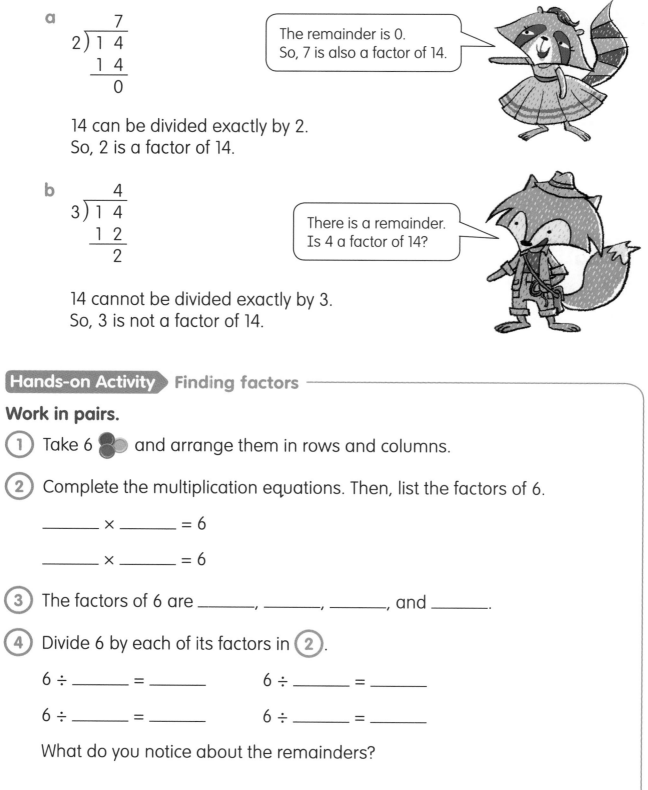

Hands-on Activity **Finding factors**

Work in pairs.

1 Take 6  and arrange them in rows and columns.

2 Complete the multiplication equations. Then, list the factors of 6.

_____ × _____ = 6

_____ × _____ = 6

3 The factors of 6 are _____, _____, _____, and _____.

4 Divide 6 by each of its factors in **2**.

6 ÷ _____ = _____   6 ÷ _____ = _____

6 ÷ _____ = _____   6 ÷ _____ = _____

What do you notice about the remainders?

_____

⑤ Take 16 🔵 and arrange them in rows and columns.

⑥ Use multiplication equations to list all the different ways in the space below. Then, list the factors of 16.

The factors of 16 are _____, _____, _____, _____, and _____.

⑦ Divide 16 by each of its factors in ⑥. Show your work in the space below.

What do you notice about the remainders?

_____

TRY Practice finding the factors of a whole number

Find each missing factor.

① What are the factors of 18?

$18 = 1 \times 18$
$18 = 2 \times 9$
$18 = 3 \times 6$

The factors of 18 are 1, 2, 3, _____, _____, and 18.

② List all the factors of 42.

$42 = 1 \times 42$
$42 = 2 \times 21$
$42 = 3 \times 14$
$42 = 6 \times 7$

The factors of 42 are 1, 2, 3, 6, _____, _____, _____, and 42.

Find all the factors of each number.

3 15

4 56

The factors of 15 are

_____.

The factors of 56 are

_____.

Find each missing factor.

5 $20 = 5 \times$ _____

6 $35 = 7 \times$ _____

7 $32 = 8 \times$ _____

8 $72 = 9 \times$ _____

Select all that apply.

9 Which of the following numbers have 5 as a factor?

    a 10   **b** 21   **c** 37   **d** 55   _____

ENGAGE

Madeline has some gray and white tiles of the same size. She has 16 gray tiles and 24 white tiles. She fits them into a rectangle exactly. How many rows of tiles can she arrange and what are the colors on each row?

LEARN Find the **common factors** of two whole numbers

1 Find the common factors of 8 and 12.

Factors of 8	**1, 2, 4**, 8
Factors of 12	**1, 2**, 3, **4**, 6, 12
Common factors of 8 and 12	1, 2, 4

The common factors of 8 and 12 are 1, 2, and 4.

2 Is 2 a common factor of 24 and 27?

a
```
    1 2
2 ) 2 4
    2
    ─
    4
    4
    ─
    0
```

b
```
    1 3
2 ) 2 7
    2
    ─
    7
    6
    ─
    1 ── There is a remainder.
```

24 can be divided exactly by 2.
2 is a factor of 24.

27 cannot be divided exactly by 2.
2 is not a factor of 27.

So, 2 is not a common factor of 24 and 27.

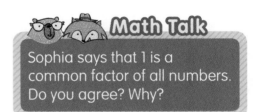

Math Talk

Sophia says that 1 is a common factor of all numbers. Do you agree? Why?

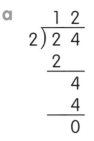 Practice finding the common factors of two whole numbers

Find each missing number.

1 Find the common factors of 9 and 36.

$9 = 1 \times 9$ $36 = 1 \times 36$

$9 = 3 \times$ _____ $36 = 2 \times$ _____

                              $36 = 3 \times$ _____

                              $36 = 4 \times$ _____

                              $36 = 6 \times$ _____

The factors of 9 are 1, _____, and 9.

The factors of 36 are 1, 2, 3, 4, _____, _____, _____, _____, and 36.

The common factors of 9 and 36 are 1, _____, and _____.

Find all the common factors of each pair of numbers.

2 45 and 48

The common factors of 45 and 48 are _____.

3 60 and 54

The common factors of 60 and 54 are _____.

Select all that apply.

4 Which of the following pairs of numbers have 3 as a common factor?

a   18 and 24   b   21 and 25

c   51 and 63   d   49 and 52   _____

MATH SHARING

Mathematical Habit 7 Make use of structure

Find a common factor of 6 and 8. Then, find the simplest form of $\frac{6}{8}$.

a   What number can be used to divide the numerator and denominator of $\frac{6}{8}$?

b   Discuss with your partner what you notice about the number used in **a**.

Which numbers between 1 and 20 only have themselves and 1 as a factor? How do you know? Explain your thinking to your partner.

LEARN Identify prime and composite numbers

1 Find all the factors of 5.

$5 = 1 \times 5$

The factors of 5 are 1 and 5.
5 has only two different factors, 1 and itself.
5 is a prime number .

A prime number has only two different factors, 1 and itself.

2 Find all the factors of 12.

$12 = 1 \times 12$
$12 = 2 \times 6$
$12 = 3 \times 4$

The factors of 12 are 1, 2, 3, 4, 6, and 12.
12 has 6 factors.
12 is a composite number .

A composite number has more than two different factors.

3 Find all the factors of 1.

$1 = 1 \times 1$

The number 1 has only 1 factor.
So, 1 is neither prime nor composite.

Math Talk

What is the least prime number? Explain.

Hands-on Activity Finding prime numbers

Work in pairs.

Use the chart below to find the prime numbers from 1 to 50.

① Cross out 1 since it is not a prime number.

② Circle 2, which is the first prime number. Cross out all the greater numbers that can be divided exactly by 2.

③ Find the first number after 2 that has not been crossed out, and circle it. That number, 3, is the next prime number. Cross out all the greater numbers that can be divided exactly by 3.

④ Take turns circling the next prime number and crossing out the numbers that can be divided exactly by it.

⑤ List the numbers that are circled. These are the prime numbers between

1 and 100: _____

_____

1	2	3	4	5	6	7	8	9	10
11	12	13	14	15	16	17	18	19	20
21	22	23	24	25	26	27	28	29	30
31	32	33	34	35	36	37	38	39	40
41	42	43	44	45	46	47	48	49	50
51	52	53	54	55	56	57	58	59	60
61	62	63	64	65	66	67	68	69	70
71	72	73	74	75	76	77	78	79	80
81	82	83	84	85	86	87	88	89	90
91	92	93	94	95	96	97	98	99	100

TRY Practice identifying prime and composite numbers

Find all the factors of each number. Then, decide whether the number is prime or composite.

1 21

21 is a _____ number.

2 33

33 is a _____ number.

3 59

59 is a _____ number.

4 77

77 is a _____ number.

Solve.

5 Write all the prime numbers from 1 to 10.

_____

6 Look at the numbers. Write each number in the correct box.

| 24 | 18 | 11 | 39 | 31 | 12 |

| 15 | 19 | 27 | 43 | 57 |

| 60 | 67 | 81 | 90 | 72 | 75 |

| 63 | 71 | 85 | 91 | 99 |

Composite Numbers	**Prime Numbers**

Math Talk

Joseph says that all prime numbers are odd numbers. Do you agree? Why or why not?

INDEPENDENT PRACTICE

Find each missing factor.

1 $45 = 5 \times$ _____

2 $50 = 10 \times$ _____

3 $56 = 7 \times$ _____

4 $63 =$ _____ $\times 7$

List all the factors of 40.

5 $40 =$ _____ $\times$ _____

$40 =$ _____ $\times$ _____

$40 =$ _____ $\times$ _____

$40 =$ _____ $\times$ _____

The factors of 40 are _____.

Find all the factors of each number.

6 35

7 24

The factors of 35 are

_____.

The factors of 24 are

_____.

Select all that apply.

8 Which of the following have 8 as a factor?

   a 4   **b** 16   **c** 32   **d** 84   _____

9 Which of the following are factor pairs of 54?

   a 2 and 27   **b** 3 and 18

   c 4 and 14   **d** 6 and 9   _____

Find the common factors of each pair of numbers.

10 24 and 52

The common factors of 24 and 52 are _____.

11 45 and 60

The common factors of 45 and 60 are _____.

Select all that apply.

12 Which of the following pairs of numbers have 4 as a common factor?

   a 12 and 42   **b** 36 and 54

   c 64 and 28   **d** 56 and 92   _____

Circle the prime numbers.

13 21   7   13   36   15   4   31   23   39   27

Underline the composite numbers.

14 45   11   30   47   71   99   81   67   53   63

6 Multiples

Learning Objectives:
- Find the multiples of a whole number.
- Make multiplication comparisons.
- Find common multiples of two whole numbers.

> **New Vocabulary**
> multiple
> common multiple

THINK

At 1 P.M., Charlotte set her alarm to go off every 2 minutes. At the same time, Jonathan set his alarm to go off every 3 minutes. At what time will their alarms first go off at the same time?

ENGAGE

Count by 2s to 30. Now, count by 4s to 30. What do you notice?
Share your observation.

LEARN Find multiples of a whole number

1. Recall the multiplication facts of 2.

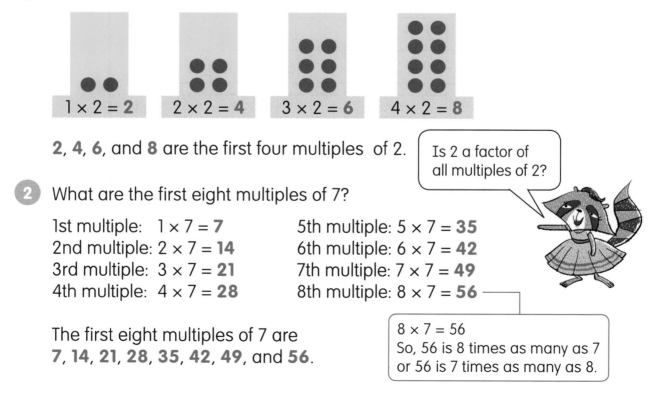

$1 \times 2 = 2$ $2 \times 2 = 4$ $3 \times 2 = 6$ $4 \times 2 = 8$

2, **4**, **6**, and **8** are the first four multiples of 2.

> Is 2 a factor of all multiples of 2?

2. What are the first eight multiples of 7?

1st multiple: $1 \times 7 = \mathbf{7}$	5th multiple: $5 \times 7 = \mathbf{35}$
2nd multiple: $2 \times 7 = \mathbf{14}$	6th multiple: $6 \times 7 = \mathbf{42}$
3rd multiple: $3 \times 7 = \mathbf{21}$	7th multiple: $7 \times 7 = \mathbf{49}$
4th multiple: $4 \times 7 = \mathbf{28}$	8th multiple: $8 \times 7 = \mathbf{56}$

The first eight multiples of 7 are
7, **14**, **21**, **28**, **35**, **42**, **49**, and **56**.

> $8 \times 7 = 56$
> So, 56 is 8 times as many as 7
> or 56 is 7 times as many as 8.

3 We can use division to check for multiples.

a Is 45 a multiple of 3?

```
      1 5
   ┌──────
 3 ) 4 5
     3
   ──────
     1 5
     1 5
   ──────
       0
```

45 can be divided exactly by 3.
3 is a factor of 45.
So, 45 is a multiple of 3.

b Is 81 a multiple of 6?

```
      1 3
   ┌──────
 6 ) 8 1
     6
   ──────
     2 1
     1 8
   ──────
       3 ──── There is a remainder.
```

81 cannot be divided exactly by 6.
6 is not a factor of 81.
So, 81 is not a multiple of 6.

Hands-on Activity ▶ Relating factors and multiples to multiplication and division

Work in pairs.

1 Use the following chart to skip count by 5s.
Then, complete the table on the next page.

1	2	3	4	5	6	7	8	9	10
11	12	13	14	15	16	17	18	19	20
21	22	23	24	25	26	27	28	29	30
31	32	33	34	35	36	37	38	39	40
41	42	43	44	45	46	47	48	49	50
51	52	53	54	55	56	57	58	59	60
61	62	63	64	65	66	67	68	69	70
71	72	73	74	75	76	77	78	79	80
81	82	83	84	85	86	87	88	89	90
91	92	93	94	95	96	97	98	99	100

Number Used to Skip Count	Numbers You Landed on
5	

2 a What do you notice about the numbers you landed on?

_____

b What do you notice about the number you used to skip count?

_____

3 Look at the numbers in ②.
How can you relate the numbers in a to the number in b?

Math Talk

Alexis says that if a number is a factor of another number, then the second number is a multiple of the first.

Do you agree? Why? Share your ideas with your partner.
Show examples to explain your reasoning.

TRY Practice finding multiples of a whole number

Find each missing number.

1 Find the next four multiples of 6.

   6, 12, 18, 24, 30, 36, 42, 48, _____ , _____, _____, _____

List the first five multiples of each number.

2 2

3 7

_____

_____

Check for multiples. Show your work.

4 Is 39 a multiple of 3? Why?

5 Is 62 a multiple of 8? Why?

Write a statement that represents the multiplication equation.

6 $35 = 5 \times 7$

   _____ is _____ times as many as _____.

Write a multiplication equation that represents the statement.

7 48 is 6 times as many as 8.

_____ = _____ × _____

ENGAGE

How do you find multiples of 4 which are also multiples of 5? Explain your thinking to your partner.

LEARN Find common multiples of two whole numbers

1 List the multiples of 4 and 5.
Then, find their common multiples.

Multiples of 4   4, 8, 12, 16, **20**, 24, 28, 32, 36, **40**, …

Multiples of 5   5, 10, 15, **20**, 25, 30, 35, **40**, 45, 50, …

The first common multiple of 4 and 5 is 20.
The second common multiple of 4 and 5 is 40.

2 Is 60 a common multiple of 3 and 8?

a
```
    2 0
3)6 0
    6
    ─
    0
```

b
```
      7
8)6 0
    5 6
    ───
      4 ──[ There is a remainder. ]
```

60 can be divided exactly by 3.
3 is a factor of 60.
So, 60 is a multiple of 3.

60 cannot be divided exactly by 8.
8 is not a factor of 60.
So, 60 is not a multiple of 8.

So, 60 is not a common multiple of 3 and 8.

Hands-on Activity ▷ Finding common multiples

Work in pairs.

(1) List the first 12 multiples of 4.
Your partner lists the first 12 multiples of 9.

4: _____

9: _____

(2) Compare the lists in (1). What is the common multiple of 4 and 9?

The common multiple of 4 and 9 is _____.

(3) Repeat (1) and (2) with 3 and 5.

3: _____

5: _____

The common multiples of 3 and 5 are _____.

TRY Practice finding common multiples of two whole numbers

List the first six multiples of each number. Then, answer the question.

(1) 4

_____

(2) 6

_____

(3) What are the common multiples of 4 and 6? _____

Find the first common multiple of each pair of numbers.

4 3 and 4

The first common multiple of 3 and 4 is _____.

5 5 and 6

The first common multiple of 5 and 6 is _____.

6 7 and 8

The first common multiple of 7 and 8 is _____.

Mathematical Habit 7 Make use of structure

1 Find the first common multiple of 2 and 3.

2 How can you use the answer in **1** to compare $\frac{1}{2}$ and $\frac{2}{3}$?

MATH SHARING

MULTIPLES BINGO!

What you need:

Players: 4

Materials: 4 Bingo cards (4 × 4 grid), 🎲

What to do:

1 Each player writes 16 different numbers from 10 to 60 in separate boxes on a Bingo card. The numbers can be in any order.

2 Player 1 rolls 🎲 twice to get two 1-digit numbers. If the number is 0 or 1, he or she rolls again. The player writes the two 1-digit numbers on a piece of paper.

3 Each player then checks his or her Bingo card and circles the common multiples of the two 1-digit numbers, if any. Check each others' cards to be sure that the correct multiples have been circled.

4 Repeat 2 and 3, taking turns rolling 🎲.

Who is the winner?

The first player to circle four numbers horizontally (⟷), vertically (↕), or diagonally (⤢ or ⬂), and call out "Bingo!" wins.

INDEPENDENT PRACTICE

List the first five multiples of each number.

1 3

_____

2 8

_____

3 9

_____

Check for multiples. Show your work.

4 Is 45 a multiple of 3? Why?

5 Is 58 a multiple of 7? Why?

Write a sentence that represents the multiplication equation.

6 $66 = 11 \times 6$

_____ is _____ times as many as _____.

Write a multiplication equation that represents the sentence.

7 72 is 9 times as many as 8.

_____ = _____ × _____.

Find the first common multiple of each pair of numbers.

8 4 and 7

The first common multiple of 4 and 7 is _____.

9 6 and 9

The first common multiple of 6 and 9 is _____.

Solve.

10 15 and 30 are common multiples of 5 and N.
N is a 1-digit number. N is not 1.
What is the number N?

The number N is _____.

7 Real-World Problems: The Four Operations

Learning Objective:
• Use bar models to solve real-world problems involving the four operations.

THINK

On Monday, 1,560 people watched a movie at the theater. On Tuesday, twice as many people watched the movie. 500 fewer people watched the movie on Wednesday than on Tuesday. How can you find the total number of people who watched the movie over the three days? Share at least two different ways with your partner.

ENGAGE

Jasmine had 120 stickers. Her brother gave her another 80 stickers. Jasmine divided the total number of stickers equally among 5 sticker albums. How many stickers are in each album? Draw a bar model to represent the problem. Share your bar model with your partner.

LEARN Solve real-world problems

1 Gianna had 723 map pins. She used 164 pins on a map to show the places she had visited. She then tried to pack the remaining pins equally into 5 bags but there were some leftovers. How many pins were left unpacked?

 STEP 1 Understand the problem.

How many map pins did Gianna have at first? How many map pins did she use? How many bags did she have? What do I need to find?

 STEP 2 Think of a plan.
I can draw a bar model.

STEP 3 Carry out the plan.

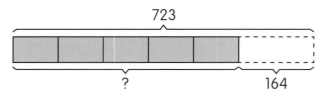

? + 164 = 723

723 − 164 = 559

After Gianna put pins on the map, she had 559 pins left.

559 ÷ 5 = 111 R 4

There were 4 pins left unpacked.

STEP 4 Check the answer.
I can work backwards to check my answer.

111 × 5 = 555
Gianna packed a total of 555 pins in bags.

555 + 4 = 559
Gianna had 559 pins left after putting pins on the map.

559 + 164 = 723
Gianna had 723 pins at first.

So, my answer is correct.

What other ways can you check your answer?

2 Mr. Cruz and Mr. Reed collected 3,546 coins in all. Mr. Cruz had twice as many coins as Mr. Reed.

a How many coins did Mr. Cruz have?

b Mr. Cruz then gave away 500 of his coins. How many coins did he have left?

a

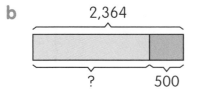

3 units = 3,546

  1 unit = 3,546 ÷ 3

      = 1,182

Mr. Reed had 1,182 coins.

2 units = 1,182 × 2

      = 2,364

Mr. Cruz had 2,364 coins.

b

2,364 − 500 = 1,864

Mr. Cruz had 1,864 coins left.

3 There were a total of 406 books in a bookcase. The bookcase had three shelves. The middle shelf held 100 more books than the top shelf. The bottom shelf held 4 times as many books as the top shelf.

a How many books were there on the top shelf?

b How many books were there on the bottom shelf?

a
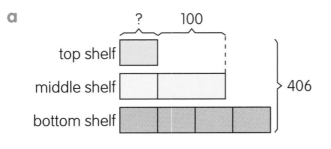

$406 - 100 = 306$

$6 \text{ units} = 306$
$1 \text{ unit} = 306 \div 6$
$\qquad = 51$

There were 51 books on the top shelf.

b
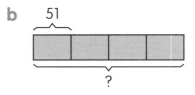

$4 \text{ units} = 51 \times 4$
$\qquad = 204$

There were 204 books on the bottom shelf.

4 Henry played 5 rounds of a game. He scored 2,085 points in each of 2 rounds. He scored 1,640 points in each remaining round. What was his total score at the end of 5 rounds?

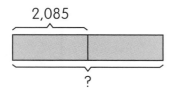

$2,085 \times 2 = 4,170$

He scored 4,170 points in 2 of the rounds.

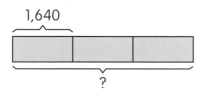

$1,640 \times 3 = 4,920$

He scored 4,920 points in the remaining rounds.

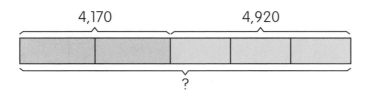

$4,170 + 4,920 = 9,090$

His total score was 9,090 points at the end of 5 rounds.

5 Carlos had 1,750 stickers. Audrey had 480 fewer stickers than Carlos. Carlos gave some stickers to Audrey. In the end, Audrey had 3 times as many stickers as Carlos. How many stickers did Carlos have in the end?

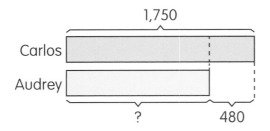

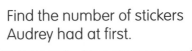

Find the number of stickers Audrey had at first.

$1,750 - 480 = 1,270$

Audrey had 1,270 stickers at first.

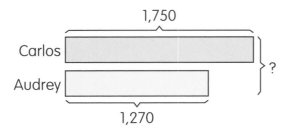

Next, find the total number of stickers Carlos and Audrey had.

$1,750 + 1,270 = 3,020$

Carlos and Audrey had a total of 3,020 stickers.

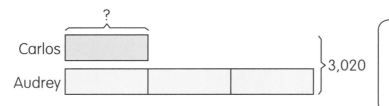

Lastly, divide the total number of stickers they had at first by 4. This will give the number of stickers Carlos had in the end.

4 units = 3,020
1 unit = 3,020 ÷ 4
       = 755

Carlos had 755 stickers in the end.

Work in groups.

Activity 1 **Completing the stories**

① Complete each story. You may use the words and numbers in the box.

28	jacket	25	basket	98	7
sweater	896	4	bag	lemons	fruit

a   The total cost of 3 sweaters and 5 jackets is $284.

Each _____ costs $_____ more than each _____.

Each _____ costs $_____.

b   A fruit vendor bought 16 baskets of _____. Each basket contained

_____ lemons. He packed the lemons in bags of _____.

He sold each bag for $_____. He received $_____.

Activity 2 **Creating real-world problems**

① Write a real-world problem involving the four operations on the next page. Use the words and numbers in the box below in your problem.

100	birds	5	trees	475	twice
stamps	12	3,200	fewer	23,600	more

② Ask another group to solve the problem and explain how to check the answers.

Real-world problem:

Solve. Show your work.

TRY Practice solving real-world problems

Solve. Use the bar model to help you.

1 Irene had $3,756 to spend on office furniture.
She bought a sofa for $1,195 and 6 chairs for $128 each.

a How much did she spend altogether?

b How much money did she have left?

a $128

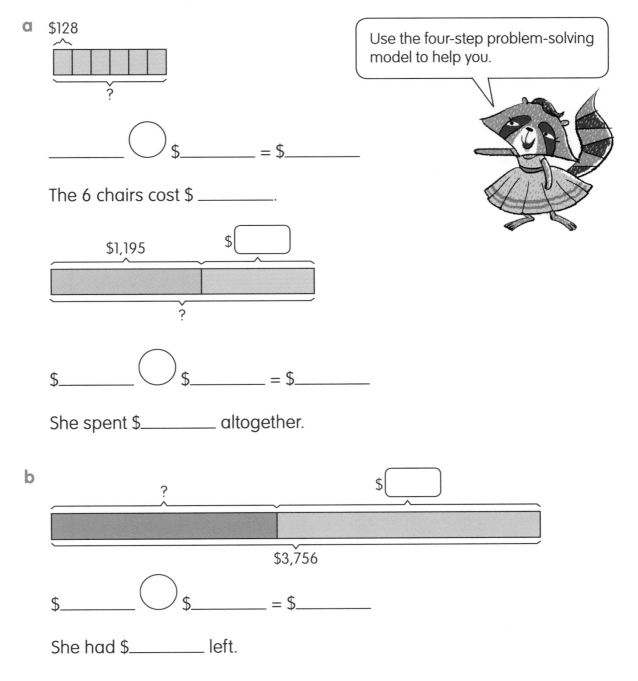

?

_____ ◯ $_____ = $_____

The 6 chairs cost $ _____.

$1,195 $ ▢

?

$_____ ◯ $_____ = $_____

She spent $_____ altogether.

b

? $ ▢

$3,756

$_____ ◯ $_____ = $_____

She had $_____ left.

Use the four-step problem-solving model to help you.

2 Nicolas had 1,240 beads and Ian had 4,730 beads. Ian gave some beads to Nicolas. In the end, Nicolas had twice as many beads as Ian.

   a How many beads did Ian have in the end?

   b How many beads did Ian give Nicolas?

a

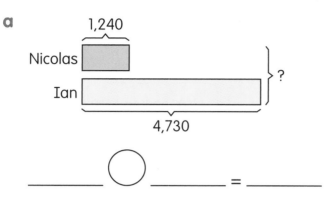

_____ ◯ _____ = _____

Nicolas and Ian had _____ beads altogether.

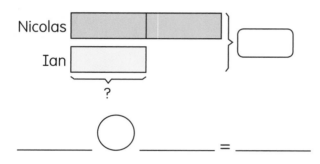

_____ ◯ _____ = _____

Ian had _____ beads in the end.

b

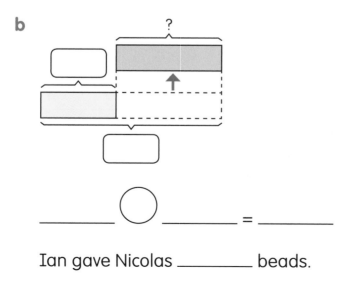

_____ ◯ _____ = _____

Ian gave Nicolas _____ beads.

3 A tailor had 5,000 buttons. He sewed 9 buttons on each shirt he made and had 2,048 buttons left. Then, he sold all of the shirts for $36 each. Find the total amount the tailor earned from selling the shirts.

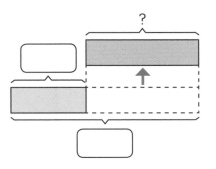

Solve. Draw a bar model to help you.

4 An empty box has a mass of 82 grams. Tristan packs 8 jars of honey in each of several boxes. The mass of each jar of honey is 420 grams. What is the total mass of 6 boxes of honey?

1 Lauren and Evan often meet each other in a local market. Lauren goes to the market every 2 days and Evan goes to the market every 3 days. Both of them meet at the market on January 1 of a calendar year. List the next four dates on which they will meet again at the market.

Use a calendar to help you.

2 Look at the dates on which they meet at the market. Find the pattern. Use the pattern to find four other dates on which they will meet.

INDEPENDENT PRACTICE

Solve. Draw a bar model to help you.

1 Sara, Hailey, and Ravi folded paper cranes to sell at a craft fair. Sara folded 325 paper cranes. Hailey folded 5 times as many paper cranes as Sara. Ravi folded 987 fewer paper cranes than Hailey.

a How many paper cranes did Hailey fold?

b How many paper cranes did Ravi and Hailey fold in all?

Kimberly made some bookmarks to sell for charity. She kept 1,022 bookmarks aside and bundled the rest equally in packs of 3. She sold all the bookmark packs for $4 each, and earned $3,704 for the charity. How many bookmarks did Kimberly make?

3 Katherine and Ivan had 96 marbles in all. Katherine lost 24 marbles to Ivan during a game. At the end of the game, Ivan had twice as many marbles as Katherine. How many marbles did Ivan have at first?

4 Amanda and Blake played a board game. In the game, Amanda had $2,740 in play money and Blake had $3,560. Amanda had to give some play money to Blake. After that, Blake had 4 times the amount of play money Amanda had. How much play money did Blake have in the end?

5 The sum of two numbers is 726. The difference between the two numbers is 102. Find the two numbers.

Is there another way you can find the numbers?

6　The mass of a teapot and 4 cups is 1,280 grams. The mass of the same teapot and 10 cups is 2,720 grams. Each cup has the same mass. What is the mass of the teapot?

Name: _____ Date: _____

Mathematical Habit 3 Construct viable arguments

Read the word problem. Then, look at Eric's solution.

> Ms. Scott had 708 pennies. She had twice as many pennies as Mr. Perez. Ms. Young had 3 times as many pennies as Mr. Perez. How many pennies did Ms. Young have?
>
> Eric's solution:
>
> $708 \times 2 = 1,416$
> $1,416 \times 3 = 4,248$
>
> Ms. Young had 4,248 pennies.

a Explain the mistake in Eric's solution.

b Show how you would solve the problem.

Problem Solving with Heuristics

1 **Mathematical Habit 2** Use mathematical reasoning

The factors of a number are 1, 2, 3, and 9. The number has 6 factors in all. What is the number?

2 **Mathematical Habit 1** Persevere in solving problems

The product of the page numbers on two facing pages in a storybook is 210. The book has 30 pages. What are the two page numbers?

3 **Mathematical Habit 4** Use mathematical models

A group of friends decided to collect pins. Valery had no pins at first. Aiden gave Valery some of his pins. He then had 3 times as many pins as Valery. After Aiden gave 24 pins to a friend and 72 pins to a neighbor, he had no pins left. How many pins did Aiden have at first?

CHAPTER WRAP-UP

? How can you multiply by a 2-digit number? How can you divide whole numbers?

Multiplication and Division

Multiplication

Multiplying by a 1-digit number:

$$\begin{array}{r} {\scriptstyle 1\ 1\ 1} \\ 1,3\ 4\ 5 \\ \times\qquad 3 \\ \hline 4,0\ 3\ 5 \end{array}$$

$1,345 \times 3 = 4,035$

Multiplying by a 2-digit number:

$$\begin{array}{r} 1\ 6 \\ \times\ 1\ 2 \\ \hline 3\ 2 \\ 1\ 6\ 0 \\ \hline 1\ 9\ 2 \end{array}$$

$16 \times 12 = 192$

Estimating products by rounding:
$2,874 \times 7$

↓

$3,000 \times 7 = 21,000$
The estimated product is 21,000.

Division

Dividing by a 1-digit number without regrouping, and with or without remainder:

$$\begin{array}{r} 1\ 3 \\ 3\overline{)3\ 9} \\ 3 \\ \hline 9 \\ 9 \\ \hline 0 \end{array}$$ ← Quotient

$39 \div 3 = 13$

Dividing by a 1-digit number with regrouping, and with or without remainder:

$$\begin{array}{r} 1\ 8 \\ 4\overline{)7\ 4} \\ 4 \\ \hline 3\ 4 \\ 3\ 2 \\ \hline 2 \end{array}$$ ← Quotient
← Remainder

$74 \div 4 = 18 \text{ R } 2$

Recall related multiplication facts to estimate quotients:
To estimate $546 \div 6$,
$6 \times 9\mathbf{0} = 54\mathbf{0}$
$6 \times 10\mathbf{0} = 60\mathbf{0}$
546 is closer to 540 than to 600.
$540 \div 6 = 90$
The estimated quotient is 90.

Factors and Multiples

Any whole number is a multiple of its factors.

$14 = 1 \times 14$
$14 = 2 \times 7$
1, 2, 7, and 14 are factors of 14.
So, 14 is a multiple of 1, 2, 7, and 14.

Prime and Composite Numbers

A prime number has only two different factors, 1 and the number itself.
$5 = 1 \times 5$
5 is a prime number.

A composite number has more than two different factors.
$6 = 1 \times 6$
$6 = 2 \times 3$
6 is a composite number.

Name: _____   Date: _____

Multiply. Show your work.

1 $167 \times 30 =$ _____

2 $690 \times 70 =$ _____

Use the area model to find the product. Show your work.

3 $2{,}102 \times 4 =$ _____

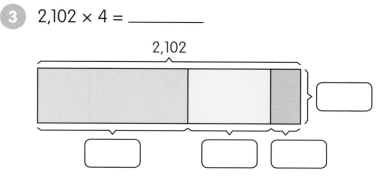

2,102

Multiply. Show your work.
Estimate to check that each answer is reasonable.

4 $8{,}007 \times 5 =$ _____

5 $96 \times 25 =$ _____

Use the area model to find the quotient. Show your work.

6 5,424 ÷ 6 = _____

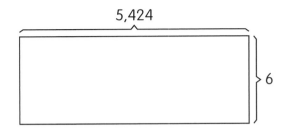

Divide. Show your work.
Estimate to check that each answer is reasonable.

7 91 ÷ 7 = _____   **8** 328 ÷ 5 = _____   **9** 5,376 ÷ 8 = _____

Find the factors of each number.

10 16   **11** 36

Write the common factors.

12 The common factors of 16 and 36 are _____.

Find the first ten multiples of each number.

13 4

_____

14 5

_____

Fill in the blank.

15 The first common multiple of 4 and 5 is _____.

Complete a statement that represents the multiplication equation.

16 $60 = 12 \times 5$

_____ is _____ times as many as _____.

Write a multiplication equation that represents the statement.

17 54 is 9 times as many as 6.

_____ = _____ × _____

Solve. Draw a bar model to help you.

18 Shop A sold 1,054 baseball caps. Shop B sold 3 times as many baseball caps as Shop A. How many baseball caps did Shop B sell?

19 Caroline has 425 football cards in her collection. She has 5 times as many football cards as Aarón. How many football cards does Aarón have?

20 A supermarket had 30 crates of apples. Each crate contained 148 apples. The supermarket sold 835 apples in the morning and 906 apples in the evening. How many apples were left?

Assessment Prep

Answer each question.

 21 Ten numbers are shown in the box.

| 11 | 23 | 24 | 31 | 39 |
| 57 | 61 | 63 | 91 | 97 |

Which list includes all the prime numbers that are shown in the box?

Ⓐ 11, 57, 63, 91, 97

Ⓑ 11, 23, 31, 61, 97

Ⓒ 24, 39, 57, 63, 91

Ⓓ 23, 31, 61, 63, 97

22 Select the **two** choices that are factor pairs for the number 36.

Ⓐ 2 and 16

Ⓑ 3 and 12

Ⓒ 4 and 8

Ⓓ 6 and 5

Ⓔ 9 and 4

23 Which number makes the equation true?

$32 \times 3 = 12 \times ?$

Ⓐ 3

Ⓑ 4

Ⓒ 6

Ⓓ 8

24 A baker made 366 muffins in the morning. He made another 110 muffins in the afternoon. He sold 154 muffins and packed the rest equally in boxes of 7 muffins each. How many boxes of muffins did he have? Write your work and answer in the space below.

Name: _____   Date: _____

Sale of Fruit

1 Cole and his friend, Zara, each ran a fruit stand in their neighborhood. When Cole and Zara compared the amount they made in June, Zara said, "You made $120! That is 3 times as much as the amount I made!" Cole wondered how much Zara made.

a Cole drew a bar model to figure out how much Zara made. Complete the bar model.

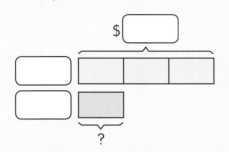

b Explain the bar model.

c What were Zara's sales, in dollars, in June?

2 Cole opened his fruit stand for 20 days in the month of June. He went to a nearby farm to buy supplies.

a If his supplies only lasted for 5 days, how many times did Cole go to the farm to buy new supplies in June? Draw a bar model to show your thinking.

b If each visit to the farm cost Cole $18, how much in total did he spend on supplies in June? Draw a bar model to show your thinking.

3 In July, Cole's sales were $160. He went to the farm 5 times to buy supplies. Each visit to the farm cost him $17. He used the money from his sales to pay for his July supplies. How much money did Cole have left? Show your work.

Rubric

Point(s)	Level	My Performance
7–8	4	• Most of my answers are correct. • I showed complete understanding of what I have learned. • I used the correct strategies to solve the problems. • I explained my answers and mathematical thinking clearly and completely.
5–6.5	3	• Some of my answers are correct. • I showed some understanding of what I have learned. • I used some correct strategies to solve the problems. • I explained my answers and mathematical thinking clearly.
3–4.5	2	• A few of my answers are correct. • I showed little understanding of what I have learned. • I used a few correct strategies to solve the problems. • I explained some of my answers and mathematical thinking clearly.
0–2.5	1	• A few of my answers are correct. • I showed little or no understanding of what I have learned. • I used a few strategies to solve the problems. • I did not explain my answers and mathematical thinking clearly.

Teacher's Comments

Backpack Supplies

Late each summer, students and their families shop for school supplies for the new school year. Schools and businesses such as grocery stores post supply lists.

What supplies did you put in your backpack this year? Did they include pocket folders? Colored pens and glue sticks? Where did you go to fill your backpack?

Task

Fill a Backpack

Work in small groups to find the cost of school supplies.

1 Ask your teacher or principal for a copy of this year's school-supply list. Use newspaper advertisements or search online for sales of the materials on your list. Record the cost of each item in a whole-dollar amount.

2 Some materials may come in packages that hold more items than you need. Write the package cost as a whole-dollar amount. Then, find the cost of each item in whole-dollar amounts.

3 If you need more than one of a certain item, multiply to find the total cost of this item.

4 Find the total cost of the supplies on your list. Then, multiply the cost by the number of people in your group.

5 Share your results with other groups. Sort costs from least to greatest.

6 Investigate community efforts where you live to help provide school supplies for all students. Discuss how you might participate in those efforts.

Chapter 3

Fractions and Mixed Numbers

How can you represent fractions greater than 1?
How can you add and subtract fractions?
How can you multiply fractions and whole numbers?

© 2020 Marshall Cavendish Education Pte Ltd

Name: _____   Date: _____

Understanding fractions and unit fractions

A fraction names equal parts of a whole.

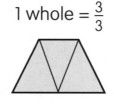 1 whole = $\frac{2}{2}$

1 whole = $\frac{3}{3}$

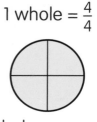 1 whole = $\frac{4}{4}$

A unit fraction names one of the equal parts of a whole.

$\frac{1}{3}$ is a unit fraction.

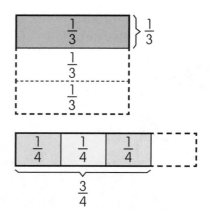

A non-unit fraction names more than one equal part of a whole.

$\frac{3}{4}$ is a non-unit fraction.

▶ **Quick Check**

Match each unit fraction with its model and name.

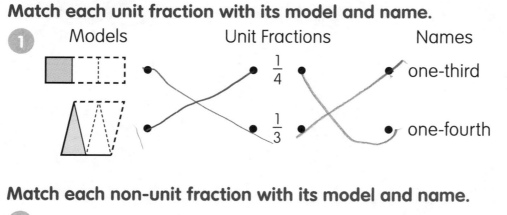

1   Models   Unit Fractions   Names

$\frac{1}{4}$ one-third

$\frac{1}{3}$ one-fourth

Match each non-unit fraction with its model and name.

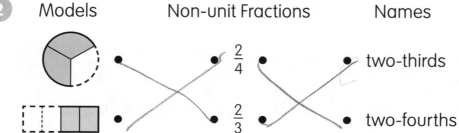

2   Models   Non-unit Fractions   Names

$\frac{2}{4}$ two-thirds

$\frac{2}{3}$ two-fourths

Making one whole with unit fractions

$\frac{1}{2} + \frac{1}{2} = \frac{2}{2}$
$\qquad\qquad = 1$

1 whole

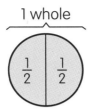

▶ **Quick Check**

Fill in each blank.

3
1 whole

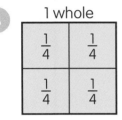

$$\frac{1}{4} + \frac{1}{4} + \frac{1}{4} + \frac{1}{4} = \frac{4}{4} = \underline{1 \text{ whole}}$$

4
1 whole

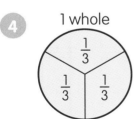

$$\frac{1}{3} + \frac{1}{3} + \frac{1}{3} = \frac{3}{3} = \underline{1 \text{ whole}}$$

Expressing fractions in terms of unit fractions

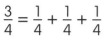

$\frac{3}{4}$ of the circle is green.

$\frac{3}{4} = \frac{1}{4} + \frac{1}{4} + \frac{1}{4}$

$\frac{1}{4}$ of the circle is white.

$\frac{3}{4}$ and $\frac{1}{4}$ make 1 whole.

▶ Quick Check

Express the shaded parts of each figure as a sum of unit fractions.
Then, complete each sentence.

5

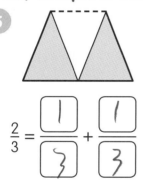

$\frac{2}{3} = \dfrac{1}{3} + \dfrac{1}{3}$

$\frac{2}{3}$ and $\dfrac{1}{3}$ make 1 whole.

6

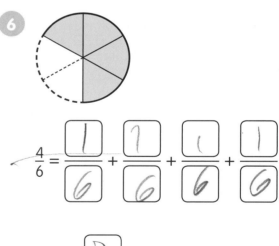

$\frac{4}{6} = \dfrac{1}{6} + \dfrac{1}{6} + \dfrac{1}{6} + \dfrac{1}{6}$

$\frac{4}{6}$ and $\dfrac{2}{6}$ make 1 whole.

Understanding like fractions

Like fractions are fractions whose wholes are divided into the same number of equal parts.

The whole is divided into 3 equal parts.
1 part out of the 3 equal parts is shaded.
$\frac{1}{3}$ of the figure is shaded.

The whole is divided into 3 equal parts.
2 parts out of the 3 equal parts are shaded.
$\frac{2}{3}$ of the figure is shaded.

The whole is divided into 3 equal parts.
3 parts out of the 3 equal parts are shaded.
$\frac{3}{3}$ of the figure is shaded.

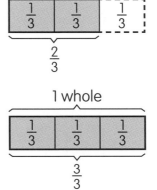

$\frac{1}{3}, \frac{2}{3}$ and $\frac{3}{3}$ are like fractions.

▶ Quick Check

Circle the like fractions.

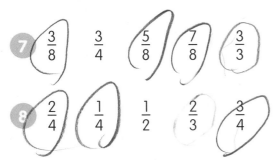

7 $\frac{3}{8}$ $\frac{3}{4}$ $\frac{5}{8}$ $\frac{7}{8}$ $\frac{3}{3}$

8 $\frac{2}{4}$ $\frac{1}{4}$ $\frac{1}{2}$ $\frac{2}{3}$ $\frac{3}{4}$

Representing fractions on a number line

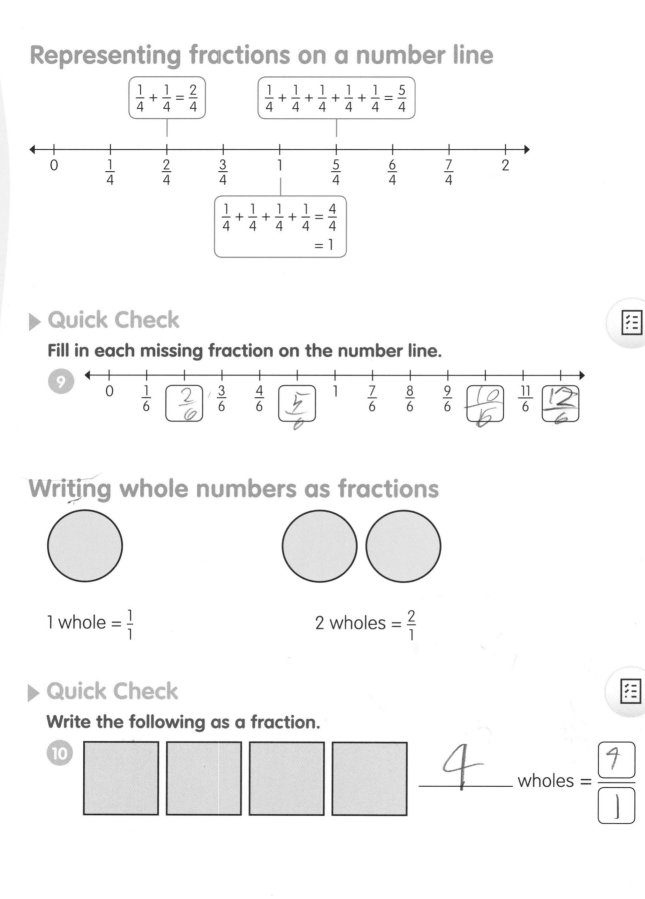

$$\frac{1}{4} + \frac{1}{4} = \frac{2}{4}$$

$$\frac{1}{4} + \frac{1}{4} + \frac{1}{4} + \frac{1}{4} + \frac{1}{4} = \frac{5}{4}$$

$$\frac{1}{4} + \frac{1}{4} + \frac{1}{4} + \frac{1}{4} = \frac{4}{4}$$
$$= 1$$

▸ **Quick Check**

Fill in each missing fraction on the number line.

9   0 $\frac{1}{6}$ $\frac{2}{6}$ $\frac{3}{6}$ $\frac{4}{6}$ $\frac{5}{6}$ 1 $\frac{7}{6}$ $\frac{8}{6}$ $\frac{9}{6}$ $\frac{10}{6}$ $\frac{11}{6}$ $\frac{12}{6}$

Writing whole numbers as fractions

1 whole = $\frac{1}{1}$

2 wholes = $\frac{2}{1}$

▸ **Quick Check**

Write the following as a fraction.

10   ____4____ wholes = $\frac{4}{1}$

Understanding fractions as part of a set

In a set of 8 triangles, $\frac{1}{4}$ of the triangles are blue.

How many triangles are blue?

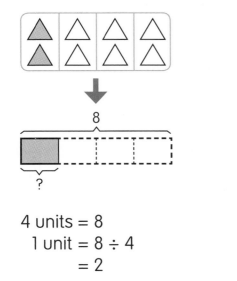

You need to find the value of $\frac{1}{4}$ of 8.

4 units = 8

1 unit = 8 ÷ 4

= 2

2 triangles are blue.

▶ Quick Check

Solve.

11 Find the value of $\frac{3}{8}$ of 16.

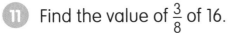

Understanding equivalent fractions

Equivalent fractions represent the same part of a whole.
You can show equivalent fractions in different ways.

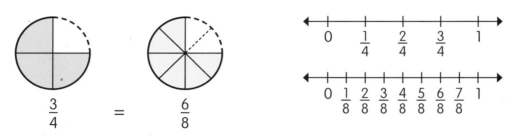

$$\frac{3}{4} = \frac{6}{8}$$

▶ **Quick Check**

Find each equivalent fraction.

12

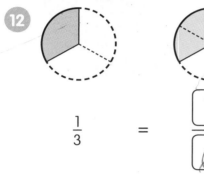

$$\frac{1}{3} = \frac{2}{6}$$

13

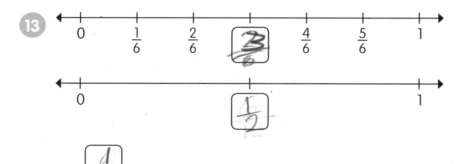

$$\frac{3}{6} = \frac{1}{2}$$

Comparing and ordering fractions

When comparing fractions with the same denominator, the greater fraction is the one with the greater numerator.

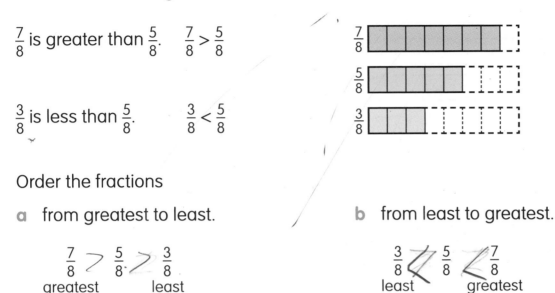

$\frac{7}{8}$ is greater than $\frac{5}{8}$. $\frac{7}{8} > \frac{5}{8}$

$\frac{3}{8}$ is less than $\frac{5}{8}$. $\frac{3}{8} < \frac{5}{8}$

Order the fractions

a   from greatest to least.

$$\frac{7}{8} > \frac{5}{8} > \frac{3}{8}$$
greatest   least

b   from least to greatest.

$$\frac{3}{8} < \frac{5}{8} < \frac{7}{8}$$
least   greatest

When comparing fractions with the same numerator, the greater fraction is the one with the lesser denominator.

$\frac{3}{4}$ is greater than $\frac{3}{6}$. $\frac{3}{4} > \frac{3}{6}$

$\frac{3}{8}$ is less than $\frac{3}{6}$. $\frac{3}{8} < \frac{3}{6}$

Order the fractions

a   from greatest to least.

$$\frac{3}{4} > \frac{3}{6} < \frac{3}{8}$$
greatest   least

b   from least to greatest.

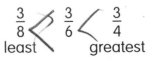

$$\frac{3}{8} < \frac{3}{6} < \frac{3}{4}$$
least   greatest

▶ **Quick Check**

Compare each pair of fractions.

14 Which is greater, $\frac{1}{4}$ or $\frac{3}{4}$?

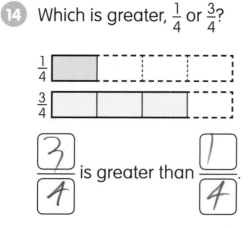

$\frac{3}{4}$ is greater than $\frac{1}{4}$.

15 Which is less, $\frac{5}{6}$ or $\frac{5}{8}$?

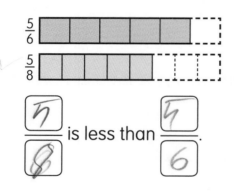

$\frac{5}{8}$ is less than $\frac{5}{6}$.

16 Order $\frac{2}{3}$, $\frac{2}{6}$, and $\frac{2}{4}$ from least to greatest.

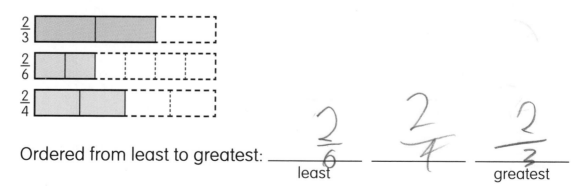

Ordered from least to greatest: $\frac{2}{6}$ _____ $\frac{2}{4}$ _____ $\frac{2}{3}$ _____
least   greatest

1 Equivalent Fractions

Learning Objectives:
- Use multiplication and division to find equivalent fractions.
- Write a fraction in simplest form.

THINK

1. What is the least fraction with denominator 12 that is greater than $\frac{5}{6}$?

2. What is the greatest fraction with denominator 9 that is greater than $\frac{5}{6}$?

ENGAGE

a. Use ⊗ or ▭ to show $\frac{1}{2}$ in two ways.

b. Write down the greatest fraction with denominator 8 that is less than $\frac{1}{2}$. Explain how you found your answer to your partner.

LEARN Find equivalent fractions

1. Look at the first three equivalent fractions of $\frac{2}{3}$.

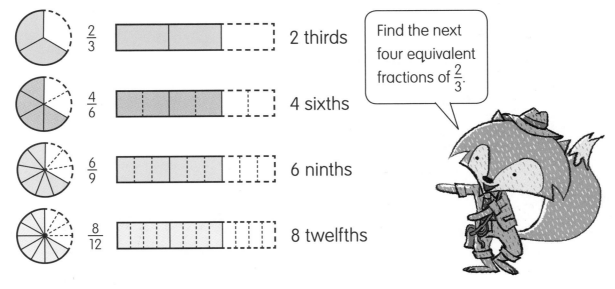

$\frac{2}{3}$ 2 thirds

$\frac{4}{6}$ 4 sixths

$\frac{6}{9}$ 6 ninths

$\frac{8}{12}$ 8 twelfths

Find the next four equivalent fractions of $\frac{2}{3}$.

All the shaded parts are equivalent.

2 You can multiply the numerator and denominator by the same number to find an equivalent fraction.

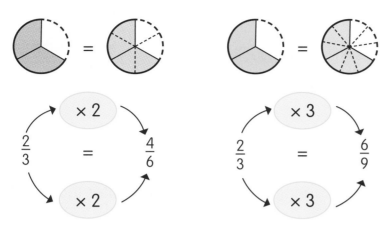

3 You can also find equivalent fractions by **simplifying** fractions. You simplify a fraction by dividing the numerator and denominator by the same number.

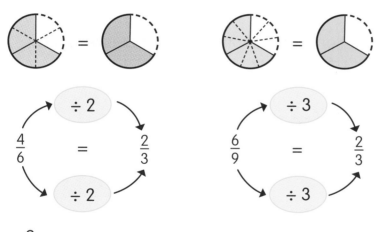

$\frac{2}{3}$ cannot be simplified further.

$\frac{2}{3}$ is the **simplest form** of $\frac{4}{6}$ and $\frac{6}{9}$.

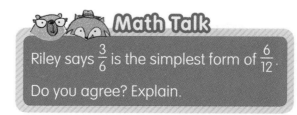

Math Talk

Riley says $\frac{3}{6}$ is the simplest form of $\frac{6}{12}$.

Do you agree? Explain.

(1) Your teacher will give you two strips of paper. Use them to form a pair of equivalent fractions. Paste the strips in the box.

Example:

$\frac{1}{2}$

$\frac{2}{4}$

(2) **Mathematical Habit 3** Construct viable arguments

Explain why the fractions are equal. Show how to use one fraction to find the other.

TRY Practice finding equivalent fractions

Fill in each blank.

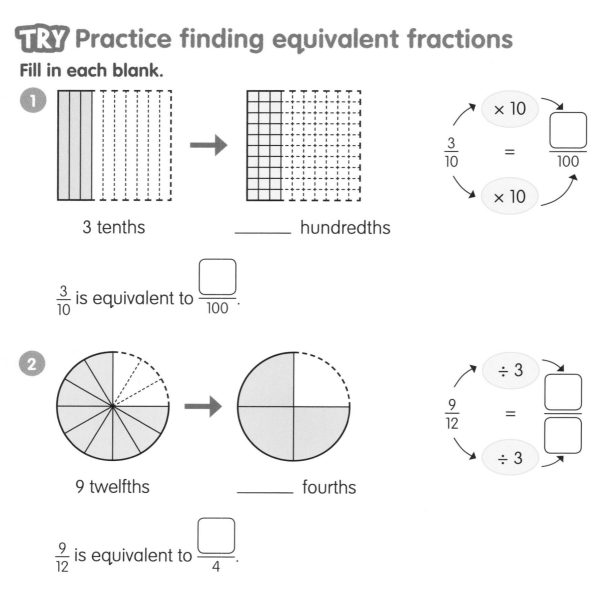

1

3 tenths   _____ hundredths

$\dfrac{3}{10}$ is equivalent to $\dfrac{\Box}{100}$.

2

9 twelfths   _____ fourths

$\dfrac{9}{12}$ is equivalent to $\dfrac{\Box}{4}$.

Use multiplication to find each equivalent fraction.

3

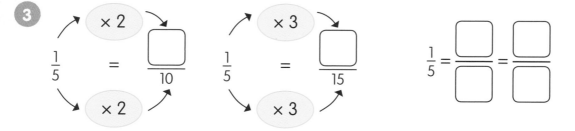

$\dfrac{1}{5} = \dfrac{\Box}{\Box} = \dfrac{\Box}{\Box}$

Use division to find each equivalent fraction.

4

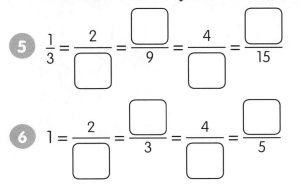

$$\frac{4}{12} = \frac{\boxed{}}{6}$$

$$\frac{4}{12} = \frac{1}{\boxed{}}$$

$$\frac{4}{12} = \frac{\boxed{}}{6} = \frac{1}{\boxed{}}$$

The simplest form of $\frac{4}{12}$ is _____.

Find the next four equivalent fractions of each fraction.

5 $\quad \dfrac{1}{3} = \dfrac{2}{\boxed{}} = \dfrac{\boxed{}}{9} = \dfrac{4}{\boxed{}} = \dfrac{\boxed{}}{15}$

6 $\quad 1 = \dfrac{2}{\boxed{}} = \dfrac{\boxed{}}{3} = \dfrac{4}{\boxed{}} = \dfrac{\boxed{}}{5}$

Write each fraction in simplest form.

7 $\quad \dfrac{8}{12} = \dfrac{\boxed{}}{3}$

8 $\quad \dfrac{3}{6} = \dfrac{1}{\boxed{}}$

9 $\quad \dfrac{8}{10} = \dfrac{\boxed{}}{\boxed{}}$

10 $\quad \dfrac{15}{100} = \dfrac{\boxed{}}{\boxed{}}$

MATCH UP!

What you need:

Players: 4
Materials: Game cards

What to do:

Put the cards face down on the table.

1. Player 1 turns over any two cards. If the cards show a pair of equivalent fractions, the player keeps the cards and takes another turn.

2. If the cards do not show a pair of equivalent fractions, the player turns the cards back over. Player 2 takes his or her turn.

3. Repeat until all pairs of equivalent fractions have been found.

Who is the winner?

The player with the most pairs of cards wins.

INDEPENDENT PRACTICE

Find each equivalent fraction.

1

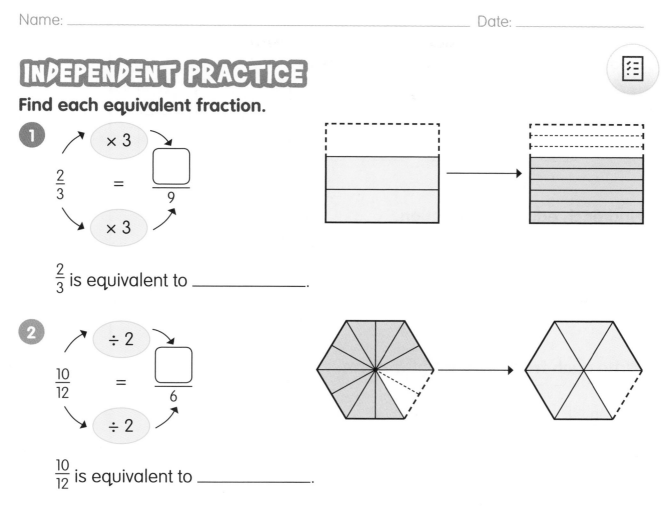

$\frac{2}{3} = \frac{\boxed{}}{9}$ (× 3, × 3)

$\frac{2}{3}$ is equivalent to _____.

2

$\frac{10}{12} = \frac{\boxed{}}{6}$ (÷ 2, ÷ 2)

$\frac{10}{12}$ is equivalent to _____.

Find each missing numerator or denominator.

3 $\frac{4}{5} = \frac{\boxed{}}{10}$

4 $\frac{3}{4} = \frac{9}{\boxed{}}$

5 $\frac{6}{10} = \frac{3}{\boxed{}}$

6 $\frac{28}{\boxed{}} = \frac{7}{25}$

We can multiply or divide to find equivalent fractions.

Find the next eight equivalent fractions.

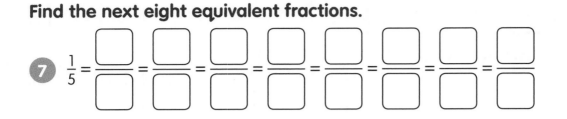

7 $\dfrac{1}{5} = \dfrac{\square}{\square} = \dfrac{\square}{\square} = \dfrac{\square}{\square} = \dfrac{\square}{\square} = \dfrac{\square}{\square} = \dfrac{\square}{\square} = \dfrac{\square}{\square} = \dfrac{\square}{\square}$

Find each equivalent fraction.

8 $\dfrac{3}{\square} = \dfrac{6}{12} = \dfrac{\square}{24}$

9 $\dfrac{4}{\square} = \dfrac{\square}{20} = \dfrac{12}{\square} = \dfrac{\square}{40}$

Write each fraction in simplest form.

10 $\dfrac{10}{12} = \dfrac{\square}{\square}$

11 $\dfrac{6}{12} = \dfrac{\square}{\square}$

12 $\dfrac{5}{100} = \dfrac{\square}{\square}$

13 $\dfrac{36}{100} = \dfrac{\square}{\square}$

Match each pair of equivalent fractions.

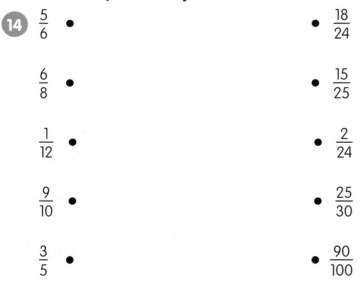

14 $\dfrac{5}{6}$ •   • $\dfrac{18}{24}$

$\dfrac{6}{8}$ •   • $\dfrac{15}{25}$

$\dfrac{1}{12}$ •   • $\dfrac{2}{24}$

$\dfrac{9}{10}$ •   • $\dfrac{25}{30}$

$\dfrac{3}{5}$ •   • $\dfrac{90}{100}$

INDEPENDENT PRACTICE

Use equivalent fractions to compare each pair of fractions.

1 Which is less, $\frac{3}{8}$ or $\frac{1}{2}$?

_____ is less than _____.

2 Which is greater, $\frac{3}{4}$ or $\frac{2}{3}$?

_____ is greater than _____.

Use the benchmark fraction $\frac{1}{2}$ to compare each pair of fractions.
Write < or >.

3 Which is less, $\frac{5}{8}$ or $\frac{3}{10}$?

$\frac{5}{8}$ ◯ $\frac{1}{2}$

$\frac{3}{10}$ ◯ $\frac{1}{2}$

So, $\frac{5}{8}$ ◯ $\frac{3}{10}$.

4 Which is greater, $\frac{3}{5}$ or $\frac{5}{12}$?

$\frac{3}{5}$ ◯ $\frac{1}{2}$

$\frac{5}{12}$ ◯ $\frac{1}{2}$

So, $\frac{3}{5}$ ◯ $\frac{5}{12}$.

Compare each pair of fractions. Write < or >.

5) $\frac{5}{12}$ ◯ $\frac{9}{10}$ 6) $\frac{2}{5}$ ◯ $\frac{1}{3}$

7) $\frac{3}{4}$ ◯ $\frac{7}{100}$ 8) $\frac{5}{6}$ ◯ $\frac{7}{8}$

Circle the greatest fraction in each set.

9) $\frac{2}{3}$ $\frac{1}{4}$ $\frac{5}{6}$ 10) $\frac{1}{2}$ $\frac{7}{100}$ $\frac{7}{10}$

Order each set of fractions from least to greatest.

11) $\frac{5}{8}$ $\frac{2}{5}$ $\frac{1}{4}$

_____   _____   _____

　least   　　　　　　　greatest

12) $\frac{3}{4}$ $\frac{1}{3}$ $\frac{5}{6}$

_____   _____   _____

　least   　　　　　　　greatest

Order each set of fractions from greatest to least.

13) $\frac{7}{10}$ $\frac{5}{12}$ $\frac{3}{4}$

_____   _____   _____

　greatest   　　　　　　least

14) $\frac{3}{8}$ $\frac{5}{6}$ $\frac{2}{3}$

_____   _____   _____

　greatest   　　　　　　least

3 Adding and Subtracting Like Fractions

Learning Objectives:
- Add like fractions.
- Subtract like fractions.

THINK

Grace and Mason shared a granola bar. Grace ate $\frac{6}{8}$ of the bar more than Mason. What fraction of the granola bar did each person eat?

ENGAGE

a Fold a rectangular piece of paper into 6 equal parts. Color 2 parts blue. What fraction is not colored?

b Color the remaining parts of the paper yellow and green such that there is twice as much yellow as green. What fraction of the paper is yellow?

LEARN Add like fractions

1 Tomas ate $\frac{1}{4}$ of a waffle. Violeta ate $\frac{2}{4}$ of it.

What fraction of the waffle did they eat in all?

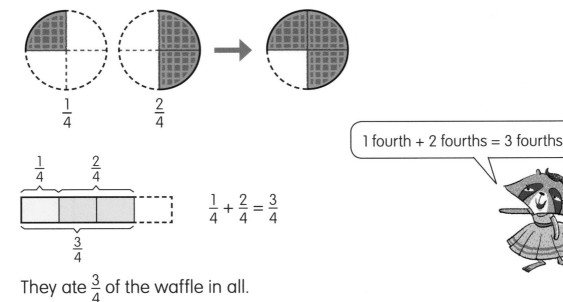

$$\frac{1}{4} + \frac{2}{4} = \frac{3}{4}$$

1 fourth + 2 fourths = 3 fourths

They ate $\frac{3}{4}$ of the waffle in all.

 **Math Talk**

Claire says the sum of $\frac{2}{5}$ and $\frac{1}{5}$ is $\frac{3}{10}$. Do you agree with Claire? Explain your reasoning to your partner.

Hands-on Activity Adding like fractions

Work in pairs.

① Add $\frac{5}{8}$ and $\frac{1}{8}$. Write the answer in simplest form.

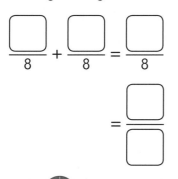

$$\frac{\square}{8} + \frac{\square}{8} = \frac{\square}{8}$$

$$= \frac{\square}{\square}$$

② Use ⊘ to check your answer.

③ Repeat ① and ② to solve each of the following problems.

a Add $\frac{2}{10}$ and $\frac{4}{10}$.

b Add $\frac{2}{6}$ and $\frac{2}{6}$.

c Add $\frac{1}{12}$ and $\frac{6}{12}$.

TRY Practice adding like fractions

Write the correct fraction in each box. Use the models to help you.

1 Faith and Aki bought a fruit tart. Faith ate $\frac{5}{10}$ of the fruit tart. Aki ate $\frac{2}{10}$ of the fruit tart. What fraction of the fruit tart did they eat in all?

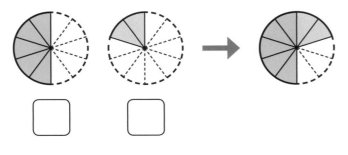

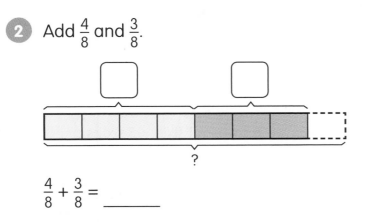

$\frac{5}{10} + \frac{2}{10} =$ _____

They ate _____ of the fruit tart in all.

2 Add $\frac{4}{8}$ and $\frac{3}{8}$.

?

$\frac{4}{8} + \frac{3}{8} =$ _____

Add. Write each answer in simplest form.

3 $\frac{2}{6} + \frac{1}{6} = \frac{\boxed{}}{6}$

= _____

4 $\frac{1}{12} + \frac{3}{12} = \frac{\boxed{}}{12}$

= _____

ENGAGE

a Fold a rectangular piece of paper into 8 equal parts. Color 3 parts blue. What fraction is not colored?

b Color the remaining parts of the paper yellow and green. The fraction of yellow parts is $\frac{1}{8}$ less than the fraction of green parts. What fraction of the paper is blue and yellow?

LEARN Subtract like fractions

1 Cameron bought a fruit pie. He gave $\frac{1}{6}$ of the fruit pie to his sister. What fraction of the pie did he have left?

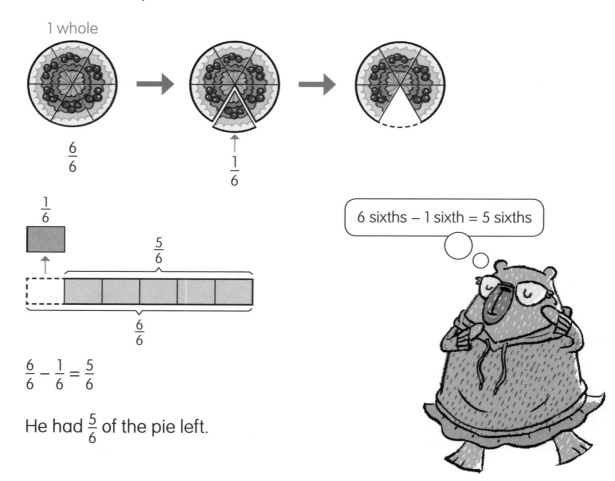

$$\frac{6}{6} - \frac{1}{6} = \frac{5}{6}$$

He had $\frac{5}{6}$ of the pie left.

> 6 sixths − 1 sixth = 5 sixths

Hands-on Activity Subtracting like fractions

Work in pairs.

(1) Subtract $\frac{1}{8}$ from $\frac{3}{8}$. Write the answer in simplest form.

$$\frac{\boxed{}}{8} - \frac{\boxed{}}{8} = \frac{\boxed{}}{8}$$

$$= \frac{\boxed{}}{\boxed{}}$$

(2) Use 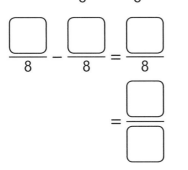 to check your answer.

(3) Repeat (1) and (2) to solve each of the following problems.

   a Subtract $\frac{2}{10}$ from $\frac{5}{10}$.

   b Subtract $\frac{2}{5}$ and $\frac{4}{5}$.

   c Subtract $\frac{4}{8}$ from 1.

TRY Practice subtracting like fractions

Write the correct fraction in each box. Use the models to help you.

1 Emma had $\frac{2}{3}$ of a pancake. She ate $\frac{1}{3}$ of the pancake. What fraction of the pancake did Emma have left? ?

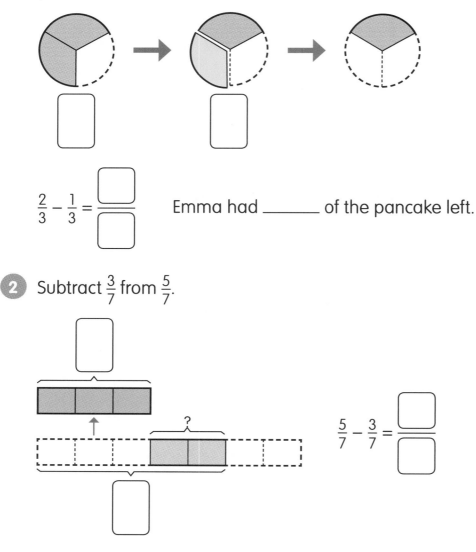

$$\frac{2}{3} - \frac{1}{3} = \frac{\boxed{}}{\boxed{}}$$

Emma had _____ of the pancake left.

2 Subtract $\frac{3}{7}$ from $\frac{5}{7}$.

$$\frac{5}{7} - \frac{3}{7} = \frac{\boxed{}}{\boxed{}}$$

Subtract. Write each answer in simplest form.

3 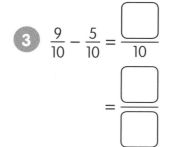 $\dfrac{9}{10} - \dfrac{5}{10} = \dfrac{\boxed{}}{10}$

$= \dfrac{\boxed{}}{\boxed{}}$

4 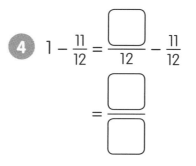 $1 - \dfrac{11}{12} = \dfrac{\boxed{}}{12} - \dfrac{11}{12}$

$= \dfrac{\boxed{}}{\boxed{}}$

INDEPENDENT PRACTICE

Add. Show your work. Write each answer in simplest form.

1 $\frac{3}{6} + \frac{2}{6} = \dfrac{\boxed{}}{\boxed{}}$

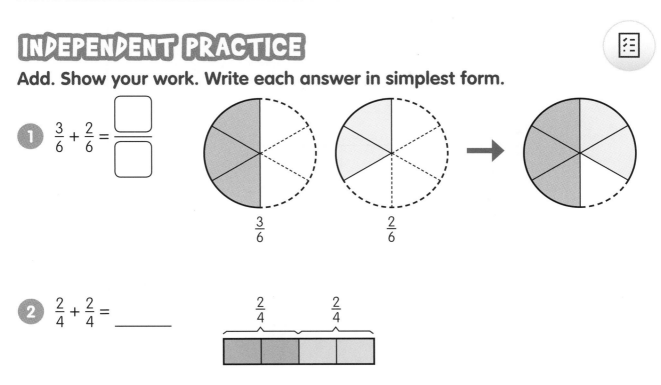

$\frac{3}{6}$ $\frac{2}{6}$

2 $\frac{2}{4} + \frac{2}{4} = \underline{\hspace{3cm}}$

$\frac{2}{4}$ $\frac{2}{4}$

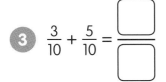

Add. Show your work. Write each answer in simplest form.

3 $\frac{3}{10} + \frac{5}{10} = \dfrac{\boxed{}}{\boxed{}}$

4 $\frac{2}{8} + \frac{6}{8} = \underline{\hspace{3cm}}$

Subtract. Show your work.

5   $\dfrac{3}{4} - \dfrac{2}{4} = \dfrac{\boxed{}}{\boxed{}}$

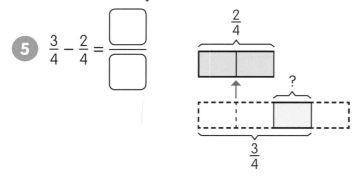

6   $1 - \dfrac{3}{5} = \dfrac{\boxed{}}{\boxed{}}$

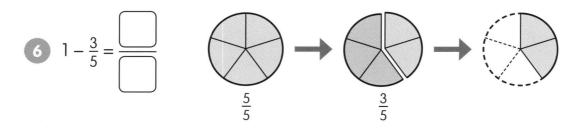

Subtract. Show your work. Write each answer in simplest form.

7   $\dfrac{11}{12} - \dfrac{7}{12} = \dfrac{\boxed{}}{\boxed{}}$

8   $1 - \dfrac{3}{6} = \dfrac{\boxed{}}{\boxed{}}$

Name: _____   Date: _____

4 Mixed Numbers

Learning Objectives:

- Express the sum of a whole number and a proper fraction as a mixed number.
- Interpret pictorial representations of mixed numbers.
- Write the fractional part of a mixed number in simplest form.
- Use a number line to identify mixed numbers.

New Vocabulary
mixed number

THINK

Count by 1s. 1, 2, 3, 4, 5, … We use these numbers to represent wholes. Are there any numbers between any two of these numbers? If there are, how can you find these numbers?

ENGAGE

a Mark the points 1, 2, 3, and $1\frac{1}{4}$ on a number line.

b Fill in the blank with the least possible number with denominator 8.

$1, 1\frac{1}{4}, 2, \underline{\hspace{1.5cm}}, 3$

What is the difference between this number and $1\frac{1}{4}$?

LEARN Write mixed numbers

1 Ms. Davis sold two pies. Then, she sold half of another pie.

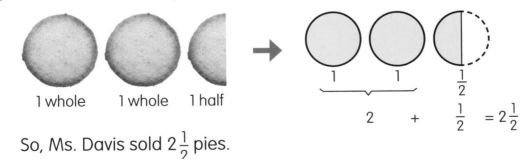

1 whole   1 whole   1 half

So, Ms. Davis sold $2\frac{1}{2}$ pies.

$2\frac{1}{2}$ is an example of a mixed number.

A mixed number includes a whole number and a fraction.

2 A jug contains $1\frac{4}{10}$ liters of strawberry milk.

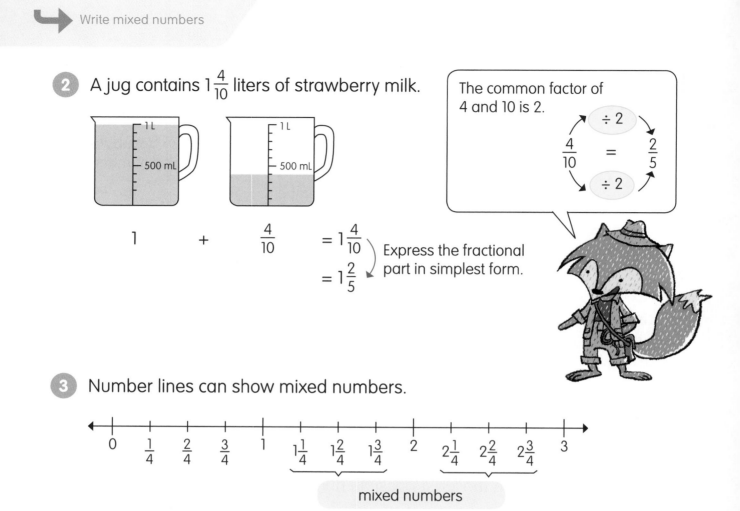

The common factor of 4 and 10 is 2.

$$\frac{4}{10} = \frac{2}{5}$$

$$1 \qquad + \qquad \frac{4}{10} \qquad = 1\frac{4}{10}$$
$$= 1\frac{2}{5}$$

Express the fractional part in simplest form.

3 Number lines can show mixed numbers.

```
0   1/4   2/4   3/4   1   1 1/4  1 2/4  1 3/4   2   2 1/4  2 2/4  2 3/4   3
```

mixed numbers

Math Talk

Look at the container.

Explain to your partner how you write the amount of water in the container.

Hands-on Activity Showing mixed numbers

Work in pairs.

(1) Use  to show $2\frac{3}{5}$.

(2) Represent the mixed number on the number line.

```
←—+—+—+—+—+—+—+—+—+—+—+—→
  1         2         3
```

(3) Repeat (1) and (2) with $3\frac{5}{6}$.

```
←—+—+—+—+—+—+—+—+—+—+—+—→
  3         4         5
```

TRY Practice writing mixed numbers

Write the mixed number that the shaded parts represent.

1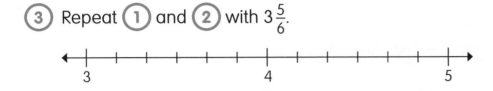

$1 + \dfrac{\boxed{}}{8} =$ _____

1 whole _____ eighths

Find each missing fraction or mixed number.

2 The mass of a box of washing powder is 3 kilograms. The mass of two bars of soap is $\frac{1}{10}$ kilogram. What is the total mass of the items?

$3 +$ _____ $=$ _____

The total mass of the items is _____ kilograms.

4 Mixed Numbers **263**

© 2020 Marshall Cavendish Education Pte Ltd

Find each missing mixed number on the number line.

3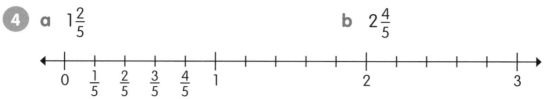

Mark an X on the number line to show each mixed number.

4 a $1\dfrac{2}{5}$ b $2\dfrac{4}{5}$

Express each mixed number in simplest form.

5 $2\dfrac{6}{8} = $ _____

6 $3\dfrac{8}{10} = $ _____

7 $4\dfrac{6}{12} = $ _____

8 $3\dfrac{10}{100} = $ _____

MATH SHARING

Mathematical Habit **6** Use precise mathematical language

Look around your house or your school for items that show mixed numbers. Record the items and the mixed numbers shown. Share your findings with your partner.

Example:
Measuring cup

INDEPENDENT PRACTICE

Use the shaded parts of each model to fill in each blank.

1

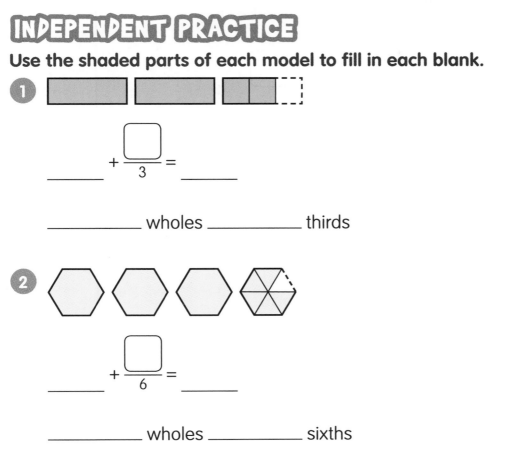

_____ + $\dfrac{\boxed{}}{3}$ = _____

_____ wholes _____ thirds

2

_____ + $\dfrac{\boxed{}}{6}$ = _____

_____ wholes _____ sixths

Write the amount of water in each tank as a mixed number in simplest form.

3

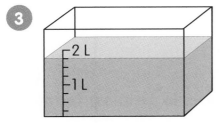

_____ liters

4

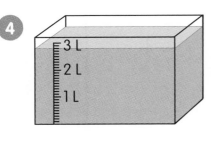

_____ liters

Find each missing mixed number on the number line.

5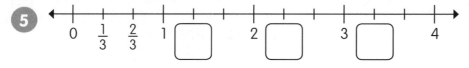

Mark an X on the number line to show each mixed number.

6 a $1\frac{1}{6}$ b $3\frac{3}{6}$

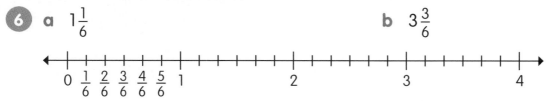

Express each mixed number in simplest form.

7 $1\frac{4}{6} =$ _____

8 $2\frac{6}{10} =$ _____

9 $3\frac{8}{12} =$ _____

10 $6\frac{5}{10} =$ _____

Fill in each missing mixed number. Write each answer in simplest form.

11

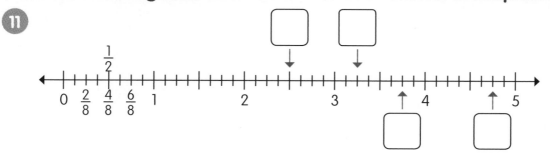

Improper Fractions

Learning Objectives:
- Interpret pictorial representations of improper fractions.
- Write an improper fraction in simplest form.
- Use a number line to identify improper fractions.

> **New Vocabulary**
> improper fraction

THINK

Four fractions are arranged in an order. Three of the fractions are $\frac{6}{5}$, $\frac{8}{9}$, and $\frac{11}{3}$. What is the possible missing fraction?

ENGAGE

Use to model each fraction of a pie.

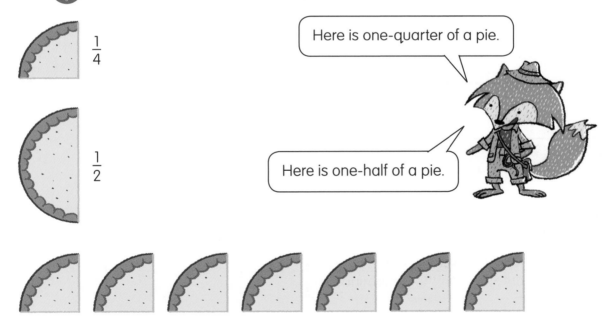

How much pie is there in all? How can you express your answer in different ways? Explain your thinking to your partner.

LEARN Write improper fractions

1 Alyssa has some strips of ribbon.

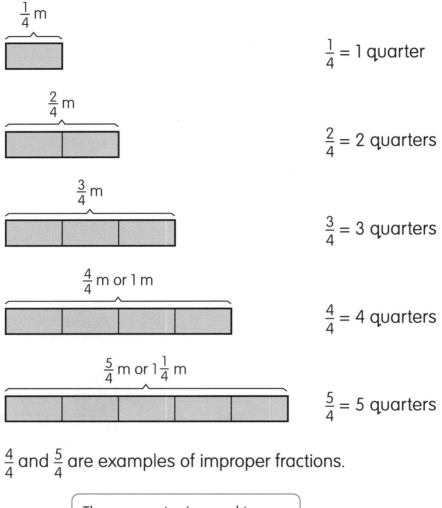

$\frac{1}{4}$ m

$\frac{1}{4}$ = 1 quarter

$\frac{2}{4}$ m

$\frac{2}{4}$ = 2 quarters

$\frac{3}{4}$ m

$\frac{3}{4}$ = 3 quarters

$\frac{4}{4}$ m or 1 m

$\frac{4}{4}$ = 4 quarters

$\frac{5}{4}$ m or $1\frac{1}{4}$ m

$\frac{5}{4}$ = 5 quarters

$\frac{4}{4}$ and $\frac{5}{4}$ are examples of improper fractions.

$\frac{4}{4}$ ──── The numerator is equal to or greater than the denominator. ──── $\frac{5}{4}$

Improper fractions are equal to or greater than 1.

2 Number lines can show improper fractions.

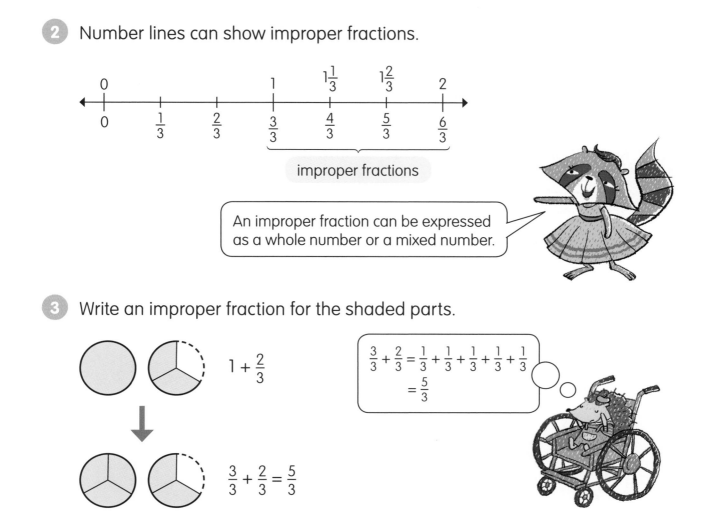

improper fractions

An improper fraction can be expressed as a whole number or a mixed number.

3 Write an improper fraction for the shaded parts.

$1 + \frac{2}{3}$

$\frac{3}{3} + \frac{2}{3} = \frac{5}{3}$

$$\frac{3}{3} + \frac{2}{3} = \frac{1}{3} + \frac{1}{3} + \frac{1}{3} + \frac{1}{3} + \frac{1}{3}$$
$$= \frac{5}{3}$$

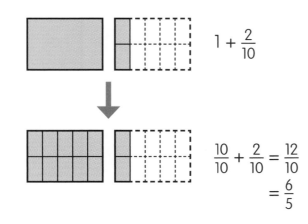

4 Write an improper fraction for the shaded parts. Express the fraction in simplest form.

$1 + \frac{2}{10}$

$$\frac{10}{10} + \frac{2}{10} = \frac{12}{10}$$
$$= \frac{6}{5}$$

Hands-on Activity Showing improper fractions

Work in pairs.

1. Use 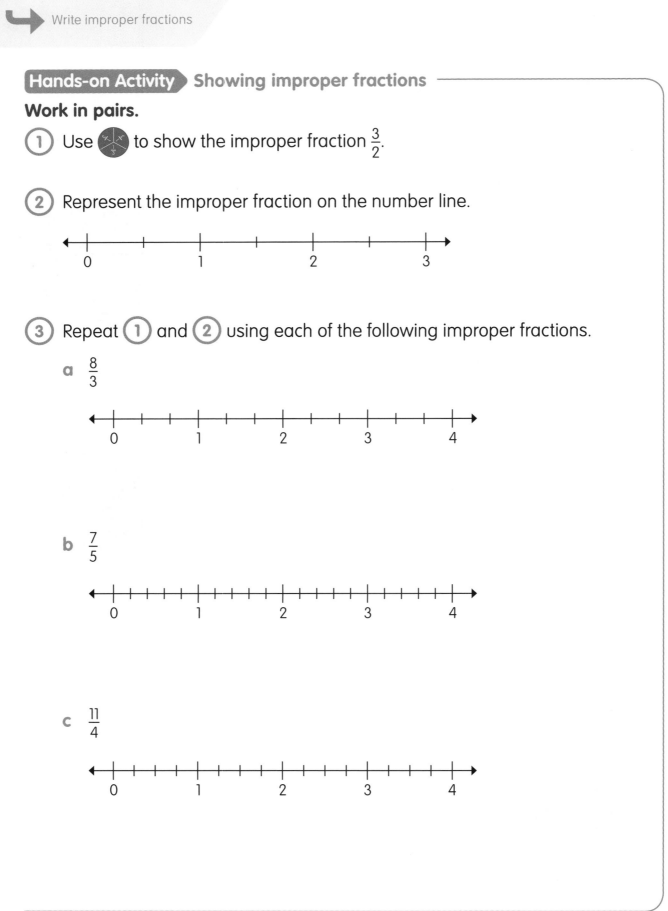 to show the improper fraction $\frac{3}{2}$.

2. Represent the improper fraction on the number line.

3. Repeat (1) and (2) using each of the following improper fractions.

   a $\frac{8}{3}$

   b $\frac{7}{5}$

   c $\frac{11}{4}$

TRY Practice writing improper fractions

Write the improper fraction that the shaded parts represent.

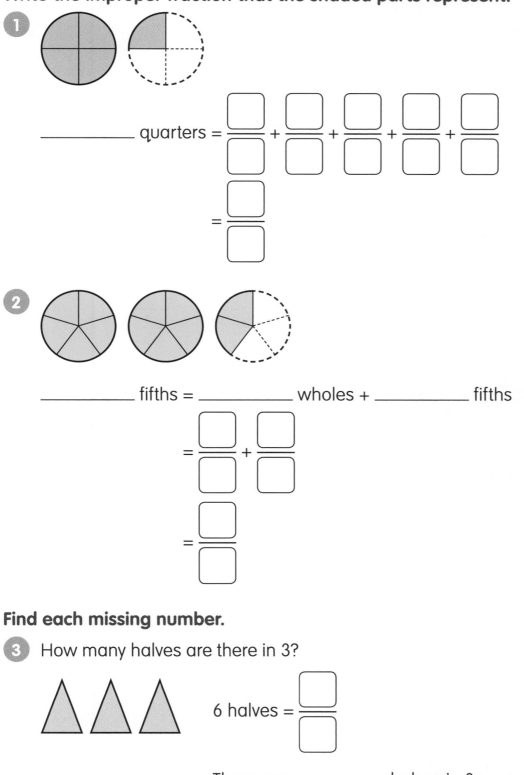

1.

_____ quarters = $\frac{\square}{\square}$ + $\frac{\square}{\square}$ + $\frac{\square}{\square}$ + $\frac{\square}{\square}$ + $\frac{\square}{\square}$

= $\frac{\square}{\square}$

2.

_____ fifths = _____ wholes + _____ fifths

= $\frac{\square}{\square}$ + $\frac{\square}{\square}$

= $\frac{\square}{\square}$

Find each missing number.

3. How many halves are there in 3?

6 halves = $\frac{\square}{\square}$

There are _____ halves in 3.

④ How many quarters are there in $1\frac{3}{4}$?

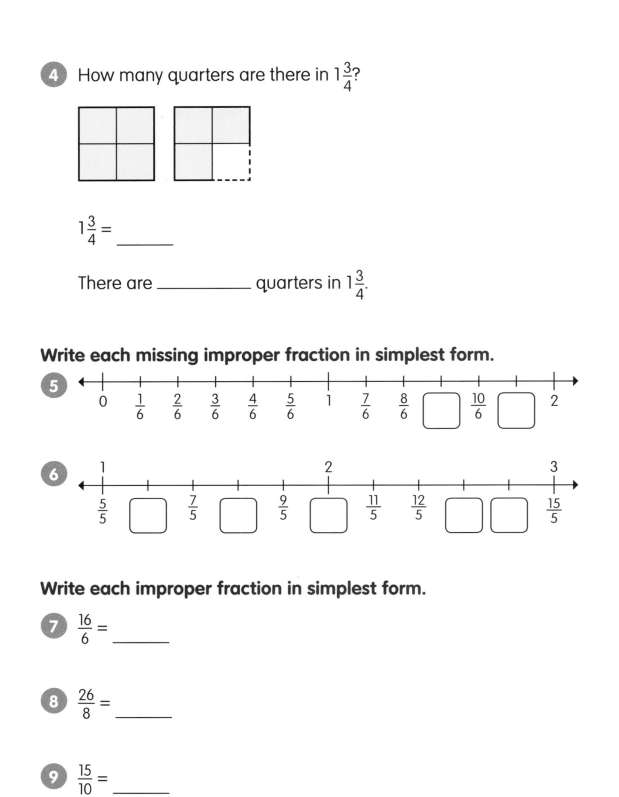

$1\frac{3}{4} =$ _____

There are _____ quarters in $1\frac{3}{4}$.

Write each missing improper fraction in simplest form.

⑤

0    $\frac{1}{6}$ $\frac{2}{6}$ $\frac{3}{6}$ $\frac{4}{6}$ $\frac{5}{6}$ 1 $\frac{7}{6}$ $\frac{8}{6}$ ☐ $\frac{10}{6}$ ☐   2

⑥

1    $\frac{5}{5}$ ☐ $\frac{7}{5}$ ☐ $\frac{9}{5}$ ☐ $\frac{11}{5}$ $\frac{12}{5}$ ☐   ☐ $\frac{15}{5}$ 3

Write each improper fraction in simplest form.

⑦ $\frac{16}{6} =$ _____

⑧ $\frac{26}{8} =$ _____

⑨ $\frac{15}{10} =$ _____

⑩ $\frac{28}{12} =$ _____

INDEPENDENT PRACTICE

Write the improper fraction that the shaded parts represent.

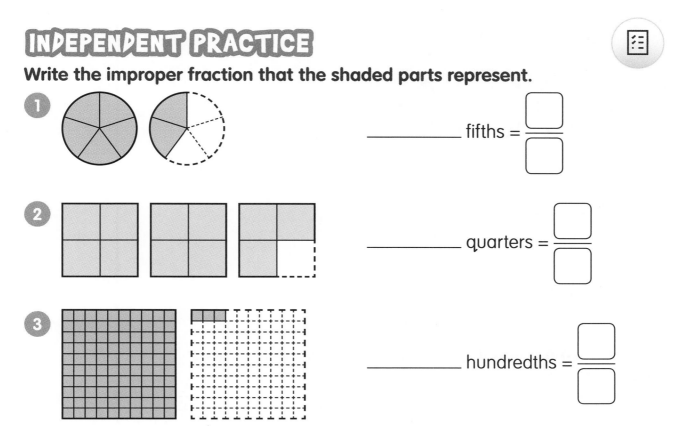

1 _____ fifths = $\dfrac{\Box}{\Box}$

2 _____ quarters = $\dfrac{\Box}{\Box}$

3 _____ hundredths = $\dfrac{\Box}{\Box}$

Find each missing number.

4 How many sixths are there in 2?

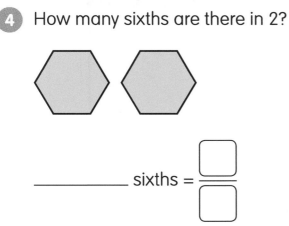

_____ sixths = $\dfrac{\Box}{\Box}$

There are _____ sixths in 2.

5 How many eighths are there in $2\frac{3}{8}$?

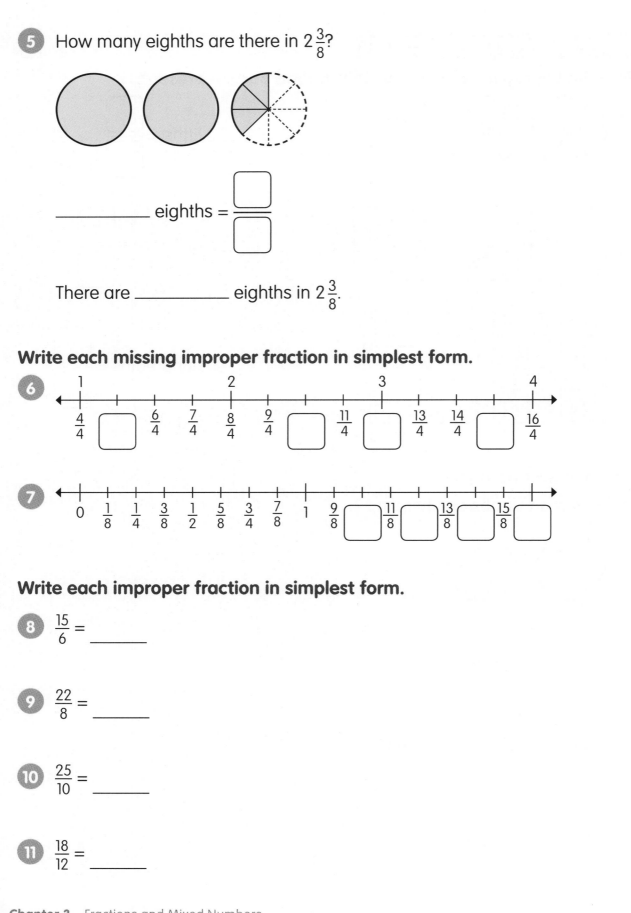

_____ eighths = $\dfrac{\boxed{}}{\boxed{}}$

There are _____ eighths in $2\frac{3}{8}$.

Write each missing improper fraction in simplest form.

6

| 1 | | | 2 | | | 3 | | | 4 |

$\dfrac{4}{4}$ $\boxed{}$ $\dfrac{6}{4}$ $\dfrac{7}{4}$ $\dfrac{8}{4}$ $\dfrac{9}{4}$ $\boxed{}$ $\dfrac{11}{4}$ $\boxed{}$ $\dfrac{13}{4}$ $\dfrac{14}{4}$ $\boxed{}$ $\dfrac{16}{4}$

7

0 $\dfrac{1}{8}$ $\dfrac{1}{4}$ $\dfrac{3}{8}$ $\dfrac{1}{2}$ $\dfrac{5}{8}$ $\dfrac{3}{4}$ $\dfrac{7}{8}$ 1 $\dfrac{9}{8}$ $\boxed{}$ $\dfrac{11}{8}$ $\boxed{}$ $\dfrac{13}{8}$ $\boxed{}$ $\dfrac{15}{8}$ $\boxed{}$

Write each improper fraction in simplest form.

8 $\dfrac{15}{6} = $ _____

9 $\dfrac{22}{8} = $ _____

10 $\dfrac{25}{10} = $ _____

11 $\dfrac{18}{12} = $ _____

6 Renaming Improper Fractions and Mixed Numbers

Learning Objectives:
- Write an improper fraction as a mixed number.
- Write a mixed number as an improper fraction.

THINK

Ella has $2\frac{1}{2}$ apples. Julia has $\frac{?}{2}$ apples. Julia has more apples than Ella but fewer than 5 apples. What are the possible values of ? if ? is a whole number?

ENGAGE

1 Use ⬤ to show $\frac{8}{3}$. How many wholes and thirds are there?

2 Without using ⬤, how can you tell how many wholes and quarters there are in $\frac{11}{4}$?

LEARN Write an improper fraction as a mixed number

1 Convert or change $\frac{3}{2}$ to a mixed number.

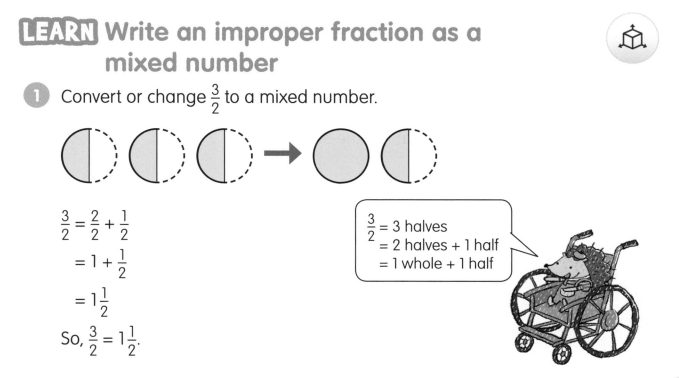

$\frac{3}{2} = \frac{2}{2} + \frac{1}{2}$

$\quad = 1 + \frac{1}{2}$

$\quad = 1\frac{1}{2}$

So, $\frac{3}{2} = 1\frac{1}{2}$.

> $\frac{3}{2}$ = 3 halves
> = 2 halves + 1 half
> = 1 whole + 1 half

2 Convert $\frac{7}{3}$ to a mixed number.

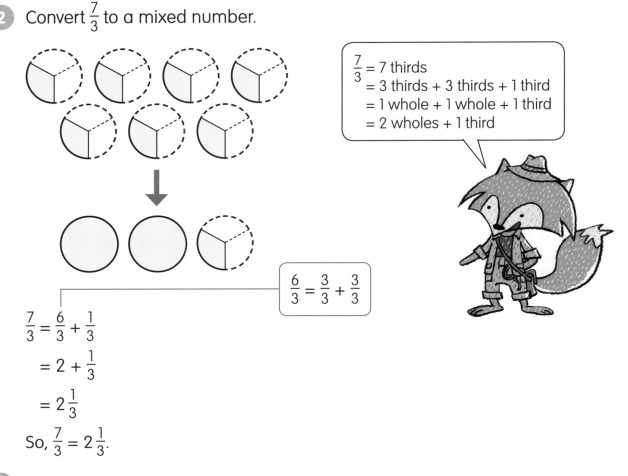

$\frac{7}{3}$ = 7 thirds
= 3 thirds + 3 thirds + 1 third
= 1 whole + 1 whole + 1 third
= 2 wholes + 1 third

$\frac{6}{3} = \frac{3}{3} + \frac{3}{3}$

$\frac{7}{3} = \frac{6}{3} + \frac{1}{3}$

$\quad = 2 + \frac{1}{3}$

$\quad = 2\frac{1}{3}$

So, $\frac{7}{3} = 2\frac{1}{3}$.

3 Number lines can show improper fractions and their mixed numbers.

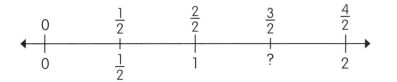

The number line shows that $\frac{3}{2}$ is the same as $1\frac{1}{2}$.

Work in groups.

(1) Use 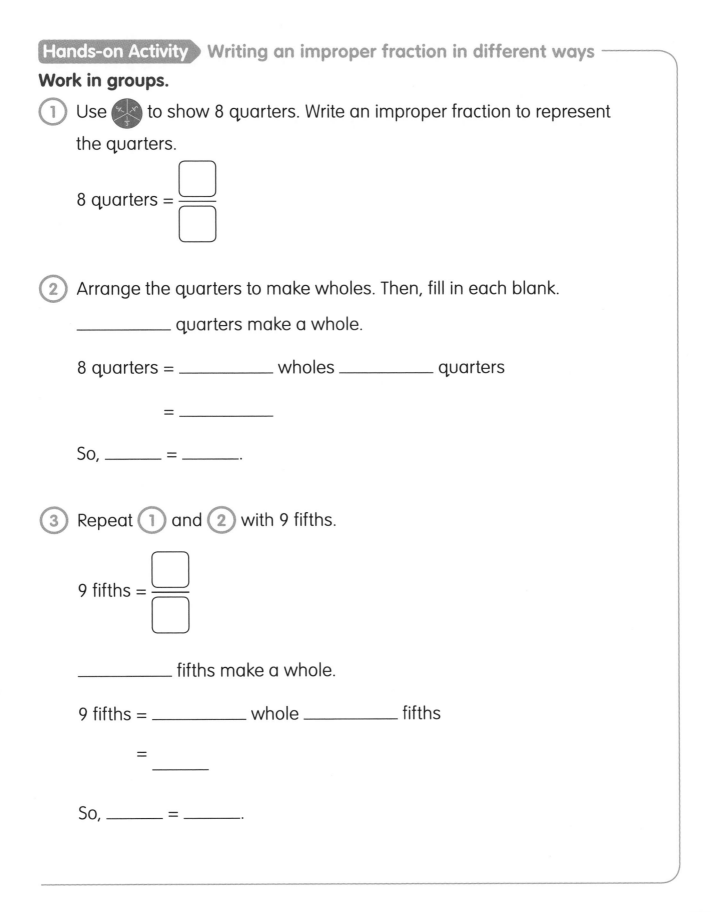 to show 8 quarters. Write an improper fraction to represent the quarters.

8 quarters = □/□

(2) Arrange the quarters to make wholes. Then, fill in each blank.

_____ quarters make a whole.

8 quarters = _____ wholes _____ quarters

= _____

So, _____ = _____.

(3) Repeat (1) and (2) with 9 fifths.

9 fifths = □/□

_____ fifths make a whole.

9 fifths = _____ whole _____ fifths

= _____

So, _____ = _____.

TRY **Practice writing an improper fraction as a mixed number**

Write each improper fraction as a mixed number.

1 $\frac{12}{5} = \frac{10}{5} + \frac{\boxed{}}{5}$

$= 2 + \dfrac{\boxed{}}{\boxed{}}$

$=$ _____

2 $\frac{13}{6} = \frac{12}{6} + \frac{\boxed{}}{6}$

$= 2 + \dfrac{\boxed{}}{\boxed{}}$

$=$ _____

Write the improper fraction as a mixed number in simplest form.

3 $\frac{14}{8}$

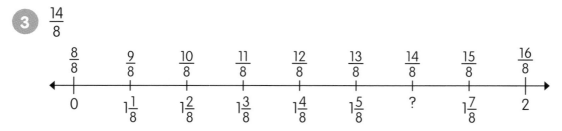

The number line shows that $\frac{14}{8}$ is the same as _____.

Convert each improper fraction to a mixed number. Express each answer in simplest form.

4 $\frac{8}{3}$

5 $\frac{11}{6}$

6 $\frac{22}{4}$

7 $\frac{26}{8}$

ENGAGE

1 Use 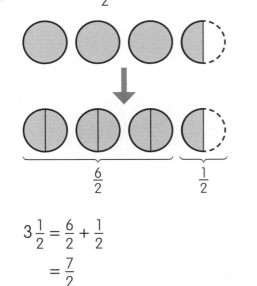 to represent $2\frac{3}{5}$ using fifths. How many fifths did you use? Then, fill in the blank.

$2\frac{3}{5} = \dfrac{\Box}{5}$

2 Use different sets of to help you find the missing number.

$3\frac{3}{4} = \dfrac{\Box}{4}$

Explain how you did it with your partner.

LEARN Write a mixed number as an improper fraction

1 Convert $3\frac{1}{2}$ to an improper fraction.

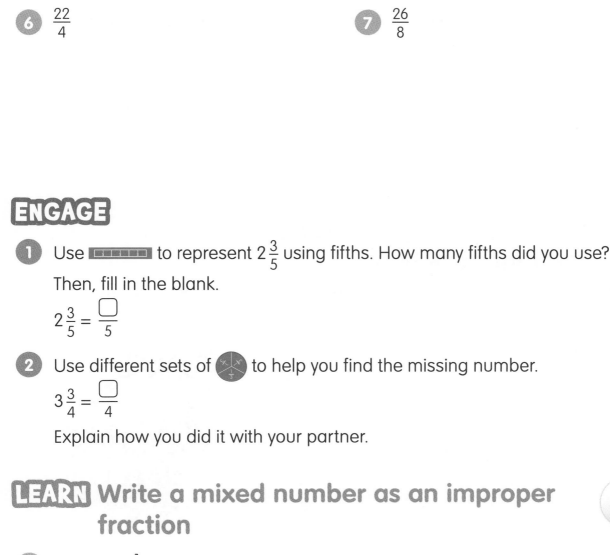

$\underbrace{}_{\frac{6}{2}}$ $\underbrace{}_{\frac{1}{2}}$

$3\frac{1}{2} = \frac{6}{2} + \frac{1}{2}$

$\qquad = \frac{7}{2}$

How many halves are there in $3\frac{1}{2}$?

2 Number lines can show mixed numbers and their improper fractions.

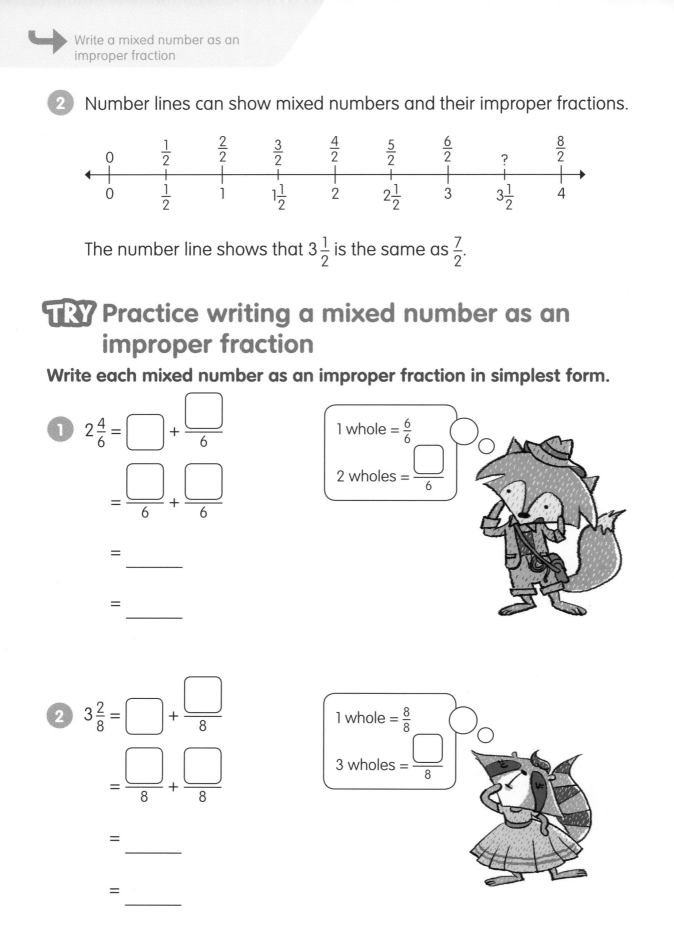

The number line shows that $3\frac{1}{2}$ is the same as $\frac{7}{2}$.

TRY Practice writing a mixed number as an improper fraction

Write each mixed number as an improper fraction in simplest form.

1 $2\frac{4}{6} = \boxed{} + \dfrac{\boxed{}}{6}$

$= \dfrac{\boxed{}}{6} + \dfrac{\boxed{}}{6}$

$= \underline{}$

$= \underline{}$

1 whole $= \dfrac{6}{6}$

2 wholes $= \dfrac{\boxed{}}{6}$

2 $3\frac{2}{8} = \boxed{} + \dfrac{\boxed{}}{8}$

$= \dfrac{\boxed{}}{8} + \dfrac{\boxed{}}{8}$

$= \underline{}$

$= \underline{}$

1 whole $= \dfrac{8}{8}$

3 wholes $= \dfrac{\boxed{}}{8}$

Convert each mixed number to an improper fraction.

3 $1\dfrac{2}{5}$

4 $4\dfrac{2}{3}$

5 $3\dfrac{4}{5}$

6 $2\dfrac{7}{10}$

7 $5\dfrac{3}{8}$

8 $6\dfrac{3}{4}$

Mathematical Habit 2 Use mathematical reasoning

Josiah converts $2\dfrac{1}{4}$ to an improper fraction in the following way.

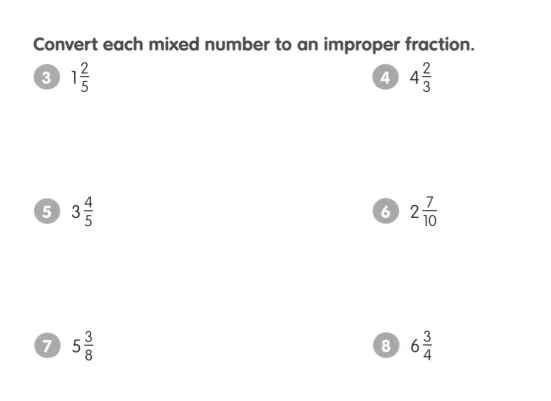

$2\dfrac{1}{4}$

2 wholes   1 quarter
= 2 x 4 quarters
= 8 quarters

8 quarters + 1 quarter = 9 quarters

So, $2\dfrac{1}{4} = \dfrac{9}{4}$.

Explain to your partner how to use Josiah's method to convert $3\dfrac{7}{10}$ to an improper fraction.

MATH SHARING

ROLL AND RENAME!

That's correct!

$$\frac{2}{2} = \frac{?}{?} + \frac{?}{2} = ?\frac{1}{2}$$

What you need:

Players: 3
Materials: Number cube

What to do:

1. Player 1 rolls the number cube two times to make an improper fraction. Then, he or she renames the improper fraction as a mixed number.

2. The other players check the answer. Player 1 will receive one point if the answer is correct.

3. Players continue to take turns rolling the number cube and writing the numbers. Play at least 4 rounds.

Who is the winner?

The player with the highest score wins!

INDEPENDENT PRACTICE

Convert each improper fraction to a mixed number.
Express each answer in simplest form.

1 $\dfrac{8}{5}$

2 $\dfrac{15}{6}$

3 $\dfrac{26}{8}$

4 $\dfrac{16}{3}$

Find the mixed number represented by each letter on the number line.

5
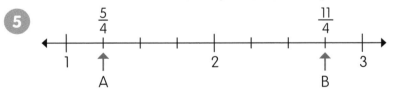

A: _____

B: _____

Convert each mixed number to an improper fraction.

6 $1\frac{1}{6}$

7 $3\frac{9}{10}$

8 $6\frac{2}{3}$

9 $1\frac{3}{100}$

Match each mixed number to its equivalent improper fraction.

10 $2\frac{3}{4}$ •

$2\frac{2}{3}$ •

$2\frac{2}{5}$ •

$6\frac{1}{3}$ •

$3\frac{4}{5}$ •

• $\frac{12}{5}$

• $\frac{19}{5}$

• $\frac{19}{3}$

• $\frac{8}{3}$

• $\frac{11}{4}$

7 Adding and Subtracting Mixed Numbers

Learning Objectives:
- Add mixed numbers with like denominators.
- Subtract mixed numbers with like denominators.

THINK

Fill in the circles with the numbers and fractions such that the sum along each side of the figure is 6.

$1, 1\frac{1}{2}, 2, 2\frac{1}{2}, 3, 3\frac{1}{2}$

ENGAGE

Use ▭▭▭▭ to model this problem.

a Jocelyn picked $1\frac{1}{5}$ pounds of strawberries. Kiri picked $1\frac{2}{5}$ pounds of strawberries. How many pounds of strawberries did they pick in all?

b If they shared the strawberries equally between them, how many pounds would each person get?

LEARN Add mixed numbers without renaming wholes

1 Layla sold $2\frac{1}{4}$ pies. David sold $1\frac{2}{4}$ pies. How many pies did they sell in all?

$2\frac{1}{4} + 1\frac{2}{4}$

$= 3\frac{1}{4} + \frac{2}{4}$

$= 3\frac{3}{4}$

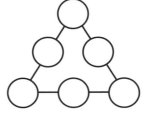

Add the whole numbers before adding the fractions.

They sold $3\frac{3}{4}$ pies in all.

Hands-on Activity Adding mixed numbers without renaming wholes

Work in pairs.

(1) Add $1\frac{1}{4}$ and $2\frac{1}{4}$. Express your answer in simplest form.

$1\frac{1}{4} + 2\frac{1}{4} = $ _____

(2) Use 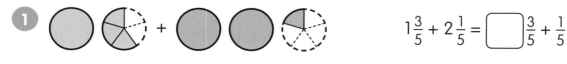 to check your answer.

(3) Repeat (1) and (2) using $3\frac{5}{8}$ and $1\frac{1}{8}$.

$3\frac{5}{8} + 1\frac{1}{8} = $ _____

TRY Practice adding mixed numbers without renaming wholes

Add.

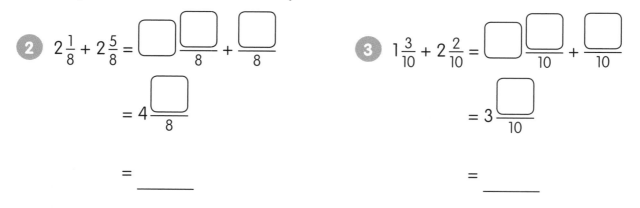

1 $1\frac{3}{5} + 2\frac{1}{5} = \boxed{}\frac{3}{5} + \frac{1}{5}$

$= $ _____

Add. Express each answer in simplest form.

2 $2\frac{1}{8} + 2\frac{5}{8} = \boxed{}\dfrac{\boxed{}}{8} + \dfrac{\boxed{}}{8}$

$= 4\dfrac{\boxed{}}{8}$

$= $ _____

3 $1\frac{3}{10} + 2\frac{2}{10} = \boxed{}\dfrac{\boxed{}}{10} + \dfrac{\boxed{}}{10}$

$= 3\dfrac{\boxed{}}{10}$

$= $ _____

ENGAGE

a Complete each number bond.

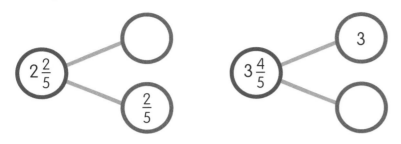

b How can you use the number bonds to help you add $2\frac{2}{5}$ and $3\frac{3}{5}$?

LEARN Add mixed numbers with renaming wholes

1 Find the sum of $2\frac{2}{4}$ and $1\frac{3}{4}$.

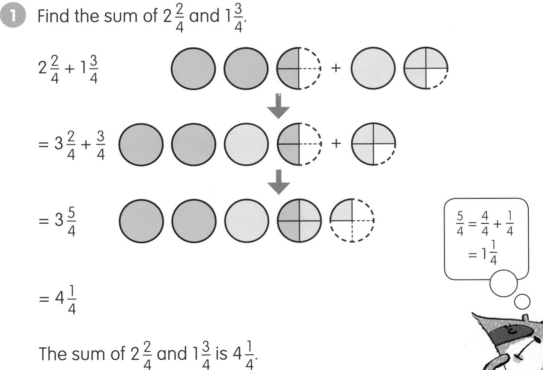

$2\frac{2}{4} + 1\frac{3}{4}$

$= 3\frac{2}{4} + \frac{3}{4}$

$= 3\frac{5}{4}$

$= 4\frac{1}{4}$

$\frac{5}{4} = \frac{4}{4} + \frac{1}{4}$
$\quad = 1\frac{1}{4}$

The sum of $2\frac{2}{4}$ and $1\frac{3}{4}$ is $4\frac{1}{4}$.

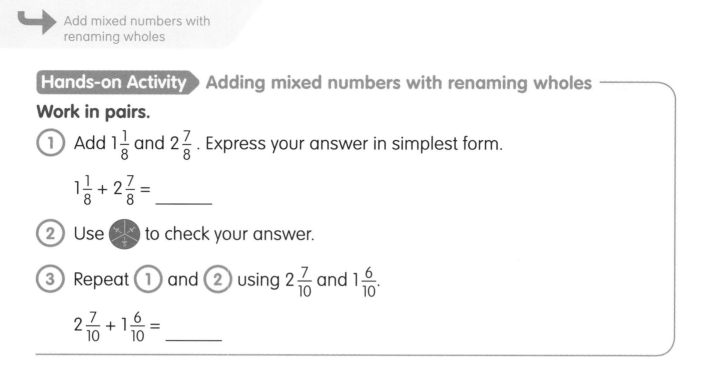

Hands-on Activity — Adding mixed numbers with renaming wholes

Work in pairs.

1. Add $1\frac{1}{8}$ and $2\frac{7}{8}$. Express your answer in simplest form.

   $$1\frac{1}{8} + 2\frac{7}{8} = \underline{\hspace{2cm}}$$

2. Use ⊘ to check your answer.

3. Repeat ① and ② using $2\frac{7}{10}$ and $1\frac{6}{10}$.

   $$2\frac{7}{10} + 1\frac{6}{10} = \underline{\hspace{2cm}}$$

TRY Practice adding mixed numbers with renaming wholes

Add. Express each answer in simplest form.

1. $2\frac{4}{5} + 3\frac{3}{5} = \boxed{}\frac{4}{5} + \frac{3}{5}$

   $= 5\dfrac{\boxed{}}{\boxed{}}$

   $= \underline{\hspace{1.5cm}}$

2. $3\frac{3}{10} + 2\frac{9}{10} = \boxed{}\boxed{}\dfrac{\boxed{}}{10} + \dfrac{\boxed{}}{10}$

   $= 5\dfrac{\boxed{}}{10}$

   $= \boxed{}\dfrac{\boxed{}}{10}$

   $= \underline{\hspace{1.5cm}}$

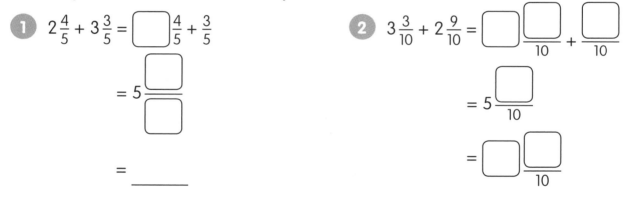

MATH SHARING

Mathematical Habit 6 Use precise mathematical language

Discuss with your partner different ways to mentally add the following.

$$1\frac{3}{8} + 1\frac{7}{8} + 2\frac{5}{8} = ?$$

ENGAGE

a Complete each number bond.

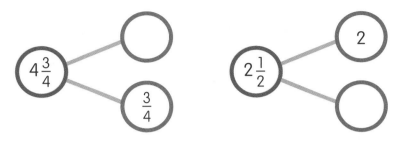

b How can you use the number bonds to help you subtract $2\frac{1}{2}$ from $4\frac{3}{4}$?

LEARN Subtract mixed numbers without renaming wholes

1 Martina had $2\frac{3}{4}$ watermelon slices. She gave away $1\frac{2}{4}$ watermelon slices.

How many watermelon slices did Martina have left?

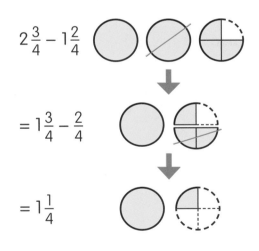

$2\frac{3}{4} - 1\frac{2}{4}$

$= 1\frac{3}{4} - \frac{2}{4}$

$= 1\frac{1}{4}$

Subtract the whole numbers before subtracting the fractions.

Martina had $1\frac{1}{4}$ watermelon slices left.

Hands-on Activity Subtracting mixed numbers without renaming wholes

Work in pairs.

1. Find the difference between $1\frac{3}{8}$ and $2\frac{5}{8}$. Express your answer in simplest form.

   $2\frac{5}{8} - 1\frac{3}{8} = $ _____

2. Use 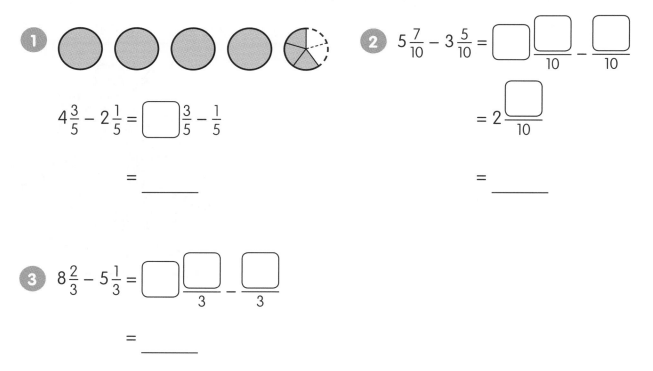 to check your answer.

3. Repeat ① and ② using $1\frac{4}{6}$ and $1\frac{2}{6}$.

   $1\frac{4}{6} - 1\frac{2}{6} = $ _____

TRY Practice subtracting mixed numbers without renaming wholes

Subtract. Express each answer in simplest form.

1.

   $4\frac{3}{5} - 2\frac{1}{5} = \boxed{}\frac{3}{5} - \frac{1}{5}$

   $= $ _____

2. $5\frac{7}{10} - 3\frac{5}{10} = \boxed{}\dfrac{\boxed{}}{10} - \dfrac{\boxed{}}{10}$

   $= 2\dfrac{\boxed{}}{10}$

   $= $ _____

3. $8\frac{2}{3} - 5\frac{1}{3} = \boxed{}\dfrac{\boxed{}}{3} - \dfrac{\boxed{}}{3}$

   $= $ _____

ENGAGE

Use 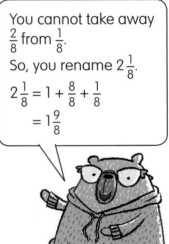 to show $2\frac{2}{4}$. How can you take away $1\frac{3}{4}$ from $2\frac{2}{4}$? Write an equation to show your answer.

LEARN Subtract mixed numbers with renaming wholes

1 Subtract $1\frac{2}{8}$ from $3\frac{1}{8}$.

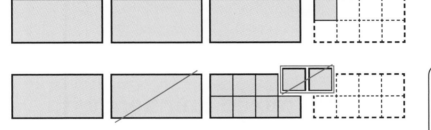

$$3\frac{1}{8} - 1\frac{2}{8} = 2\frac{1}{8} - \frac{2}{8}$$
$$= 1\frac{9}{8} - \frac{2}{8}$$
$$= 1\frac{7}{8}$$

You cannot take away $\frac{2}{8}$ from $\frac{1}{8}$.
So, you rename $2\frac{1}{8}$.
$$2\frac{1}{8} = 1 + \frac{8}{8} + \frac{1}{8}$$
$$= 1\frac{9}{8}$$

2 Find the difference between 4 and $1\frac{7}{12}$.

$$4 - 1\frac{7}{12} = 3 - \frac{7}{12}$$
$$= 2\frac{12}{12} - \frac{7}{12}$$
$$= 2\frac{5}{12}$$

The difference between 4 and $1\frac{7}{12}$ is $2\frac{5}{12}$.

Hands-on Activity Subtracting mixed numbers with renaming wholes

Work in pairs.

① Find the difference between $1\frac{8}{10}$ and $2\frac{3}{10}$. Express your answer in simplest form.

$$2\frac{3}{10} - 1\frac{8}{10} = \underline{\hspace{2cm}}$$

② Use 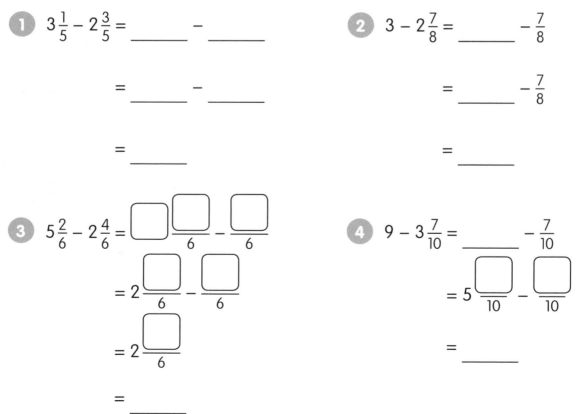 to check your answer.

③ Repeat ① and ② using 4 and $1\frac{7}{8}$.

$$4 - 1\frac{7}{8} = \underline{\hspace{2cm}}$$

TRY Practice subtracting mixed numbers with renaming wholes

Subtract. Express each answer in simplest form.

① $3\frac{1}{5} - 2\frac{3}{5} = \underline{\hspace{2cm}} - \underline{\hspace{2cm}}$

$= \underline{\hspace{1.5cm}} - \underline{\hspace{1.5cm}}$

$= \underline{\hspace{2cm}}$

② $3 - 2\frac{7}{8} = \underline{\hspace{2cm}} - \frac{7}{8}$

$= \underline{\hspace{1.5cm}} - \frac{7}{8}$

$= \underline{\hspace{2cm}}$

③ $5\frac{2}{6} - 2\frac{4}{6} = \boxed{}\ \dfrac{\boxed{}}{6} - \dfrac{\boxed{}}{6}$

$= 2\dfrac{\boxed{}}{6} - \dfrac{\boxed{}}{6}$

$= 2\dfrac{\boxed{}}{6}$

$= \underline{\hspace{1.5cm}}$

④ $9 - 3\frac{7}{10} = \underline{\hspace{2cm}} - \frac{7}{10}$

$= 5\dfrac{\boxed{}}{10} - \dfrac{\boxed{}}{10}$

$= \underline{\hspace{1.5cm}}$

INDEPENDENT PRACTICE

Add. Show your work. Express each answer in simplest form.

1 $3\frac{1}{10} + 1\frac{2}{10} = $ _____

2 $2\frac{5}{12} + 4\frac{2}{12} = $ _____

3 $1\frac{2}{10} + 3\frac{7}{10} = $ _____

4 $3\frac{1}{6} + 1\frac{3}{6} = $ _____

5 $2\frac{5}{12} + 4\frac{7}{12} = $ _____

6 $2\frac{5}{8} + 1\frac{6}{8} = $ _____

7 $5\frac{3}{5} + 4\frac{4}{5} = $ _____

8 $3\frac{5}{6} + 6\frac{5}{6} = $ _____

Subtract. Show your work. Express each answer in simplest form.

⑨ $4\frac{6}{8} - 2\frac{1}{8} = $ _____

⑩ $3\frac{4}{5} - 1\frac{3}{5} = $ _____

⑪ $5\frac{5}{6} - 4\frac{3}{6} = $ _____

⑫ $6\frac{9}{10} - 3\frac{1}{10} = $ _____

⑬ $2\frac{2}{8} - 1\frac{5}{8} = $ _____

⑭ $4\frac{1}{4} - 1\frac{3}{4} = $ _____

⑮ $7\frac{5}{10} - 3\frac{7}{10} = $ _____

⑯ $12 - 2\frac{4}{5} = $ _____

8 Multiplying Fractions and Whole Numbers

Learning Objectives:
- Represent a fraction as a multiple of a unit fraction.
- Multiply a whole number and a fraction, and relate the product to a multiple of a unit fraction.

THINK

Find the missing number in $\frac{3}{8} \times \boxed{?} = 27$.

ENGAGE

How many one-fifths does it take to make $\frac{7}{5}$? Write an equation to show the number of $\frac{1}{5}$ in $\frac{7}{5}$.

How can you relate your equation to factors and multiples? Explain your thinking to your partner.

LEARN Represent a fraction as a multiple of a unit fraction

1. A pie was cut into 5 equal pieces. Emilio bought $\frac{2}{5}$ of the pie. How many pieces of the pie did Emilio buy?

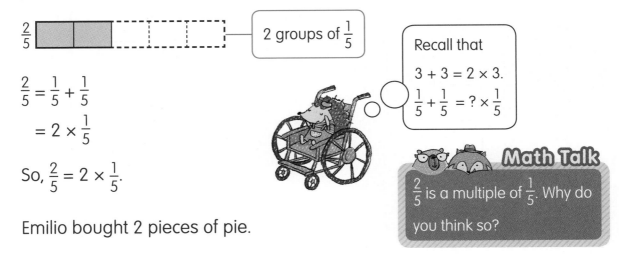

$\frac{2}{5}$ [ ] — 2 groups of $\frac{1}{5}$

Recall that
$3 + 3 = 2 \times 3$.
$\frac{1}{5} + \frac{1}{5} = ? \times \frac{1}{5}$

$\frac{2}{5} = \frac{1}{5} + \frac{1}{5}$

$\quad = 2 \times \frac{1}{5}$

So, $\frac{2}{5} = 2 \times \frac{1}{5}$.

Emilio bought 2 pieces of pie.

Math Talk

$\frac{2}{5}$ is a multiple of $\frac{1}{5}$. Why do you think so?

2 Write $\frac{7}{4}$ as a product of a whole number and a unit fraction.

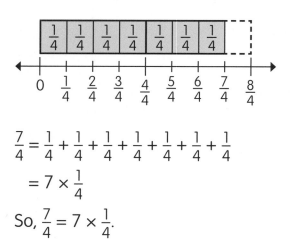

| $\frac{1}{4}$ | $\frac{1}{4}$ | $\frac{1}{4}$ | $\frac{1}{4}$ | $\frac{1}{4}$ | $\frac{1}{4}$ | $\frac{1}{4}$ | |

$$\frac{7}{4} = \frac{1}{4} + \frac{1}{4} + \frac{1}{4} + \frac{1}{4} + \frac{1}{4} + \frac{1}{4} + \frac{1}{4}$$

$$= 7 \times \frac{1}{4}$$

So, $\frac{7}{4} = 7 \times \frac{1}{4}$.

TRY Practice representing a fraction as a multiple of a unit fraction

Write each fraction as a sum of its unit fractions. Then, write it as a product of a whole number and a unit fraction.

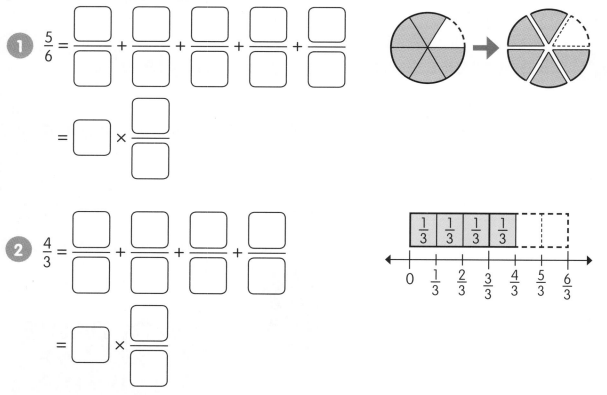

1 $\frac{5}{6} = \dfrac{\square}{\square} + \dfrac{\square}{\square} + \dfrac{\square}{\square} + \dfrac{\square}{\square} + \dfrac{\square}{\square}$

$= \square \times \dfrac{\square}{\square}$

2 $\frac{4}{3} = \dfrac{\square}{\square} + \dfrac{\square}{\square} + \dfrac{\square}{\square} + \dfrac{\square}{\square}$

$= \square \times \dfrac{\square}{\square}$

ENGAGE

Use 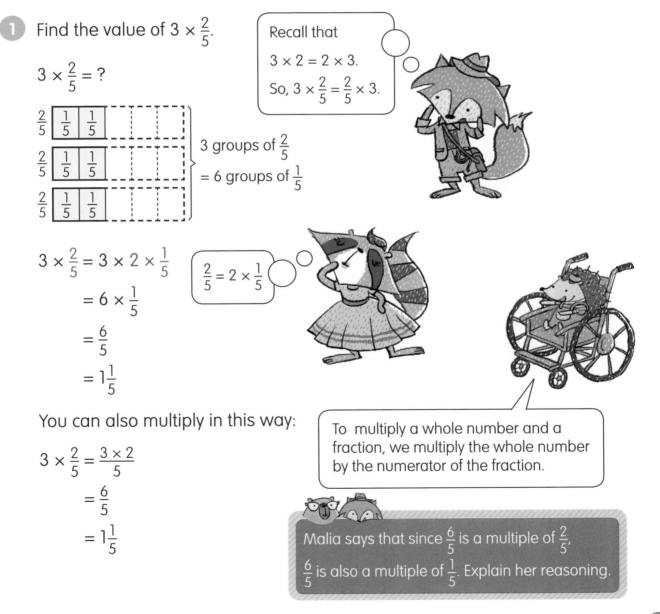 to show 4 groups of 2. What is 4 groups of 2? Write an equation to show your answer. Now, draw ⊕ to show 4 groups of two-thirds. What is 4 groups of $\frac{2}{3}$? Write an equation to show your answer. How can you relate the two equations? Explain your thinking to your partner.

What is another way to find 4 groups of $\frac{2}{3}$? Use it to find 5 groups of $\frac{3}{4}$.

LEARN Multiply a whole number and a fraction

1 Find the value of $3 \times \frac{2}{5}$.

$$3 \times \frac{2}{5} = ?$$

Recall that
$3 \times 2 = 2 \times 3$.
So, $3 \times \frac{2}{5} = \frac{2}{5} \times 3$.

3 groups of $\frac{2}{5}$
= 6 groups of $\frac{1}{5}$

$$3 \times \frac{2}{5} = 3 \times 2 \times \frac{1}{5}$$

$\frac{2}{5} = 2 \times \frac{1}{5}$

$$= 6 \times \frac{1}{5}$$
$$= \frac{6}{5}$$
$$= 1\frac{1}{5}$$

You can also multiply in this way:

$$3 \times \frac{2}{5} = \frac{3 \times 2}{5}$$
$$= \frac{6}{5}$$
$$= 1\frac{1}{5}$$

To multiply a whole number and a fraction, we multiply the whole number by the numerator of the fraction.

Malia says that since $\frac{6}{5}$ is a multiple of $\frac{2}{5}$, $\frac{6}{5}$ is also a multiple of $\frac{1}{5}$. Explain her reasoning.

Hands-on Activity Multiplying a whole number and a fraction

Work in pairs.

1. Use 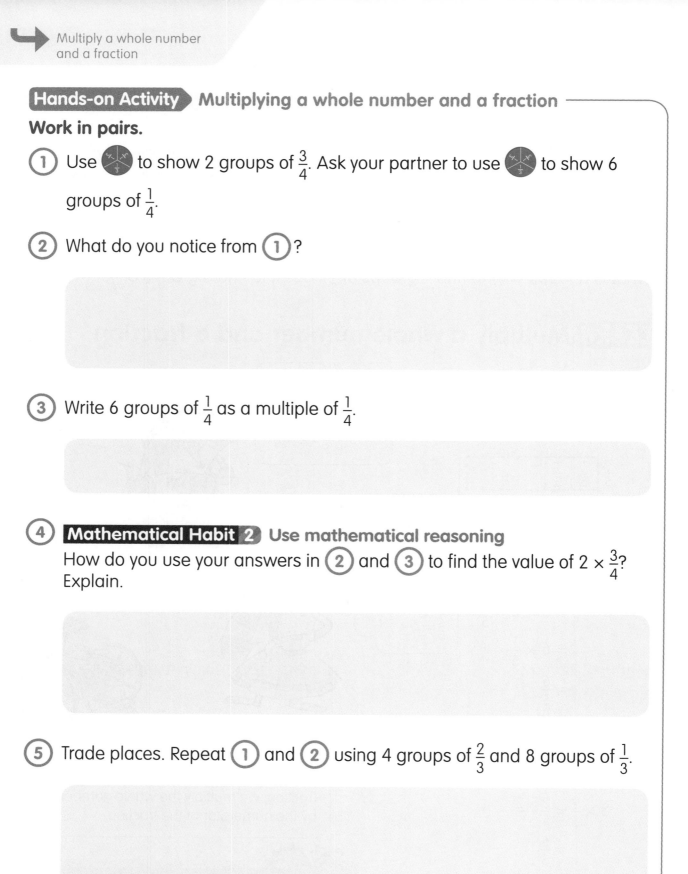 to show 2 groups of $\frac{3}{4}$. Ask your partner to use to show 6 groups of $\frac{1}{4}$.

2. What do you notice from 1?

3. Write 6 groups of $\frac{1}{4}$ as a multiple of $\frac{1}{4}$.

4. **Mathematical Habit 2** Use mathematical reasoning
   How do you use your answers in 2 and 3 to find the value of $2 \times \frac{3}{4}$? Explain.

5. Trade places. Repeat 1 and 2 using 4 groups of $\frac{2}{3}$ and 8 groups of $\frac{1}{3}$.

TRY Practice multiplying a whole number and a fraction

Write the given expression as a product of a whole number and a unit fraction.

1. $2 \times \dfrac{3}{4} = \boxed{} \times \dfrac{\boxed{}}{\boxed{}}$

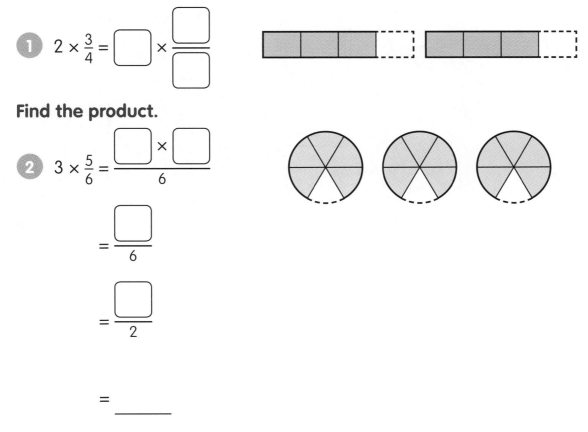

Find the product.

2. $3 \times \dfrac{5}{6} = \dfrac{\boxed{} \times \boxed{}}{6}$

   $= \dfrac{\boxed{}}{6}$

   $= \dfrac{\boxed{}}{2}$

   $= \underline{}$

Multiply. Show your work. Write each answer as a mixed number in simplest form.

3. $12 \times \dfrac{3}{8}$

4. $2 \times \dfrac{5}{3}$

ROLL AND MULTIPLY!

What you need:

Players: 4
Materials: Number cube
Fraction cards

What to do:

1. Shuffle the fraction cards and place the deck facedown on the table.

2. Player 1 turns over the top card of the deck, and then rolls the number cube. He or she finds the product of the whole number from the number cube and the fraction on the fraction card.

3. The other players check the product. If the answer is correct, Player 1 keeps the fraction card. If it is wrong, the card is returned to the bottom of the deck.

4. Players take turns repeating 2 and 3 until there are no cards left in the deck.

Who is the winner?

The player with the greatest number of cards at the end of the game wins!

Name: _____ Date: _____

Write each fraction as a product of a whole number and a unit fraction.

1 $\dfrac{4}{6} = \boxed{} \times \dfrac{\boxed{}}{\boxed{}}$

2 $\dfrac{8}{5} = \boxed{} \times \dfrac{\boxed{}}{\boxed{}}$

Write the given expression as a product of a whole number and a unit fraction.

3 $3 \times \dfrac{6}{8} = \boxed{} \times \dfrac{\boxed{}}{\boxed{}}$

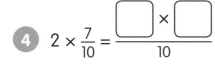

Find the product.

4 $2 \times \dfrac{7}{10} = \dfrac{\boxed{} \times \boxed{}}{10}$

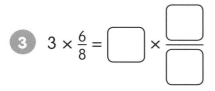

$= \dfrac{\boxed{}}{10}$

$= \dfrac{\boxed{}}{5}$

$= \boxed{} \dfrac{\boxed{}}{\boxed{}}$

Find each product. Show your work. Write each answer as a fraction or mixed number in simplest form.

5 $3 \times \frac{1}{6}$

6 $11 \times \frac{2}{3}$

7 $\frac{11}{12} \times 2$

8 $\frac{3}{4} \times 6$

9 $2 \times \frac{5}{4}$

10 $\frac{8}{5} \times 3$

Name: _____ Date: _____

Real-World Problems: Fractions

Learning Objectives:
- Solve real-world problems involving adding and subtracting like fractions.
- Solve real-world problems by adding and subtracting like fractions using data in a line plot.
- Solve real-world problems involving multiplying whole numbers and fractions.

 THINK

Sofia buys 8 bowls. The mass of each bowl is $\frac{3}{5}$ kilogram. Sofia wants to pack the bowls in a box. She can use a box that holds up to 4 kilograms, or a box that holds up to 5 kilograms. Which box should she choose?

ENGAGE

Hugo baked a pie. He gave $\frac{2}{4}$ of the pie of his friend and $\frac{1}{4}$ of the pie to his neighbor. Draw a bar model to show the fraction of pie Hugo had left.

Share your bar model with your partner.

What is another question you can ask? Share the question with your partner and solve it.

LEARN Solve real-world problems involving adding and subtracting like fractions

1. Brady ate $\frac{2}{5}$ of a yogurt bar. Robert ate $\frac{1}{5}$ of the yogurt bar. What fraction of the yogurt bar did they eat in all?

   STEP 1 Understand the problem.

   > What fraction of the yogurt bar did each of them eat? What do I need to find?

   STEP 2 Think of a plan.
   I can draw a bar model.

STEP 3 Carry out the plan.

$$\frac{2}{5} + \frac{1}{5} = \frac{3}{5}$$

They ate $\frac{3}{5}$ of the yogurt bar in all.

STEP 4 Check the answer.
I can use subtraction to check my answer.

I can subtract $\frac{1}{5}$ from $\frac{3}{5}$.
$$\frac{3}{5} - \frac{1}{5} = \frac{2}{5}$$
So, my answer is correct.

What other ways can you check your answer?

2 A tailor buys $2\frac{3}{4}$ meters of blue ribbon and some red ribbon. The length of the red ribbon is $1\frac{2}{4}$ meters longer than the blue ribbon. What is the length of the red ribbon?

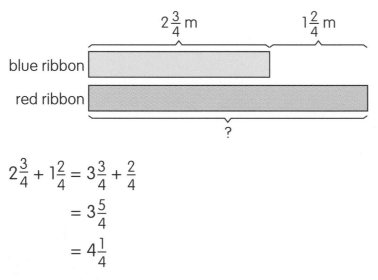

$2\frac{3}{4} + 1\frac{2}{4} = 3\frac{3}{4} + \frac{2}{4}$

$= 3\frac{5}{4}$

$= 4\frac{1}{4}$

The length of the red ribbon is $4\frac{1}{4}$ meters.

3 Lucas bought some meat. He cooked $\frac{2}{8}$ of the meat and stored the rest in the freezer. What fraction of the meat did Lucas store in the freezer?

$1 - \frac{2}{8} = \frac{8}{8} - \frac{2}{8}$

$= \frac{6}{8}$

$= \frac{3}{4}$

Always write your final answer in simplest form.

Lucas stored $\frac{3}{4}$ of the meat in the freezer.

TRY Practice solving real-world problems involving adding and subtracting like fractions

Solve. Use the bar model to help you.

1. Zoey used $3\frac{1}{3}$ cups of flour to make a loaf of bread. She used $2\frac{2}{3}$ cups of flour to make a pie. How much more flour did she use to make the loaf of bread?

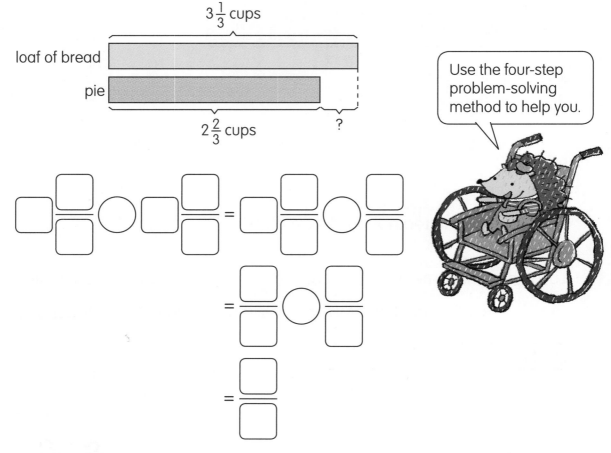

She used _____ cup more flour to make the loaf of bread.

2 Ms. Morgan painted a wall with three different colours. She painted $\frac{2}{10}$ of the wall blue, $\frac{5}{10}$ of the wall yellow, and the rest of the wall green.

a What fraction of the wall did she paint blue and yellow?

b What fraction of the wall did she paint green?

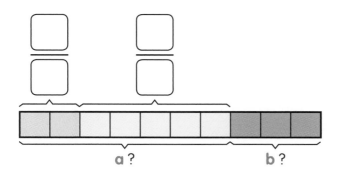

a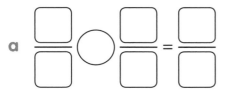

She painted _____ of the wall blue and yellow.

b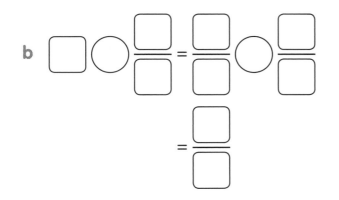

She painted _____ of the wall green.

3 Nathan bought 3 different packets of meat. The mass of the first packet was $2\frac{1}{5}$ kilograms. The mass of the second packet was $\frac{4}{5}$ kilogram less than the first packet. The mass of the third packet was $1\frac{3}{5}$ kilograms more than the second packet. Find the mass of the third packet of meat.

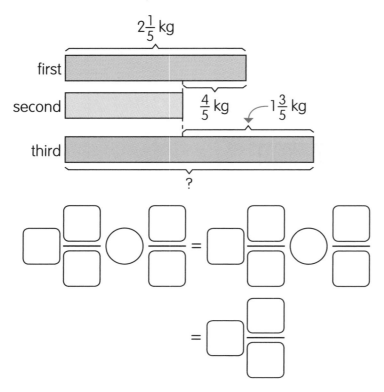

The mass of the second packet was _____ kilograms.

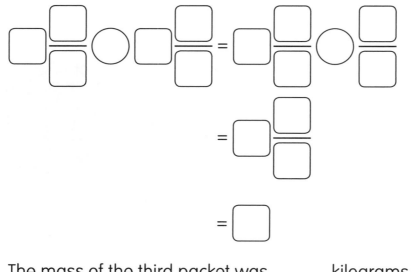

The mass of the third packet was _____ kilograms.

ENGAGE

Measure the lengths of 20 pencils in inches. Write the length of each pencil to the nearest tenth of an inch. How can you record your data using a chart? What other ways can you represent the data?

LEARN Solve real-world problems involving data in a line plot

1 A science class measures the lengths of beetles in the school garden and records their data in a tally chart.

Length (in.)	Tally	Number of Beetles
$\frac{1}{8}$	|||	3
$\frac{2}{8}$	||	2
$\frac{3}{8}$			1
$\frac{4}{8}$	||	2
$\frac{5}{8}$	||||	4
$\frac{6}{8}$		0
$\frac{7}{8}$			1
1							5

Then, they show the data in a line plot.

They want to look for patterns in the data.
Each ✗ represents 1 beetle.

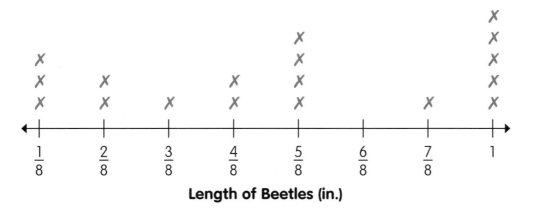

Length of Beetles (in.)

The data in the line plot tell the class that most of the beetles they

measured are $\frac{1}{8}$ inch, $\frac{5}{8}$ inch, or 1 inch. This may mean that the class is

measuring 3 or more different kinds of beetles.

What is the difference in length between the shortest and longest beetles?

The shortest beetles are $\frac{1}{8}$ inch long.

The longest beetles are 1 inch long.

$$1 - \frac{1}{8} = \frac{8}{8} - \frac{1}{8}$$
$$= \frac{7}{8}$$

The difference in length between the shortest and longest beetles is

$\frac{7}{8}$ inch.

Use the line plot on the previous page to answer the question.

1. What is the sum of the lengths of the beetles that are $\frac{2}{8}$ inch and $\frac{3}{8}$ inch long?

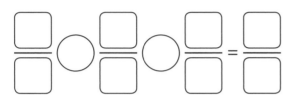

   The sum of the lengths of the beetles that are $\frac{2}{8}$ inch and $\frac{3}{8}$ inch long is

   _____ inch.

ENGAGE

Andrea drank $\frac{1}{4}$ of a bottle of water. Her brother drank twice as much water from the bottle as Andrea. Draw a bar model to show how much water they drank in all. Share your bar model with your partner.

LEARN Solve real-world problems involving multiplying by a fraction

1. Mr. Hill baked a pumpkin pie and cut it into 5 equal slices. He ate a slice and gave a slice each to his students, José, Mai, and Kyle. What fraction of the whole pie did they eat?

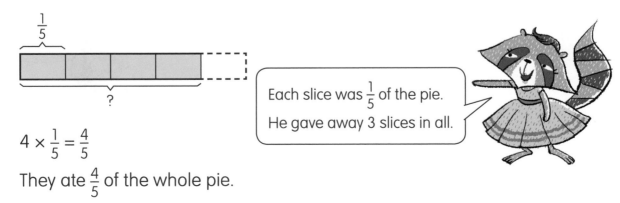

Each slice was $\frac{1}{5}$ of the pie.
He gave away 3 slices in all.

$4 \times \frac{1}{5} = \frac{4}{5}$

They ate $\frac{4}{5}$ of the whole pie.

2 A librarian stacked 7 books on a table. Each book was $\frac{3}{4}$ inch thick.
Find the total height of the stack of books.

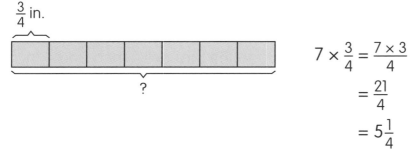

$$7 \times \frac{3}{4} = \frac{7 \times 3}{4}$$
$$= \frac{21}{4}$$
$$= 5\frac{1}{4}$$

The total height of the stack of books was $5\frac{1}{4}$ inches.

TRY Practice solving real-world problems involving multiplying by a fraction

Solve. Use the bar model to help you.

1 Leah wants to make 10 bowls of salad for a party. She uses $\frac{1}{8}$ kilogram of carrot sticks for each bowl. What is the total mass of carrot sticks that she must prepare?

Use the four-step problem-solving method to help you.

$$\boxed{} \bigcirc \frac{\boxed{}}{\boxed{}} = \frac{\boxed{}}{\boxed{}}$$
$$= 1\frac{2}{8}$$
$$= 1\frac{1}{4}$$

She must prepare a total of _____ kilograms of carrot sticks for the party.

2 Chloe made 3 jugs of lemonade for a party. At the end of the party, each jug had $\frac{3}{10}$ liter of lemonade left. She poured all the remaining lemonade into cups. Each cup contained $\frac{1}{10}$ liter of lemonade.

a How much lemonade did she have left?

b How many cups did she use?

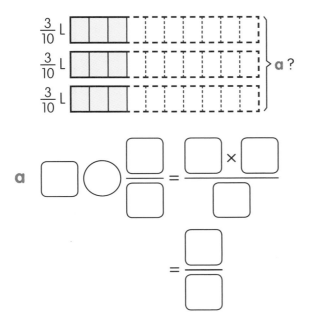

a

She had _____ liter of lemonade left.

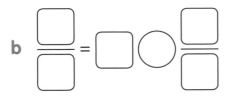

b

She used _____ cups.

3 Alan buys 5 apples and a melon. The mass of each apple is $\frac{2}{5}$ kilogram. The mass of the melon is $\frac{4}{5}$ kilogram. Find the total mass of the apples and the melon.

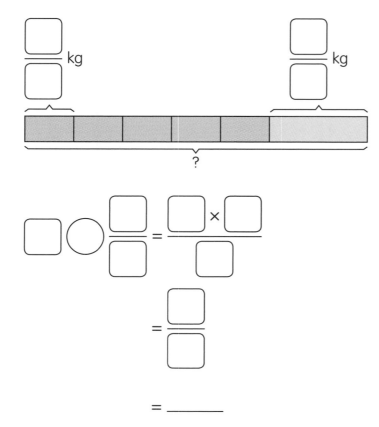

The mass of the apples is _____ kilograms.

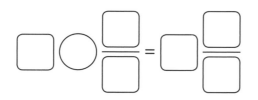

The total mass of the apples and the melon is _____ kilograms.

INDEPENDENT PRACTICE

Solve. Use the bar model to help you.

1. Whitney measures the lengths of three ropes. Rope A is $\frac{1}{8}$ meter long. Rope B is $\frac{5}{8}$ meter long and Rope C is $\frac{3}{8}$ meter long. What is the total length of three ropes?

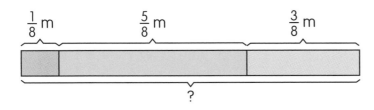

Solve. Draw a bar model to help you.

2. A grocer sold $4\frac{2}{3}$ kilograms of potatoes on Monday. He sold $2\frac{2}{3}$ kilograms of potatoes on Tuesday. What is the total mass of potatoes he sold in the two days? Express your answer as a mixed number in simplest form.

3 Bruno took $1\frac{1}{6}$ hours to complete his homework. Sarah took $\frac{2}{6}$ hour less than Bruno to complete her homework. How long did Sarah take to complete her homework?

Use the data in the table to complete the line plot in ④.
Then, answer exercises ⑤ to ⑨.

Zoe planted some seeds. After two months, she recorded the heights of the plants.

Height (ft)	Number of Plants
0	2
$\frac{1}{4}$	1
$\frac{1}{2}$	4
$\frac{3}{4}$	3
1	2
$1\frac{1}{4}$	1

4

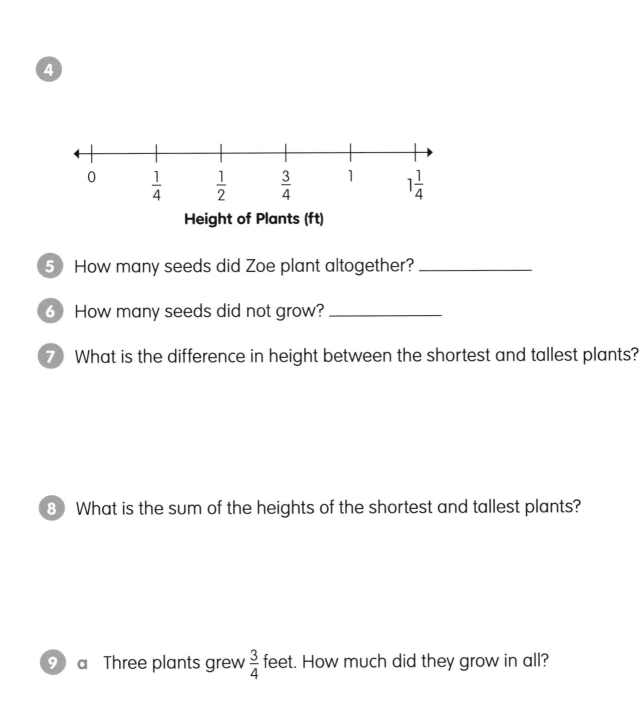

Height of Plants (ft)

5 How many seeds did Zoe plant altogether? _____

6 How many seeds did not grow? _____

7 What is the difference in height between the shortest and tallest plants?

8 What is the sum of the heights of the shortest and tallest plants?

9 **a** Three plants grew $\frac{3}{4}$ feet. How much did they grow in all?

b Which two plants have a total height as your answer in **a**?

Solve. Draw a bar model to help you.

10 Ethan walks $\frac{5}{8}$ kilometer to the bus stop each morning. How far does he walk in 5 days?

11 Mr. Brown spends $\frac{2}{3}$ hour gardening every day. How long does he spend gardening in one week?

12 Mr. Lopez mixed $\frac{3}{10}$ liter of orange juice and $\frac{4}{10}$ liter of pineapple juice to make 1 portion of a fruit punch. He made 4 portions in all. How much orange juice and pineapple juice did he use in all?

Mr. Johnson has a muffin recipe that uses $\frac{3}{4}$ cup of milk. He wants to make 3 times as many muffins, but he has only 2 cups of milk. How much more milk does he need?

Mathematical Habit 3 Construct viable arguments

A recipe for an apple pie uses $\frac{3}{4}$ cup of flour. Jackson wants to make 2 apple pies. He only has a $\frac{1}{4}$-cup measuring cup. He says he has to use the cup 6 times to get the amount of flour he needs.

Show why his reasoning is correct.

Problem Solving with Heuristics

1 **Mathematical Habit 8** Look for patterns

What fraction of the figure is shaded? Express your answer in simplest form.

2 **Mathematical Habit 2** **Use mathematical reasoning**

Fill in each box with the digits 2, 3, 4, 6, 8, or 9 to form two mixed numbers that have the greatest possible difference. Each digit can be used only once. Then, find the difference. Express the answer in simplest form.

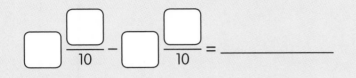

3 **Mathematical Habit 2** Use mathematical reasoning

Find the missing whole number that makes the equation true.

$$\frac{4}{5} \times 6 = \boxed{} \times \frac{2}{5}$$

CHAPTER WRAP-UP

Fractions and Mixed Numbers

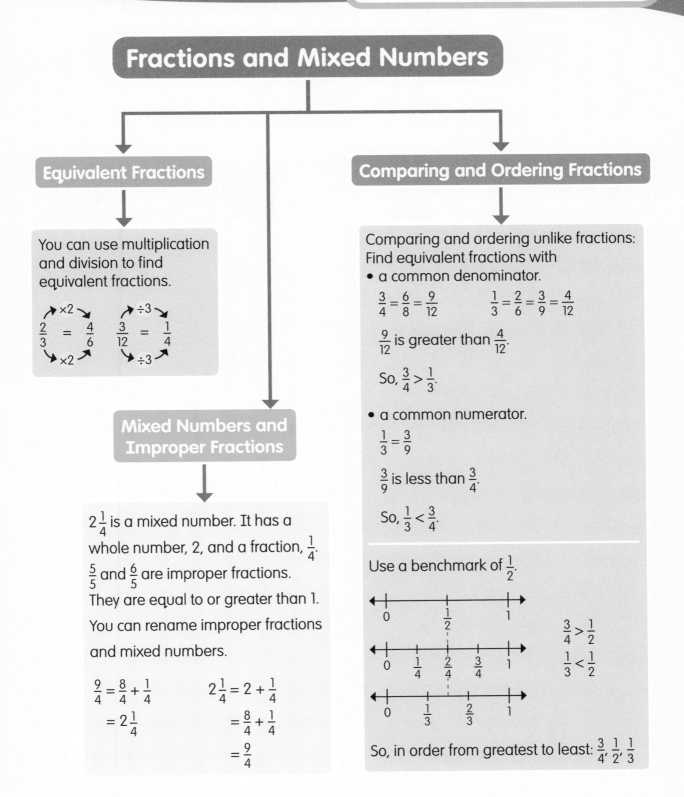

Equivalent Fractions

You can use multiplication and division to find equivalent fractions.

$$\frac{2}{3} \xrightarrow{\times 2} = \frac{4}{6} \xleftarrow{\times 2}$$

$$\frac{3}{12} \xrightarrow{\div 3} = \frac{1}{4} \xleftarrow{\div 3}$$

Mixed Numbers and Improper Fractions

$2\frac{1}{4}$ is a mixed number. It has a whole number, 2, and a fraction, $\frac{1}{4}$.

$\frac{5}{5}$ and $\frac{6}{5}$ are improper fractions. They are equal to or greater than 1.

You can rename improper fractions and mixed numbers.

$$\frac{9}{4} = \frac{8}{4} + \frac{1}{4}$$
$$= 2\frac{1}{4}$$

$$2\frac{1}{4} = 2 + \frac{1}{4}$$
$$= \frac{8}{4} + \frac{1}{4}$$
$$= \frac{9}{4}$$

Comparing and Ordering Fractions

Comparing and ordering unlike fractions: Find equivalent fractions with
- a common denominator.

$$\frac{3}{4} = \frac{6}{8} = \frac{9}{12} \qquad \frac{1}{3} = \frac{2}{6} = \frac{3}{9} = \frac{4}{12}$$

$\frac{9}{12}$ is greater than $\frac{4}{12}$.

So, $\frac{3}{4} > \frac{1}{3}$.

- a common numerator.

$$\frac{1}{3} = \frac{3}{9}$$

$\frac{3}{9}$ is less than $\frac{3}{4}$.

So, $\frac{1}{3} < \frac{3}{4}$.

Use a benchmark of $\frac{1}{2}$.

$$\frac{3}{4} > \frac{1}{2}$$
$$\frac{1}{3} < \frac{1}{2}$$

So, in order from greatest to least: $\frac{3}{4}, \frac{1}{2}, \frac{1}{3}$

Fractions and Mixed Numbers

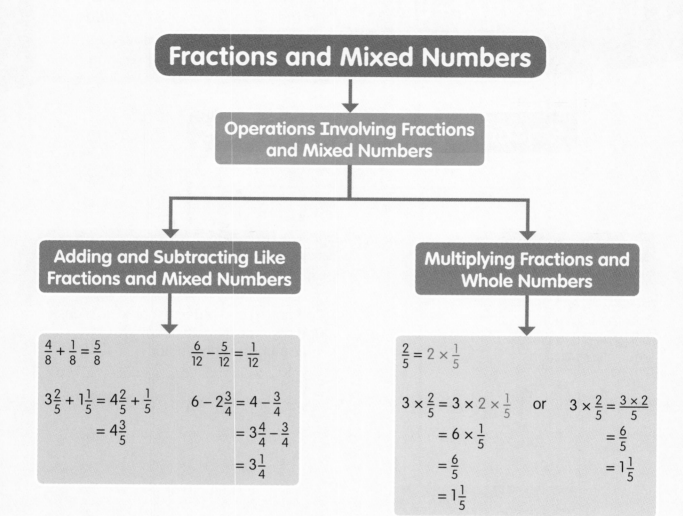

Operations Involving Fractions and Mixed Numbers

Adding and Subtracting Like Fractions and Mixed Numbers

$$\frac{4}{8} + \frac{1}{8} = \frac{5}{8}$$

$$\frac{6}{12} - \frac{5}{12} = \frac{1}{12}$$

$$3\frac{2}{5} + 1\frac{1}{5} = 4\frac{2}{5} + \frac{1}{5}$$
$$= 4\frac{3}{5}$$

$$6 - 2\frac{3}{4} = 4 - \frac{3}{4}$$
$$= 3\frac{4}{4} - \frac{3}{4}$$
$$= 3\frac{1}{4}$$

Multiplying Fractions and Whole Numbers

$$\frac{2}{5} = 2 \times \frac{1}{5}$$

$$3 \times \frac{2}{5} = 3 \times 2 \times \frac{1}{5} \quad \text{or} \quad 3 \times \frac{2}{5} = \frac{3 \times 2}{5}$$
$$= 6 \times \frac{1}{5} \qquad\qquad\qquad = \frac{6}{5}$$
$$= \frac{6}{5} \qquad\qquad\qquad\quad = 1\frac{1}{5}$$
$$= 1\frac{1}{5}$$

Name: _____   Date: _____

Find the first four equivalent fractions of $\frac{1}{4}$.

1 $\frac{1}{4} = \dfrac{\boxed{2}}{\boxed{4}} = \dfrac{\boxed{3}}{\boxed{4}} = \dfrac{\boxed{4}}{\boxed{4}} = \dfrac{\boxed{5}}{\boxed{4}}$

Find each missing numerator or denominator.

2 $\dfrac{2}{\boxed{}} = \dfrac{4}{10} = \dfrac{\boxed{}}{20}$

3 $\dfrac{\boxed{}}{6} = \dfrac{4}{12} = \dfrac{10}{\boxed{}}$

Write each fraction in simplest form.

4 $\dfrac{2}{10} = \dfrac{\boxed{}}{\boxed{}}$

5 $\dfrac{3}{6} = \dfrac{\boxed{}}{\boxed{}}$

6 $\dfrac{6}{8} = \dfrac{\boxed{}}{\boxed{}}$

7 $\dfrac{9}{12} = \dfrac{\boxed{}}{\boxed{}}$

Use equivalent fractions to compare each pair of fractions. Write > or <.

8 $\dfrac{5}{6} \bigcirc \dfrac{2}{3}$

9 $\dfrac{3}{4} \bigcirc \dfrac{5}{6}$

Use the benchmark fraction $\frac{1}{2}$ to compare each pair of fractions. Write > or <.

10 $\dfrac{1}{4} \bigcirc \dfrac{3}{8}$

11 $\dfrac{1}{3} \bigcirc \dfrac{4}{5}$

Order the fractions from greatest to least.

12 $\dfrac{3}{10} \qquad \dfrac{4}{5} \qquad \dfrac{1}{4}$

_____   _____   _____
   greatest   least

Order the fractions from least to greatest.

13) $\frac{1}{2}$ $\frac{3}{8}$ $\frac{4}{5}$

_____   _____   _____

least   greatest

Add or subtract. Show your work. Write each answer in simplest form.

14) $\frac{5}{12} + \frac{4}{12} =$

15) $\frac{9}{10} - \frac{3}{10} =$

Write the mixed number and improper fraction that the shaded parts represent. Write each answer in simplest form.

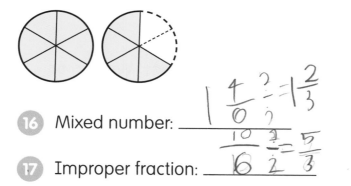

16) Mixed number: _____

17) Improper fraction: _____

Find each missing mixed number or improper fraction.

18)

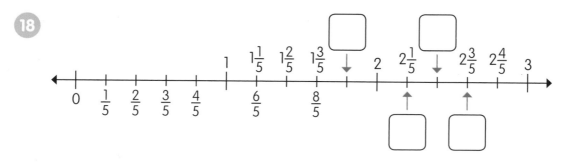

Draw a model to represent the mixed number. Then, express the mixed number as an improper fraction.

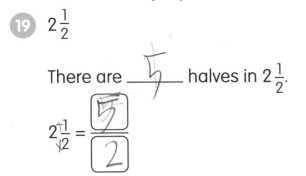

19. $2\frac{1}{2}$

There are ___5___ halves in $2\frac{1}{2}$.

$2\frac{1}{2} = \dfrac{\boxed{5}}{\boxed{2}}$

Express each improper fraction as a mixed number.

20. $\frac{9}{4}$

$2\frac{1}{4}$

21. $\frac{23}{8}$

$2\frac{7}{8}$

Express each mixed number as an improper fraction.

22. $3\frac{1}{4}$ $\quad\dfrac{13}{4}$

23. $2\frac{2}{3}$

$\dfrac{8}{3}$

Add or subtract. Show your work. Express each answer as a mixed number in simplest form.

24. $2\frac{3}{6} + 1\frac{5}{6} =$ $4\frac{2}{6} = 4\frac{1}{3}$

25. $6\frac{2}{5} - 4\frac{4}{5} =$ $1\frac{3}{5}$

5
$\cancel{6}\ \frac{2}{5}\ \frac{5}{5} + 2 = 7$
$\qquad\qquad\qquad\dfrac{7}{5}$
$- 4\ \dfrac{4}{5}$
$\overline{\qquad\qquad}$
$1\ \dfrac{3}{5}$

Multiply. Show your work. Express each answer as a fraction or mixed number in simplest form.

26 $6 \times \frac{1}{8} =$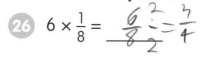

27 $5 \times \frac{3}{10} =$

Use the data in the table to make a line plot. Then, answer questions 28 to 32.

The table shows the heights of the fence posts that a garden shop has in stock.

Height of Fence Posts (m)	Number of Posts
$\frac{3}{4}$	5
$1\frac{1}{4}$	3
$1\frac{1}{2}$	2
2	5

28

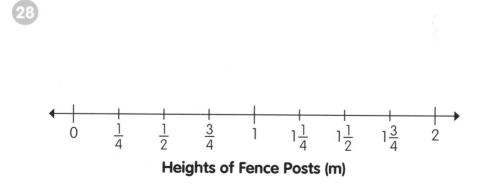

Heights of Fence Posts (m)

29 How many posts does the garden shop have?

30 What is the difference in height between the tallest post and the shortest post?

31 There are 2 posts which are $1\frac{1}{2}$ meters tall. What is their total height?

32 If the $\frac{3}{4}$-meter posts are placed one on top of the other, what will the total height be?

Solve. Draw a bar model to help you.

33 Jason had $1\frac{3}{5}$ meters of ribbon. He bought another $2\frac{2}{5}$ meters of ribbon. What was the total length of ribbon that Jason had?

34 Thomas has 8 packets of milk. Each packet contains $\frac{2}{5}$ liter of milk. After pouring all the milk into a container, he uses $1\frac{4}{5}$ liters of the milk to make a dessert. How much milk does he have left?

35 Mr. Garcia had some blueberries. He sold $2\frac{3}{4}$ kilograms of the blueberries and packed the rest equally into 9 bags. Each bag contained $\frac{1}{4}$ kilogram of blueberries. Find the mass of blueberries that Mr. Garcia had at first.

Assessment Prep

Answer each question.

36 Which **two** fractions are equivalent to $\frac{1}{3}$?

   (A) $\frac{2}{3}$

   (B) $\frac{2}{6}$

   (C) $\frac{3}{6}$

   (D) $\frac{3}{12}$

   (E) $\frac{4}{12}$

37 Which expression is equivalent to $4 \times \frac{5}{8}$?

   (A) $8 \times \frac{1}{5}$

   (B) $9 \times \frac{1}{8}$

   (C) $20 \times \frac{1}{8}$

   (D) $32 \times \frac{1}{5}$

38 Trinity divides her backyard into 10 equal plots. She plants roses in 3 of the plots and plants sunflowers in 6 of the plots. Which **two** expressions represent the fraction of the backyard that Trinity plants the two types of flowers in?

   (A) $3 + 6$

   (B) $\frac{3}{6} + \frac{6}{6}$

   (C) $\frac{3}{10} + \frac{6}{10}$

   (D) $\frac{10}{3} + \frac{10}{6}$

   (E) $\frac{1}{10} + \frac{1}{10} + \frac{1}{10} + \frac{1}{10} + \frac{1}{10} + \frac{1}{10} + \frac{1}{10} + \frac{1}{10} + \frac{1}{10}$

39 Alex makes a fruit tart. He gives $\frac{1}{2}$ of the fruit tart to Destiny and $\frac{2}{5}$ of the fruit tart to Sean.

Part A

Sean says his portion is bigger than Destiny's portion because the numerator 2 is greater than the numerator 1.

- Explain why Sean's reasoning is incorrect.
- Explain how you can use equivalent fractions to show whose portion is bigger.
- Write a comparison using < or > to compare $\frac{1}{2}$ and $\frac{2}{5}$.

Write your explanation and comparison in the space below.

Part B

Alex cuts a chicken pie into 12 equal pieces. He eats $\frac{1}{4}$ of the pie. Use the model below to show $\frac{1}{4}$ of the pie.

Name: _____ Date: _____

Picnics and Pies

 Emily made some apple sauce for a class picnic.

Her recipe used $\frac{1}{3}$ cup of sugar for each batch.

This is equivalent to $\frac{?}{12}$. Find the missing number.

2 Emily made 5 batches of apple sauce. How much sugar did she use in all?

3 Emily filled some jars equally with the apple sauce. She ate $\frac{3}{10}$ of a jar of apple sauce. Wyatt ate $\frac{2}{10}$ of a jar of apple sauce. How much apple sauce did they eat in all?

4 Anna made 3 mini apple pies of the same size for the picnic. She ate $\frac{1}{2}$ of an apple pie. Brandon ate $\frac{7}{12}$ of an apple pie and Adam ate $\frac{3}{8}$ of an apple pie.

a Who ate more pie, Anna or Adam?

b Order the amount of pie eaten from greatest to least. Explain how you determined the order.

5 Brandon made 4 chicken pies of the same size for the picnic. He gave $1\frac{4}{6}$ pies to Anna and $1\frac{1}{6}$ pies to Emily.

a How many pies did he give away in all?

b How many pies did he have left?

© 2020 Marshall Cavendish Education Pte Ltd

Rubric

Point(s)	Level	My Performance
7–8	4	• Most of my answers are correct. • I showed complete understanding of what I have learned. • I used the correct strategies to solve the problems. • I explained my answers and mathematical thinking clearly and completely.
5–6.5	3	• Some of my answers are correct. • I showed some understanding of what I have learned. • I used some correct strategies to solve the problems. • I explained my answers and mathematical thinking clearly.
3–4.5	2	• A few of my answers are correct. • I showed little understanding of what I have learned. • I used a few correct strategies to solve the problems. • I explained some of my answers and mathematical thinking clearly.
0–2.5	1	• A few of my answers are correct. • I showed little or no understanding of what I have learned. • I used a few strategies to solve the problems. • I did not explain my answers and mathematical thinking clearly.

Teacher's Comments

Tell Stories Through Art

A textile [TEK-style] artist uses cloth and other materials to make art, such as weavings, carpets, and quilts. Some artists use their art to tell stories.

Task

Story Quilt

Work as a class and then in pairs or groups to make a story quilt.

1 Visit a library or go online to learn more about the work of Faith Ringgold and the stories her textiles tell.

2 As a class, discuss ideas for a story quilt. Tell your story in ten parts. Write your story plan on the board. Then, organize into groups. Assign $\frac{1}{10}$ of the story to each pair or group.

3 Collect a large square of art paper or cloth and colored pencils, markers, or paint.

4 Design a border for your square. Use a color or pattern to make each quarter of the border different.

5 Use pencils, markers, or paint to tell your part of the story inside the border.

6 Put your story pieces together to make a quilt.

Long Jump Results – Girls

Olivia Jones	3.75 meters
Amy Lee	3.8 meters
Morgan Clark	3.82 meters

How do I read 3.75? What do the digits 7 and 5 stand for?

How are fractions and decimals related?

Name: _____ Date: _____

Knowing fractions with a denominator of 10 and 100

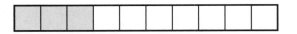

$\frac{3}{10}$ of the figure is shaded.

$\frac{3}{10}$ is read as three-tenths.

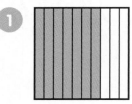

$\frac{7}{100}$ of the figure is shaded.

$\frac{7}{100}$ is read as seven-hundredths.

▶ **Quick Check**

Write the fraction represented by the shaded parts in each figure.

1

_____

2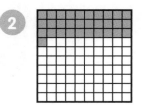

_____

Knowing improper fractions and mixed numbers with a denominator of 10 and 100

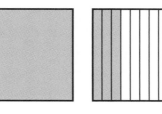

The shaded parts show $\frac{23}{10}$ or $2\frac{3}{10}$.

$2\frac{3}{10}$ is read as two and three tenths.

The shaded parts show $\frac{113}{100}$ or $1\frac{13}{100}$.

$1\frac{13}{100}$ is read as one and 13 hundredths.

▶ Quick Check

Write the mixed number represented by the shaded parts in each figure.

3 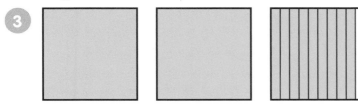 _____

4  _____

Finding equivalent fractions

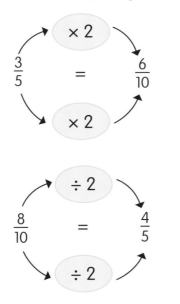

$$\frac{3}{5} = \frac{6}{10}$$

$$\frac{8}{10} = \frac{4}{5}$$

▶ **Quick Check**

Find each missing numerator and denominator.

5 $\dfrac{2}{5} = \dfrac{\boxed{}}{10}$

6 $\dfrac{6}{10} = \dfrac{3}{\boxed{}}$

7 $\dfrac{1}{2} = \dfrac{\boxed{}}{10}$

8 $\dfrac{7}{10} = \dfrac{\boxed{}}{100}$

9 $\dfrac{90}{100} = \dfrac{9}{\boxed{}}$

Rounding numbers to the nearest ten

If the digit in the ones place is 1, 2, 3, or 4, round the number to the lesser ten.

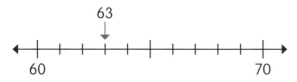

63 is between 60 and 70.
It is nearer to 60 than to 70.
63 is 60 when rounded to the nearest ten.

If the digit in the ones place is 5, 6, 7, 8, or 9, round the number to the greater ten.

38 is between 30 and 40.
It is nearer to 40 than to 30.
38 is 40 when rounded to the nearest ten.

▶ Quick Check

Round each number to the nearest ten.

10 29   _____

11 45   _____

12 183   _____

13 307   _____

Adding like fractions

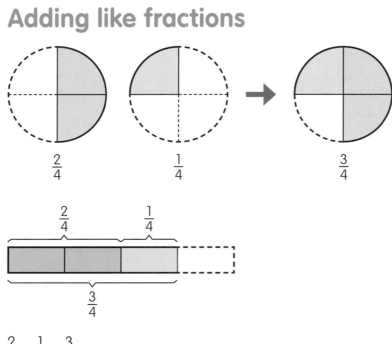

$$\frac{2}{4} + \frac{1}{4} = \frac{3}{4}$$

▶ **Quick Check**

Add. Express each answer in simplest form.

14 $\frac{1}{5} + \frac{2}{5} =$ _____

15 $\frac{5}{12} + \frac{2}{12} =$ _____

16 $\frac{4}{8} + \frac{2}{8} =$ _____

17 $\frac{3}{10} + \frac{5}{10} =$ _____

1 Understanding Tenths

Learning Objective:
- Read and write tenths in decimal form.

THINK

Find four possible sets for each missing number. $\boxed{?}.7 = 2\frac{\boxed{?}}{10}$

ENGAGE

1 Divide a strip of paper into 10 equal parts. Label each part as fractions. If $\frac{1}{10}$ is written as 0.1 and $\frac{2}{10}$ as 0.2, how do you write $\frac{7}{10}$ as a decimal?

2 Color $\frac{8}{10}$ on two identical strips of paper. Write a fraction to represent the sum of the colored parts. What decimal can you write to represent the sum?

LEARN Express tenths as decimals

1 Benjamin divides a strip of paper into 10 equal parts.

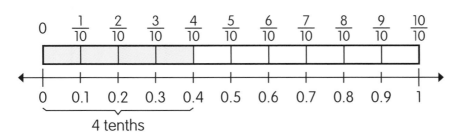

You can write 1 tenth as $\frac{1}{10}$ or 0.1.

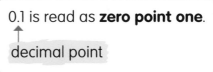

0.1 is read as **zero point one**.

decimal point

You can write 4 tenths as $\frac{4}{10}$ or 0.4.
0.1 and 0.4 are decimals.

0.4 is read as zero point four.

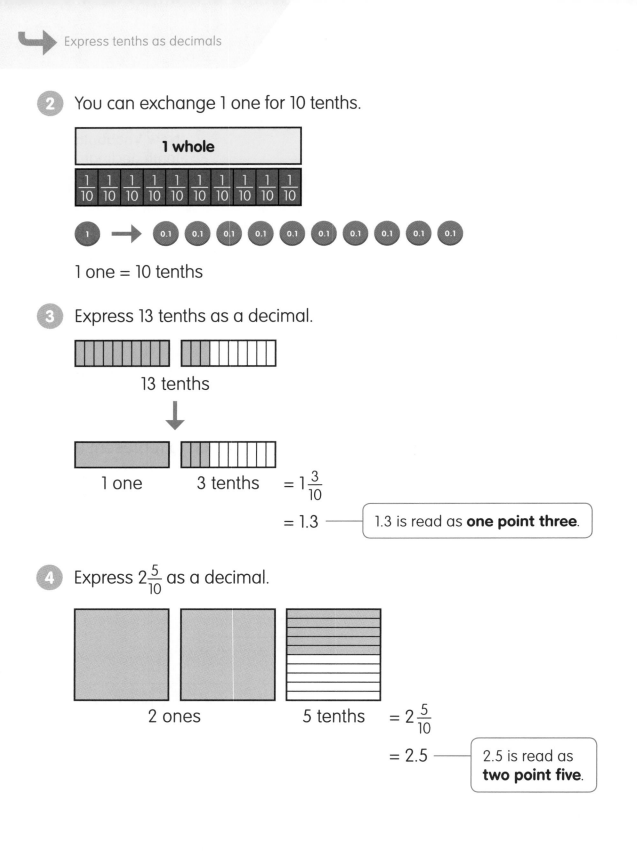

2 You can exchange 1 one for 10 tenths.

1 whole

$\frac{1}{10}$ $\frac{1}{10}$ $\frac{1}{10}$ $\frac{1}{10}$ $\frac{1}{10}$ $\frac{1}{10}$ $\frac{1}{10}$ $\frac{1}{10}$ $\frac{1}{10}$ $\frac{1}{10}$

1 → 0.1 0.1 0.1 0.1 0.1 0.1 0.1 0.1 0.1 0.1

1 one = 10 tenths

3 Express 13 tenths as a decimal.

13 tenths

1 one   3 tenths $= 1\frac{3}{10}$

$= 1.3$ —— 1.3 is read as **one point three**.

4 Express $2\frac{5}{10}$ as a decimal.

2 ones   5 tenths $= 2\frac{5}{10}$

$= 2.5$ —— 2.5 is read as **two point five**.

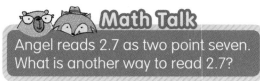

Math Talk

Angel reads 2.7 as two point seven.
What is another way to read 2.7?

5 Represent 2.8 on a place-value chart.

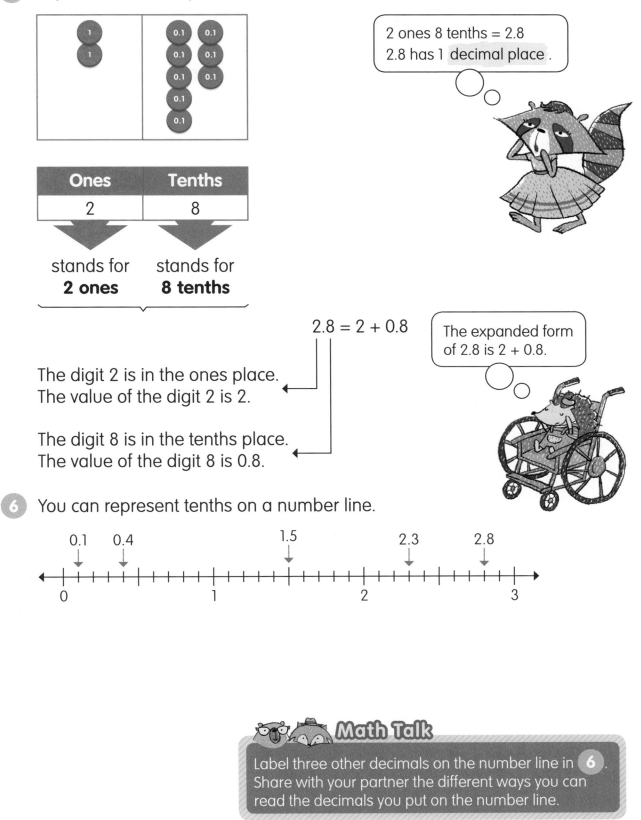

Ones	Tenths
2	8

stands for **2 ones**   stands for **8 tenths**

2 ones 8 tenths = 2.8
2.8 has 1 decimal place .

2.8 = 2 + 0.8

The digit 2 is in the ones place.
The value of the digit 2 is 2.

The digit 8 is in the tenths place.
The value of the digit 8 is 0.8.

The expanded form of 2.8 is 2 + 0.8.

6 You can represent tenths on a number line.

0.1   0.4   1.5   2.3   2.8

0   1   2   3

🦝🦊 **Math Talk**

Label three other decimals on the number line in **6**.
Share with your partner the different ways you can
read the decimals you put on the number line.

Hands-on Activity

Work in pairs.

Activity 1   Representing decimals on a number line

(1) Express $\frac{2}{10}$ as a decimal. Use  and the number line to represent the decimal.

(2) Repeat (1) using the following fraction and mixed number.

a $\frac{7}{10}$

b $1\frac{9}{10}$

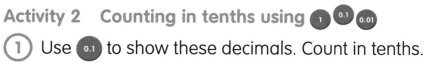

Activity 2   Counting in tenths using ⬤ ⬤ ⬤

(1) Use 🔘 to show these decimals. Count in tenths.

   a   0.5   b   0.9   c   1.2

© 2020 Marshall Cavendish Education Pte Ltd

TRY Practice expressing tenths as decimals

Write the decimal represented by the shaded parts in each figure.

1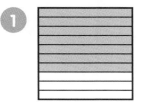

_____

2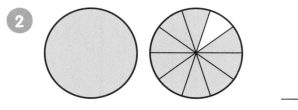

_____

Express the following as a decimal.

3   _____

Express each of the following as a decimal.

4 9 tenths = _____

5 18 tenths = _____

6 $\frac{5}{10}$ = _____

7 $2\frac{6}{10}$ = _____

Write the correct decimal in each box.

8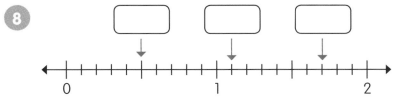

Express the total volume of water as a mixed number and a decimal.

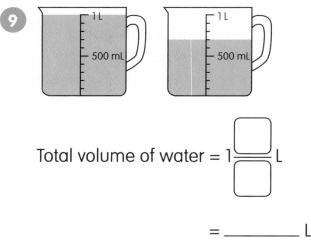

9

Total volume of water = 1 $\frac{\square}{\square}$ L

= _____ L

Find each missing number.

10 In 23.6, the digit _____ is in the tens place.

11 In 95.4, the value of the digit 4 is _____.

12 In 80.7, the value of the digit 8 is _____.

13 In 52.3, the digit _____ is in the tenths place.

14 In 134.9, the digit _____ is in the ones place.

Find each missing number.

15 9 + 0.8 = _____

16 10 + 3 + 0.2 = _____

17 18.7 = 10 + _____ + 0.7

18 37.6 = 30 + 7 + _____

19 _____ + 2 + 0.4 = 12.4

20 40 + _____ = 40.9

Name: _____ Date: _____

INDEPENDENT PRACTICE

Write the decimal represented by the shaded parts in each figure.

1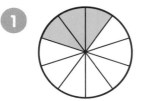

_____

2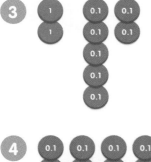

_____

Express each of the following as a decimal.

3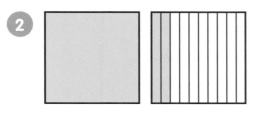

_____

4

_____

Express each of the following as a decimal.

5 7 tenths = _____

6 16 tenths = _____

7 $\frac{4}{10}$ = _____

8 $3\frac{9}{10}$ = _____

Write the correct decimal in each box.

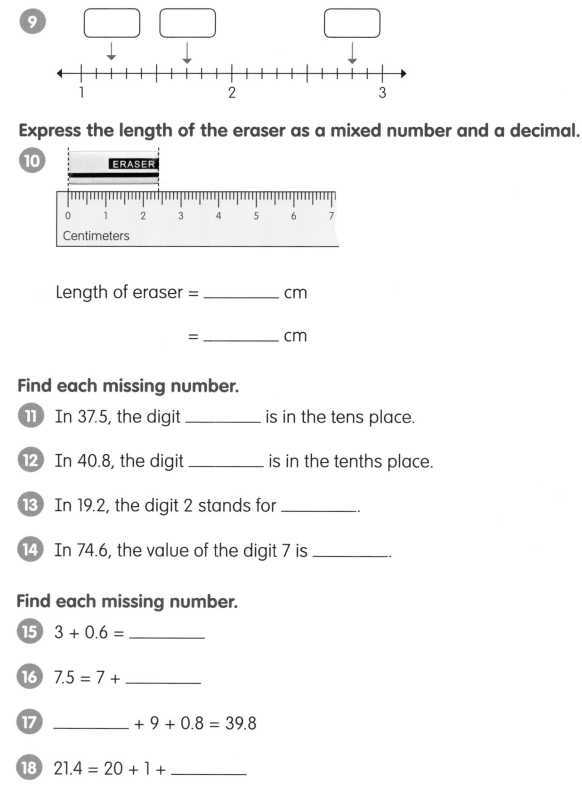

9

Express the length of the eraser as a mixed number and a decimal.

10

Length of eraser = _____ cm

= _____ cm

Find each missing number.

11 In 37.5, the digit _____ is in the tens place.

12 In 40.8, the digit _____ is in the tenths place.

13 In 19.2, the digit 2 stands for _____.

14 In 74.6, the value of the digit 7 is _____.

Find each missing number.

15 3 + 0.6 = _____

16 7.5 = 7 + _____

17 _____ + 9 + 0.8 = 39.8

18 21.4 = 20 + 1 + _____

Name: _____ Date: _____

Understanding Hundredths

Learning Objective:
• Read and write hundredths in decimal form.

THINK

Find four possible sets of answers for each blank.

$4.\boxed{?}5 = \boxed{?} + \dfrac{5}{100} =$ _____ hundredths

ENGAGE

a Shade 1 square of a hundred square grid. What fraction represents the part you shaded? Now, shade 10 squares. What is the new fraction? What is another way to write the fractions?

b Shade four sets of $\dfrac{7}{10}$ on four hundred square grids. How many squares have you shaded? Write the sum of fractions in different ways.

LEARN Express hundredths as decimals

1 Divide a square into 10 equal parts.

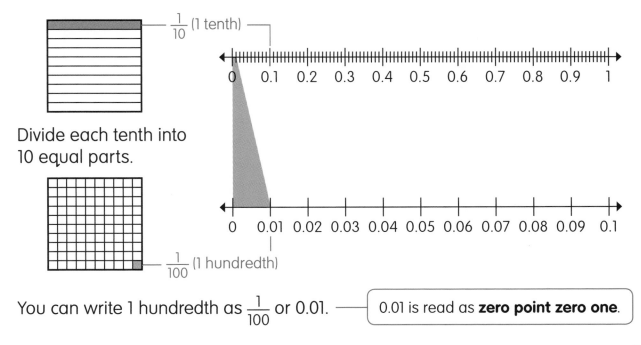

$\dfrac{1}{10}$ (1 tenth)

Divide each tenth into 10 equal parts.

$\dfrac{1}{100}$ (1 hundredth)

You can write 1 hundredth as $\dfrac{1}{100}$ or 0.01. ——— 0.01 is read as **zero point zero one**.

2 Shade 3 out of the 100 equal parts.

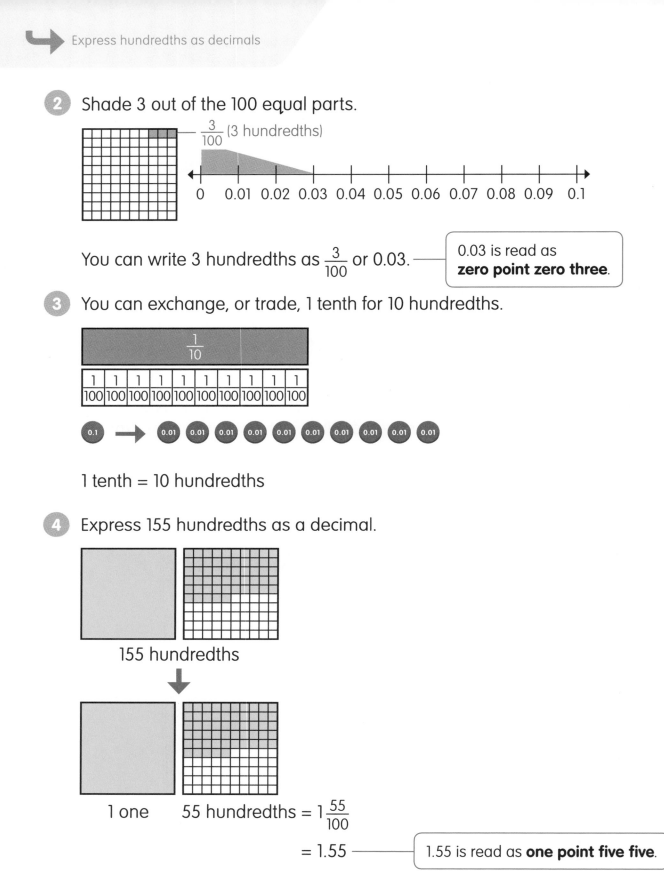

$\frac{3}{100}$ (3 hundredths)

You can write 3 hundredths as $\frac{3}{100}$ or 0.03.

0.03 is read as **zero point zero three**.

3 You can exchange, or trade, 1 tenth for 10 hundredths.

1 tenth = 10 hundredths

4 Express 155 hundredths as a decimal.

155 hundredths

1 one   55 hundredths = $1\frac{55}{100}$

$= 1.55$

1.55 is read as **one point five five**.

5 Express $2\frac{53}{100}$ as a decimal.

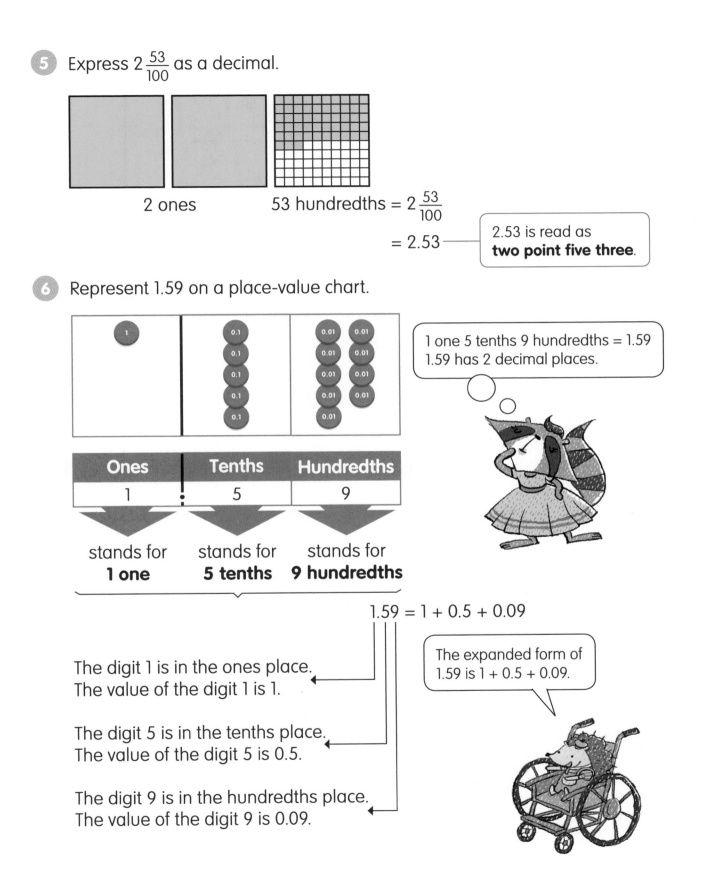

2 ones

53 hundredths = $2\frac{53}{100}$

= 2.53

2.53 is read as **two point five three**.

6 Represent 1.59 on a place-value chart.

1 one 5 tenths 9 hundredths = 1.59
1.59 has 2 decimal places.

Ones	Tenths	Hundredths
1	5	9

stands for **1 one**

stands for **5 tenths**

stands for **9 hundredths**

1.59 = 1 + 0.5 + 0.09

The expanded form of 1.59 is 1 + 0.5 + 0.09.

The digit 1 is in the ones place.
The value of the digit 1 is 1.

The digit 5 is in the tenths place.
The value of the digit 5 is 0.5.

The digit 9 is in the hundredths place.
The value of the digit 9 is 0.09.

7 You can represent hundredths on a number line.

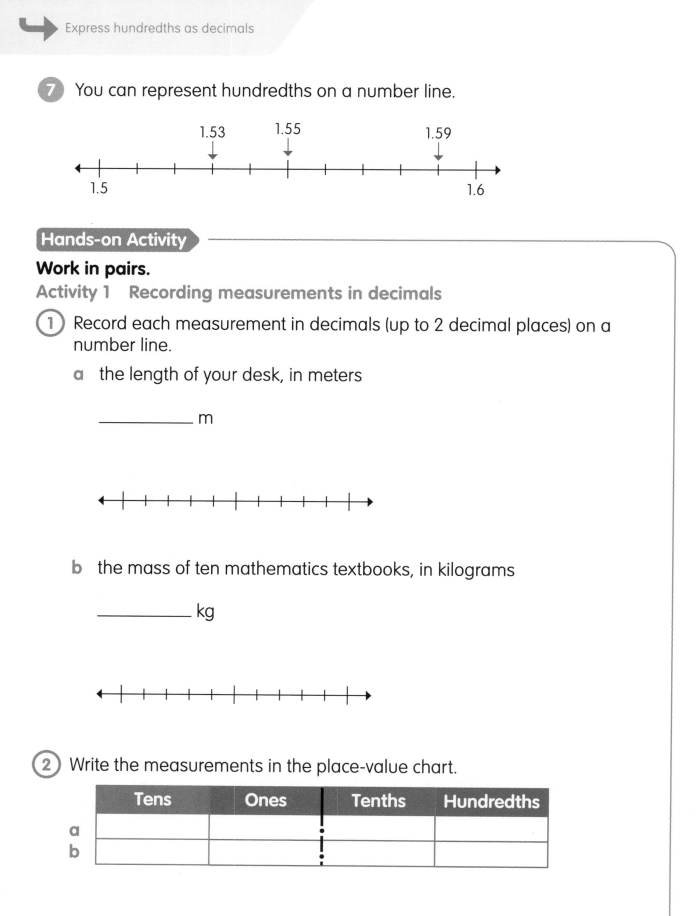

Hands-on Activity

Work in pairs.

Activity 1   Recording measurements in decimals

1 Record each measurement in decimals (up to 2 decimal places) on a number line.

a the length of your desk, in meters

_____ m

b the mass of ten mathematics textbooks, in kilograms

_____ kg

2 Write the measurements in the place-value chart.

	Tens	Ones	Tenths	Hundredths
a				
b				

Activity 2 Writing a decimal in expanded form

(1) Use  to show 8.51, 3.74, 6.08, and 5.11.

(2) Write each decimal in the place-value chart and in expanded form.

a 8.51

Ones	Tenths	Hundredths

8.51 = _____ + _____ + _____

b 3.74

Ones	Tenths	Hundredths

3.74 = _____ + _____ + _____

c 6.08

Ones	Tenths	Hundredths

6.08 = _____ + _____

d 5.11

Ones	Tenths	Hundredths

5.11 = _____ + _____ + _____

TRY Practice expressing hundredths as decimals

Write the decimal represented by the shaded parts in the figure.

1 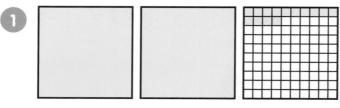 _____

Express the following as a decimal.

2  _____

Express each of the following as a decimal.

3 71 hundredths = _____

4 148 hundredths = _____

5 $\frac{26}{100}$ = _____

6 $2\frac{4}{100}$ = _____

Write the correct decimal in each box.

7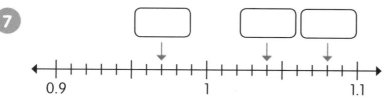

Fill in each blank.

8 In 5.39, the digit _____ is in the tenths place.

9 In 3.47, the value of the digit 7 is _____.

10 In 4.61, the value of the digit 4 is _____.

Find each missing number.

11 $7 + 0.8 + 0.02 =$ _____

12 $10 + 5 + 0.7 +$ _____ $= 15.71$

13 $34.09 = 30 + 4 +$ _____

ENGAGE

Use  to show 1 dollar and 60 cents. Use two hundred square grids and number lines to show the amount. Why do you write money in decimal form? Explain your thinking to your partner.

LEARN Use decimals to write dollars and cents

1 You can write money amounts as decimals.

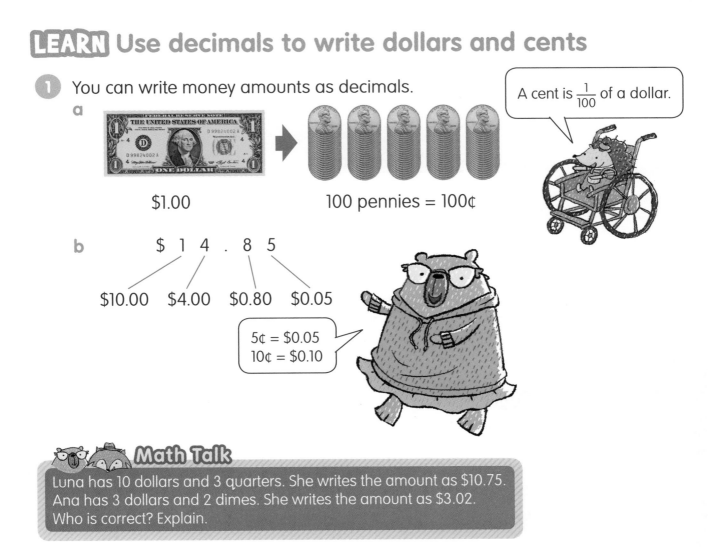

a

$1.00   100 pennies = 100¢

A cent is $\frac{1}{100}$ of a dollar.

b $ 1 4 . 8 5

$10.00 $4.00 $0.80 $0.05

5¢ = $0.05
10¢ = $0.10

Math Talk

Luna has 10 dollars and 3 quarters. She writes the amount as $10.75.
Ana has 3 dollars and 2 dimes. She writes the amount as $3.02.
Who is correct? Explain.

TRY Practice using decimals to write dollars and cents

Express each amount in dollars.

1 2¢ = $_____

2 30¢ = $_____

3 63¢ = $_____

4 120¢ = $_____

Express each amount in decimal form.

5 5 dollars 18 cents = $_____

6 7 dollars 45 cents = $_____

7 18 dollars = $_____

8 33 dollars 5 cents = $_____

9 20 dollars 6 cents = $_____

10 10 dollars 99 cents = $_____

11 15 dollars 1 cent = $_____

12 25 dollars 70 cents = $_____

© 2020 Marshall Cavendish Education Pte Ltd

MATH SHARING

Mathematical Habit 2 Use mathematical reasoning
Choose a decimal in tenths between 0 and 1, for example, 0.2.
Regroup 0.2 into hundredths and write it as a decimal.
Repeat the steps with two other decimals in tenths.
What do you notice?

INDEPENDENT PRACTICE

Write the decimal represented by the shaded parts in each figure.

1 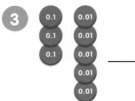 _____

2 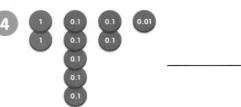 _____

Express each of the following as a decimal.

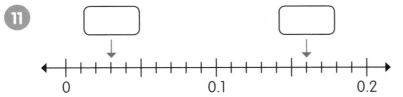

3 _____

4 _____

Express each of the following as a decimal.

5 4 hundredths = _____

6 17 hundredths = _____

7 209 hundredths = _____

8 $\frac{69}{100}$ = _____

9 $4\frac{5}{100}$ = _____

10 $8\frac{13}{100}$ = _____

Write the correct decimal in each box.

11

Mark an X on the number line to show the decimal.

12 3.45

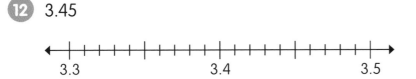

Find each missing number.

13 In 836.21, the digit _____ is in the hundreds place, and the digit

_____ is in the hundredths place.

14 In 19.05, the digit 5 stands for _____.

15 In 3.49, the digit 4 stands for _____.

16 In 50.26, the value of the digit 6 is _____.

Find each missing number.

17 8 + 0.04 = _____

18 13 + 0.9 + _____ = 13.96

19 2.75 = 2 + _____ + 0.05

20 34.08 = 30 + 4 + _____

Express each amount in dollars.

21 9¢ = $_____

22 80¢ = $_____

23 35¢ = $_____

24 278¢ = $_____

Express each amount in decimal form.

25 9 dollars 14 cents = $_____

26 2 dollars 40 cents = $_____

27 34 dollars = $_____

28 56 dollars 9 cents = $_____

3 Comparing and Ordering Decimals

Learning Objectives:
• Compare and order decimals.
• Complete number patterns.

THINK

Five decimals are ordered from least to greatest. Two decimals are missing from the list. What are the possible decimals?

1.2   1.5   1.8

ENGAGE

1. Compare 12 and 2. Which is greater? Now, compare 0.12 and 0.2. Which is greater? Use hundred square grids and number lines to help you explain your thinking.

2. Fill in the blank with **greater than** or **less than**.

   0.58 is _____ 0.9.

LEARN Compare and order decimals

1. Compare 1.2 and 2.3. Which is greater?

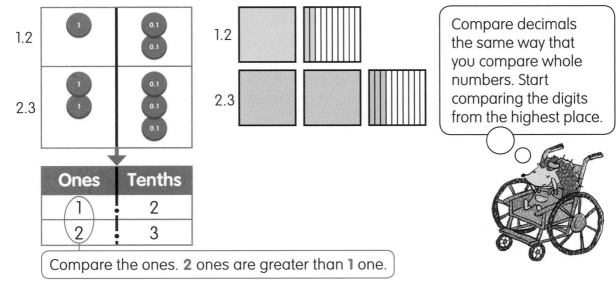

> Compare decimals the same way that you compare whole numbers. Start comparing the digits from the highest place.

Ones	Tenths
1	2
2	3

Compare the ones. **2** ones are greater than **1** one.

So, 2.3 is greater than 1.2.

2 Which is less, 2.3 or 2.24?

▶ **Method 1**

Ones	Tenths	Hundredths
②	③	
②	②	4

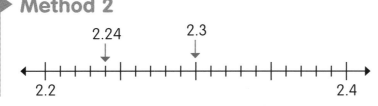

Compare the ones. They are the same.   Compare the tenths. **2** tenths are less than **3** tenths.

▶ **Method 2**

2.24   2.3

2.2   2.4

So, 2.24 is less than 2.3.

3 Order 0.62, 0.26, and 0.6 from least to greatest.

Ones	Tenths	Hundredths
0	6	2
0	2	6
0	6	0

STEP 1 Compare the ones. They are the same.

STEP 2 Compare the tenths. **2** tenths are less than **6** tenths. So, 0.26 is the least.

STEP 3 Compare the hundredths of the remaining numbers 0.62 and 0.6. **2** hundredths are greater than **0** hundredths. 0.62 is greater than 0.6. So, 0.62 is the greatest.

From least to greatest, the decimals are:

0.26   0.6   0.62
least   greatest

Work in pairs.

Activity 1   Comparing decimals using  and a number line

(1)   Use 🔵 🔵 🔵 to show 8.5 and 9.2. Then, mark 8.5 and 9.2 on the number line.

```
←——+—+—+—+—+—+—+—+—+—+—+—+—+—+—+—+—+—+—+—+—+—→
   8              9              10
```

(2)   Ask your partner to use "greater than" or "less than" to describe the decimals.

(3)   Trade places. Repeat (1) and (2) with 13.28 and 13.47.

```
←—+—+—+—+—+—+—+—+—+—+—+—+—+—+—+—+—+—+—+—+—+—+—+—+—+—+—+—+—+—+—+→
  13.2          13.3           13.4           13.5
```

Activity 2   Using 🔵 🔵 🔵 to describe, compare, and order decimals

(1)   Use 🔵 🔵 🔵 to show 1.54, 1.45, and 1.52.

(2)   Ask your partner to use "greater than," "less than," "greatest," "least," or "the same as" to describe the decimals.

(3)   Order the decimals from greatest to least.

_____   _____   _____
   greatest   least

(4)   Trade places. Repeat (1) to (3) using 4.13, 4.31, and 4.3.

_____   _____   _____
   greatest   least

TRY Practice comparing and ordering decimals

Shade each figure to show the decimal. Then, circle the greater decimal.

①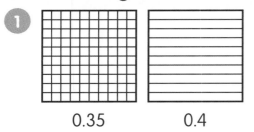

0.35   0.4

Compare the decimals. Write greater than or less than.

②

Ones	Tenths	Hundredths
0	3	3
0	0	3

0.03 is _____ 0.33.

Compare each pair of decimals. Write <, >, or =.

③ 8.21 ◯ 8.23   ④ 0.02 ◯ 0.12

⑤ 6.3 ◯ 6.30   ⑥ 4.24 ◯ 4.42

Circle the greatest decimal.

⑦ 0.58   0.54   0.61   0.06   ⑧ 2.07   2.4   2.74   2.47

Order each set.

⑨ Order 0.18, 0.08, and 0.81 from least to greatest.

_____   _____   _____
   least   greatest

⑩ Order 0.13, $\frac{3}{10}$, and 0.31 from greatest to least.

_____   _____   _____
   greatest   least

ENGAGE

1 Use 🔵 🔵 🔵 to show 0.13. Then, show and explain to your partner how to find each of the following.

    a one hundredth more than 0.13   **b** one tenth more than 0.13

2 Are the numbers arranged in a pattern?
7.53, 7.55, 7.53, 7.56, 7.26, 7.29
Explain your thinking.

LEARN Find missing numbers in a number pattern

1 **a** What is 0.1 more than 2.3?   **b** What is 0.1 less than 2.3?

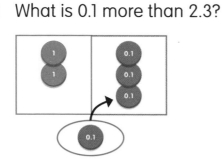

    0.1 more than 2.**3** is 2.**4**.   0.1 less than 2.**3** is 2.**2**.

2 Complete the number pattern.

   + 0.1 + 0.1 + 0.1 + 0.1 + 0.1 + 0.1 + 0.1 + 0.1 + 0.1 + 0.1

0.41   0.51   0.61   0.71   **?**   0.91   **?**   1.11   1.21   1.31   1.41

What is 0.1 more than 0.7**1**? = **0.81**   **1.01** = What is 0.1 more than 0.9**1**?

3 **a** What is 0.01 more than 1.34?   **b** What is 0.01 less than 1.34?

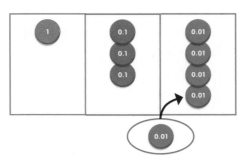

    0.01 more than 1.3**4** is 1.3**5**.   0.01 less than 1.3**4** is 1.3**3**.

4 Complete the number pattern.

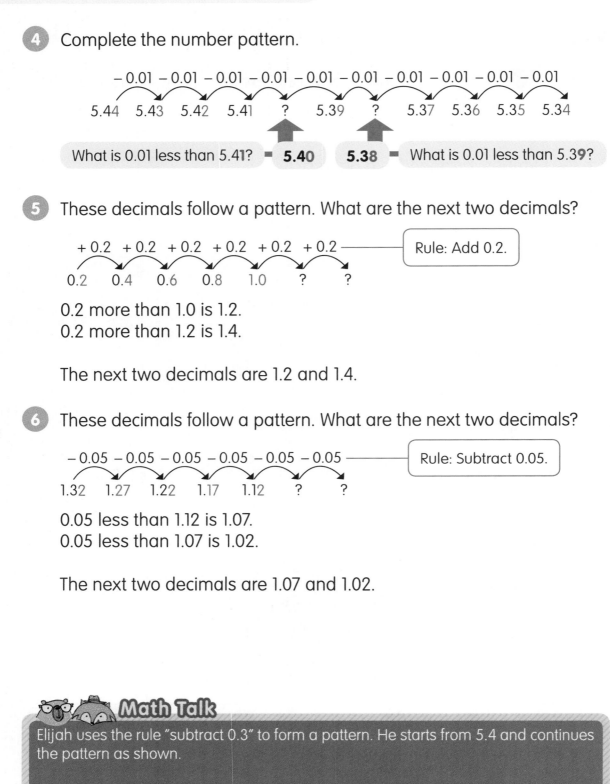

– 0.01 – 0.01 – 0.01 – 0.01 – 0.01 – 0.01 – 0.01 – 0.01 – 0.01 – 0.01

5.44 5.43 5.42 5.41 ? 5.39 ? 5.37 5.36 5.35 5.34

What is 0.01 less than 5.41? **5.40**   **5.38** What is 0.01 less than 5.39?

5 These decimals follow a pattern. What are the next two decimals?

+ 0.2 + 0.2 + 0.2 + 0.2 + 0.2 + 0.2

0.2 0.4 0.6 0.8 1.0 ? ?

Rule: Add 0.2.

0.2 more than 1.0 is 1.2.
0.2 more than 1.2 is 1.4.

The next two decimals are 1.2 and 1.4.

6 These decimals follow a pattern. What are the next two decimals?

– 0.05 – 0.05 – 0.05 – 0.05 – 0.05 – 0.05

1.32 1.27 1.22 1.17 1.12 ? ?

Rule: Subtract 0.05.

0.05 less than 1.12 is 1.07.
0.05 less than 1.07 is 1.02.

The next two decimals are 1.07 and 1.02.

Math Talk

Elijah uses the rule "subtract 0.3" to form a pattern. He starts from 5.4 and continues the pattern as shown.

5.4 5.1 4.8 4.5 4.2 3.8 3.5 3.2

Look at the digits in the tenths place in each decimal. Discuss with your partner how you can tell that there is a mistake in the pattern.

Hands-on Activity

Work in pairs.

Activity 1   Representing a decimal more than or less than a given decimal

1. Use (1) (0.1) (0.01) to show 4.62 to your partner.

2. Ask your partner to use (1) (0.1) (0.01) to show his or her answers to each of the following questions.

   a   0.1 more than the number   b   0.1 less than the number

   c   0.01 more than the number   d   0.01 less than the number

   e   0.12 more than the number   f   0.12 less than the number

3. Trade places. Repeat (1) and (2) using each of the following decimals.

   a   3.18   b   6.89   c   1.94

Activity 2   Forming and continuing number patterns

1. Order the following decimals to form a number pattern.
   0.8   1.2   0.4   1.6

2. Write the next three numbers in the pattern.

   _____ _____ _____ _____ _____ _____ _____

3. Repeat (1) and (2) using each of the following sets of decimals.

   a   5.17   5.12   5.22   5.07

   _____ _____ _____ _____ _____ _____ _____

   b   1.03   1.48   1.33   1.18

   _____ _____ _____ _____ _____ _____ _____

TRY Practice finding missing numbers in a number pattern

Answer each question.

1. What is 0.1 more than 1.26? _____

2. What is 0.01 more than 1.26? _____

3. What is 0.5 more than 1.26? _____

4. What is 0.1 less than 4.05? _____

5. What is 0.01 less than 4.05? _____

6. What is 0.14 less than 4.05? _____

Fill in each blank.

7. _____ is 0.1 more than 23.3.

8. _____ is 0.01 less than 3.40.

9. _____ is 0.06 more than 0.36.

10. 0.25 less than 9.07 is _____.

Complete each number pattern.

11. 0.1   0.3   0.5   0.7   0.9   _____

12. 1.10   1.12   1.14   1.16   1.18   _____

13. 5.28   5.26   5.24   _____   5.20   5.18

14. 9.98   9.95   9.92   _____   9.86   9.83

15. 0.12   0.25   0.38   _____   0.64   0.77

INDEPENDENT PRACTICE

Compare each pair of decimals. Write the greater decimal.

1 13.8 or 15.4 _____

2 3.46 or 3.64 _____

Compare each pair of decimals. Write the lesser decimal.

3 28.3 or 28.9 _____

4 7.15 or 7.06 _____

Compare each pair of decimals. Write <, >, or =.

5 0.7 $\bigcirc$ 2.77

6 9.5 $\bigcirc$ 9.05

7 1.96 $\bigcirc$ 1.36

8 4.30 $\bigcirc$ 4.3

Circle the greatest decimal.

9 6.53   6.13   6.35   6.31

Circle the least decimal.

10 9.01   9.1   8.91   8.19

Order each set of decimals.

11 Order 0.51, 0.57, and 1.02 from greatest to least.

_____   _____   _____
  greatest   least

12 Order 4.32, 2.43, and 3.24 from least to greatest.

_____   _____   _____
  least   greatest

13 Order 0.49, 0.4, and 0.53 from greatest to least.

_____   _____   _____
  greatest   least

Answer each question.

14 What is 0.1 more than 3.4? _____

15 What is 0.01 more than 3.4? _____

16 What is 0.5 more than 3.4? _____

17 What is 0.1 less than 0.57? _____

18 What is 0.01 less than 0.57? _____

19 What is 0.03 less than 0.57? _____

Fill in each blank.

20 _____ is 0.1 less than 3.8.

21 _____ is 0.01 more than 0.66.

22 _____ is 0.2 more than 2.9.

23 0.05 less than 0.63 is _____.

Complete each number pattern.

24 0.8   0.9   1.0   1.1   1.2   _____

25 2.2   2.5   2.8   3.1   _____   3.7

26 8.19   8.18   8.17   8.16   8.15   _____

27 9.65   9.60   9.55   9.50   9.45   _____

28 6.23   6.21   6.19   _____   6.15   6.13

29 3.34   3.36   3.38   3.40   _____   _____

4 Rounding Decimals

Learning Objectives:
- Round decimals to the nearest whole number.
- Round decimals to the nearest tenth, or 1 decimal place.

THINK

Draw a number line and label 3.1, 3.2, and 3.3. Mark and label the decimals that round to 3.2. Find the least and the greatest decimal that round to 3.2.

ENGAGE

Santino and Lillian want to buy some wood pegs for a project. They need wood pegs of lengths 5.8 inches, 5.2 inches, 5.4 inches, and 5.6 inches. A shop only sells wood pegs with lengths in whole numbers. Using rounding, Santino suggests buying two 5-inch pegs and two 6-inch pegs. Lillian suggests buying four 6-inch pegs. Who is correct? Draw a number line to explain your thinking.

LEARN Round a decimal to the nearest whole number

1. Round 9.61 to the nearest whole number.

9.61 ——

| 9 | 9.5 | 10 |

> 9.61 is between 9 and 10. The digit in the tenths place is 6. So, 9.61 is nearer to 10 than to 9.

9.61 is 10 when rounded to the nearest whole number.

2. Owen is 1.45 meters tall.
Round 1.45 meters to the nearest meter.

1.45 ——

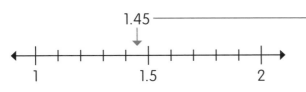

| 1 | 1.5 | 2 |

> The digit in the tenths place is 4. So, 1.45 is nearer to 1 than to 2.

1.45 meters is 1 meter when rounded to the nearest meter.

3 Round 8.5 to the nearest whole number.

8.5

8.5 is exactly halfway between 8 and 9.

Round to the greater whole number when the digit 5 is in the tenths place.

8   8.5   9

8.5 is 9 when rounded to the nearest whole number.

TRY Practice rounding a decimal to the nearest whole number

Find each missing number.

1 Round 34.45 to the nearest whole number.

34.45

34   35

34.45 is between _____ and 35.

34.45 is nearer to _____ than to _____.

34.45 is _____ when rounded to the nearest whole number.

Round each decimal to the nearest whole number.

2 0.7 _____

3 4.3 _____

4 41.5 _____

5 23.04 _____

6 8.61 _____

7 99.82 _____

ENGAGE

Draw a number line with endpoints 0.3 and 0.4. Which tenth is 0.34 nearer to? Extend the number line to 0.5. Mark all the points in the hundredths that are nearer to 0.4 than to 0.3 or 0.5.

LEARN Round a decimal to the nearest tenth or 1 decimal place

1. A cup contains 0.83 liter of water. Round 0.83 liter to 1 decimal place.

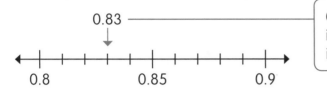

> 0.83 is between 0.8 and 0.9. The digit in the hundredths place is 3. So, 0.83 is nearer to 0.8 than to 0.9.

0.83 liter is 0.8 liter when rounded to 1 decimal place.

2. Round 1.75 to the nearest tenth.

1.75

1.7   1.8

> 1.75 is exactly halfway between 1.7 and 1.8.

> Rounding to the nearest tenth is the same as rounding to 1 decimal place.

1.75 is 1.8 when rounded to the nearest tenth.

3. Round 2.98 to 1 decimal place.

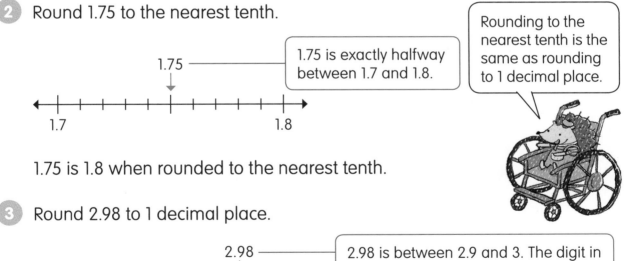

2.98

2.9   2.95   3

> 2.98 is between 2.9 and 3. The digit in the hundredths place is 8. So, 2.98 is nearer to 3 than to 2.9.

2.98 is 3.0 when rounded to 1 decimal place.

> 3 is written as 3.0 to 1 decimal place.

Hands-on Activity Rounding distances to the nearest tenth of a meter

Work in groups of four.

(1) Place a measuring tape on the floor, metric side up.

(2) Take turns walking 5 steps along the measuring tape. Measure each distance walked in meters to 2 decimal places.

(3) Record the readings in the table below.

(4) Round each distance to the nearest tenth of a meter (1 decimal place).

| Name of Student | Distance (m) | |
	Actual Reading	Rounded Reading

TRY Practice rounding a decimal to the nearest tenth or 1 decimal place

Find each missing number.

1 Round 0.36 to the nearest tenth.

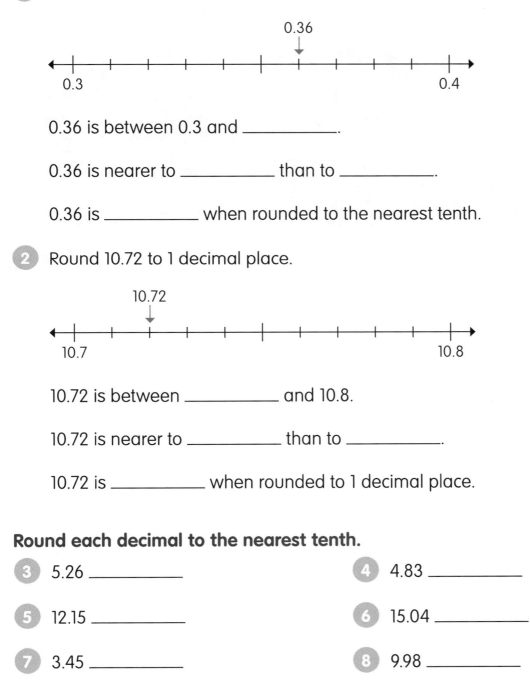

0.36 is between 0.3 and _____.

0.36 is nearer to _____ than to _____.

0.36 is _____ when rounded to the nearest tenth.

2 Round 10.72 to 1 decimal place.

10.72 is between _____ and 10.8.

10.72 is nearer to _____ than to _____.

10.72 is _____ when rounded to 1 decimal place.

Round each decimal to the nearest tenth.

3 5.26 _____

4 4.83 _____

5 12.15 _____

6 15.04 _____

7 3.45 _____

8 9.98 _____

ROUND IT FAST!

9.1

9.07

What you need:

Players: 4
Materials: Rounding decimal cards

What to do:

1. Shuffle the cards and place the deck facedown on the table.

2. Turn over the top card.

3. The fastest player to correctly round the decimal shown to the given place keeps the card.

4. Turn over the next card in the deck to continue the game. Play until there are no more cards left in the deck.

Who is the winner?

The player with the greatest number of cards in the end wins!

INDEPENDENT PRACTICE

Find each missing number.

1 Round 3.7 to the nearest whole number.

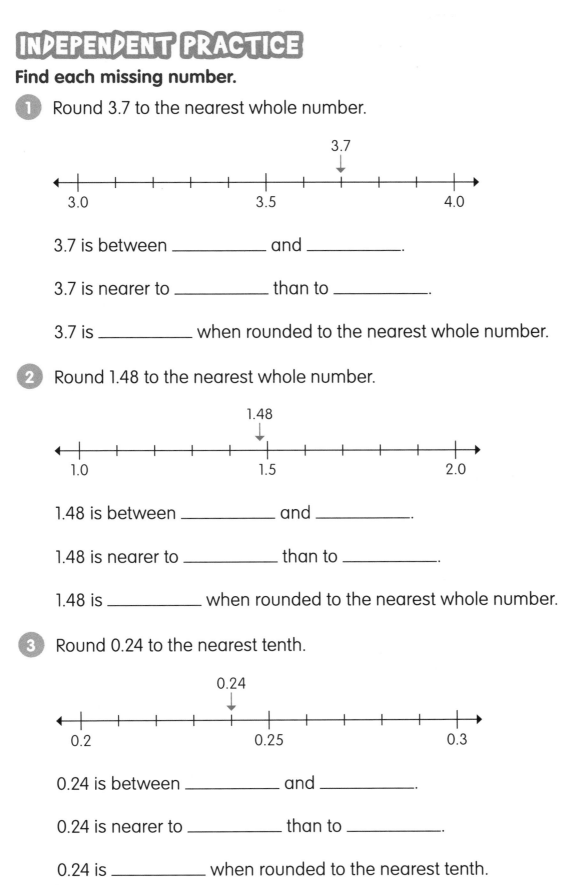

3.7 is between _____ and _____.

3.7 is nearer to _____ than to _____.

3.7 is _____ when rounded to the nearest whole number.

2 Round 1.48 to the nearest whole number.

1.48 is between _____ and _____.

1.48 is nearer to _____ than to _____.

1.48 is _____ when rounded to the nearest whole number.

3 Round 0.24 to the nearest tenth.

0.24 is between _____ and _____.

0.24 is nearer to _____ than to _____.

0.24 is _____ when rounded to the nearest tenth.

4 Round 5.17 to 1 decimal place.

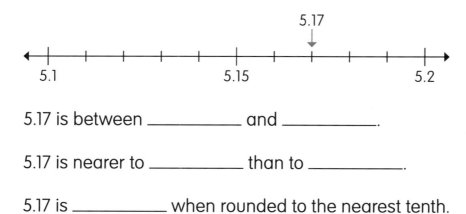

5.17 is between _____ and _____.

5.17 is nearer to _____ than to _____.

5.17 is _____ when rounded to the nearest tenth.

Round each decimal to the nearest whole number and the nearest tenth.

	Decimal	Rounded to the Nearest	
		Whole Number	**Tenth**
5	3.49		
6	4.85		
7	12.32		
8	10.71		
9	7.94		
10	9.95		
11	6.14		
12	5.55		

Fractions and Decimals

Learning Objectives:

- Express a fraction as a decimal.
- Express a decimal as a fraction.
- Add tenths and hundredths.

THINK

Find three possible sets of digits that make the equation true. $\frac{1}{10} + \frac{\boxed{?}}{100} = 0.\boxed{?}8$

ENGAGE

a Draw a number line with endpoints 0 and 1. Mark a point to show $\frac{1}{2}$ on your number line. What decimal does the point represent? Explain your thinking to your partner.

b Now, mark $\frac{4}{5}$ on the same number line. How did you do it? Explain your thinking to your partner.

LEARN Express a fraction as a decimal

1 Express $\frac{1}{5}$ as a decimal.

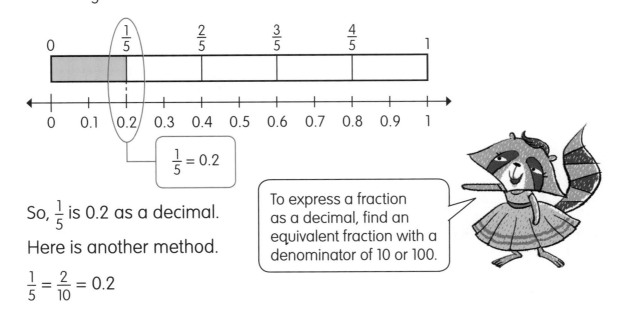

$$\frac{1}{5} = 0.2$$

So, $\frac{1}{5}$ is 0.2 as a decimal.

Here is another method.

$$\frac{1}{5} = \frac{2}{10} = 0.2$$

To express a fraction as a decimal, find an equivalent fraction with a denominator of 10 or 100.

2 Express $3\frac{4}{5}$ as a decimal.

$3\frac{4}{5} = 3\frac{8}{10}$

$\qquad = 3.8$

So, $3\frac{4}{5}$ is 3.8 as a decimal.

$\frac{4}{5} = \frac{8}{10}$

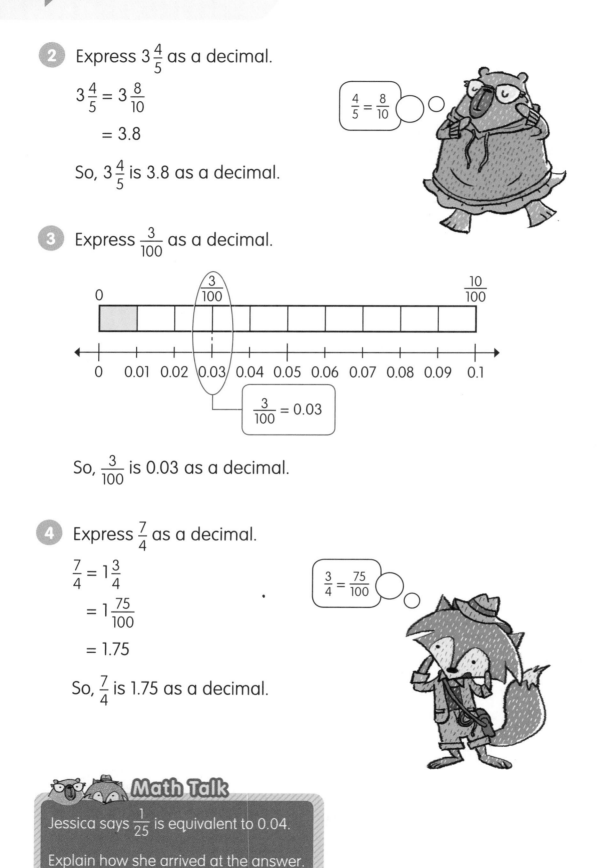

3 Express $\frac{3}{100}$ as a decimal.

$\frac{3}{100} = 0.03$

So, $\frac{3}{100}$ is 0.03 as a decimal.

4 Express $\frac{7}{4}$ as a decimal.

$\frac{7}{4} = 1\frac{3}{4}$

$\qquad = 1\frac{75}{100}$

$\qquad = 1.75$

So, $\frac{7}{4}$ is 1.75 as a decimal.

$\frac{3}{4} = \frac{75}{100}$

Math Talk

Jessica says $\frac{1}{25}$ is equivalent to 0.04.

Explain how she arrived at the answer.

TRY Practice expressing a fraction as a decimal

Express each fraction or mixed number as a decimal.

1. $\dfrac{3}{5} = \dfrac{\boxed{}}{10}$

   $= \underline{\hspace{2cm}}$

2. $\dfrac{1}{4} = \dfrac{\boxed{}}{100}$

   $= \underline{\hspace{2cm}}$

3. $2\dfrac{1}{2} = 2\dfrac{\boxed{}}{\boxed{}}$

   $= \underline{\hspace{2cm}}$

4. $3\dfrac{4}{25} = 3\dfrac{\boxed{}}{100}$

   $= \underline{\hspace{2cm}}$

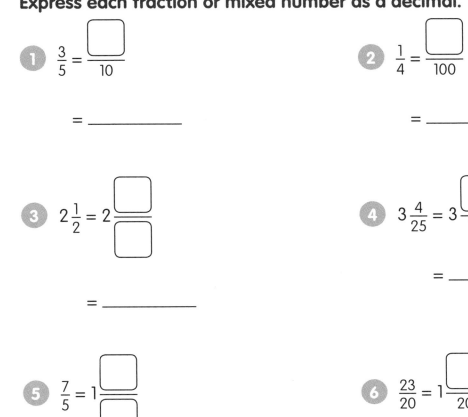

5. $\dfrac{7}{5} = 1\dfrac{\boxed{}}{\boxed{}}$

   $= 1\dfrac{\boxed{}}{\boxed{}}$

   $= \underline{\hspace{2cm}}$

6. $\dfrac{23}{20} = 1\dfrac{\boxed{}}{20}$

   $= 1\dfrac{\boxed{}}{100}$

   $= \underline{\hspace{2cm}}$

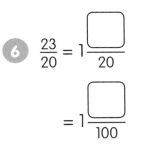

ENGAGE

a Draw a number line with endpoints 0 and 1. Mark a point to show 0.4 on your number line. What other ways can you represent 0.4? Explain your thinking to your partner.

b Now, mark 0.12 on the same number line. What other ways can you represent 0.12? Explain your thinking to your partner.

LEARN Express a decimal as a fraction

1 Express 0.8 as a fraction in simplest form.

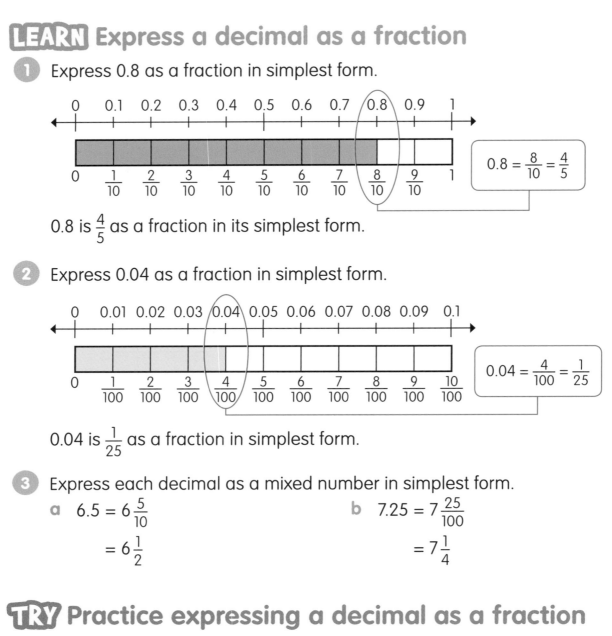

$$0.8 = \frac{8}{10} = \frac{4}{5}$$

0.8 is $\frac{4}{5}$ as a fraction in its simplest form.

2 Express 0.04 as a fraction in simplest form.

$$0.04 = \frac{4}{100} = \frac{1}{25}$$

0.04 is $\frac{1}{25}$ as a fraction in simplest form.

3 Express each decimal as a mixed number in simplest form.

a $6.5 = 6\frac{5}{10}$

       $= 6\frac{1}{2}$

b $7.25 = 7\frac{25}{100}$

       $= 7\frac{1}{4}$

TRY Practice expressing a decimal as a fraction

Express each decimal as a fraction or mixed number in simplest form.

1 $0.4 = \dfrac{\boxed{}}{\boxed{}}$

    $= \dfrac{\boxed{}}{\boxed{}}$

2 $0.6 = \dfrac{\boxed{}}{\boxed{}}$

    $= \dfrac{\boxed{}}{\boxed{}}$

3 2.8 = $\boxed{}\dfrac{\boxed{}}{\boxed{}}$

= _____

4 3.75 = $\boxed{}\dfrac{\boxed{}}{\boxed{}}$

= _____

5 4.15 = $\boxed{}\dfrac{\boxed{}}{\boxed{}}$

= _____

6 6.72 = $\boxed{}\dfrac{\boxed{}}{\boxed{}}$

= _____

ENGAGE

Use two different colors to represent $\frac{1}{10}$ and $\frac{1}{100}$ on a hundred square grid.

How can you find the total fraction of the grid that is colored? How can you write your answer in another way? Explain your thinking to your partner.

LEARN Add tenths and hundredths

1 A table is $\frac{7}{10}$ meter long. A bench is $\frac{81}{100}$ meter long. Find the total length of the table and the bench. Express your answer as a decimal.

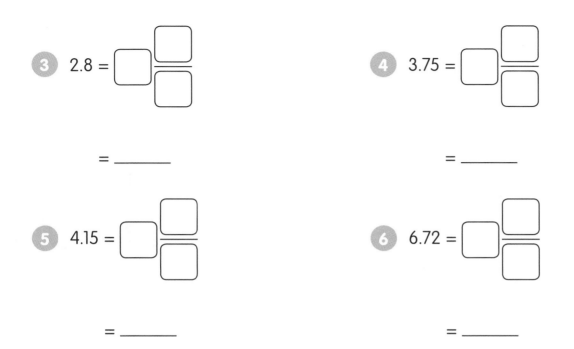

$$\frac{7}{10} + \frac{81}{100} = \frac{70}{100} + \frac{81}{100}$$
$$= \frac{151}{100}$$
$$= 1\frac{51}{100}$$
$$= 1.51$$

Find an equivalent fraction of $\frac{7}{10}$ with a denominator of 100.

$\frac{7}{10} = \frac{70}{100}$

The total length of the table and the bench is 1.51 meters.

2 Liam uses fractions to find the sum of 0.54 and 0.9.

$$0.54 + 0.9 = \frac{54}{100} + \frac{9}{10}$$

$$= \frac{54}{100} + \frac{90}{100}$$

$$= \frac{144}{100}$$

$$= 1\frac{44}{100}$$

$$= 1.44$$

Express each decimal as a fraction with a denominator of 100. Then, add.

$$0.54 = \frac{54}{100} \qquad 0.9 = \frac{9}{10}$$

$$= \frac{90}{100}$$

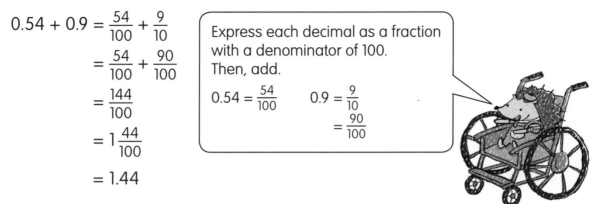

The sum of 0.9 and 0.54 is 1.44.

TRY Practice adding tenths and hundredths

Add. Express each answer as a decimal.

1 $\frac{3}{10} + \frac{49}{100}$

2 $\frac{65}{100} + \frac{4}{10}$

Express each decimal as a fraction.
Then, add. Express the answer as a decimal.

3 0.67 + 0.8

4 0.7 + 0.43

DECIMAL SNAP!

The table cards show: 0.35, 0.26, 0.9, 0.6, 0.44, 0.5, 0.55, 0.76, 0.18, 0.12, 0.1, 0.05, 4.75, 3.2, 3.02, 0.1, and $\frac{1}{2}$

What you need:

Players: 4 or 5
Materials: Decimal cards, Fraction cards

What to do:

1. Place all the decimal cards face up on the table.
2. Shuffle the fraction cards and place the deck facedown on the table.
3. Turn over the top card.
4. Check to see if the fraction on the card is equivalent to any of the decimal cards on the table.
5. The fastest player to find a match will say, "Decimal Snap!" and collect the two cards.
6. The other players check the answer. If the answer is wrong, the fraction card is put at the bottom of the card deck, and the decimal card is returned to the table.
7. Turn over the next fraction card to continue the game. Play until no more matches can be found.

Who is the winner?

The player who collects the greatest number of matching cards wins!

Example

A number has two decimal places.
It is 1.7 when rounded to the nearest tenth.
What could the number be?
Van draws a number line to find the number.

1.64 **1.65** **1.66** **1.67** **1.68** **1.69** 1.70 **1.71** **1.72** **1.73** **1.74** 1.75

The numbers in **green** are the possible answers.

A number has two decimal places.
It is 4.2 when rounded to one decimal place.

 What could the number be? List the possible answers.

 Which of these numbers is the greatest?

 Which of these numbers is the least?

INDEPENDENT PRACTICE

Find each missing fraction or decimal.

1

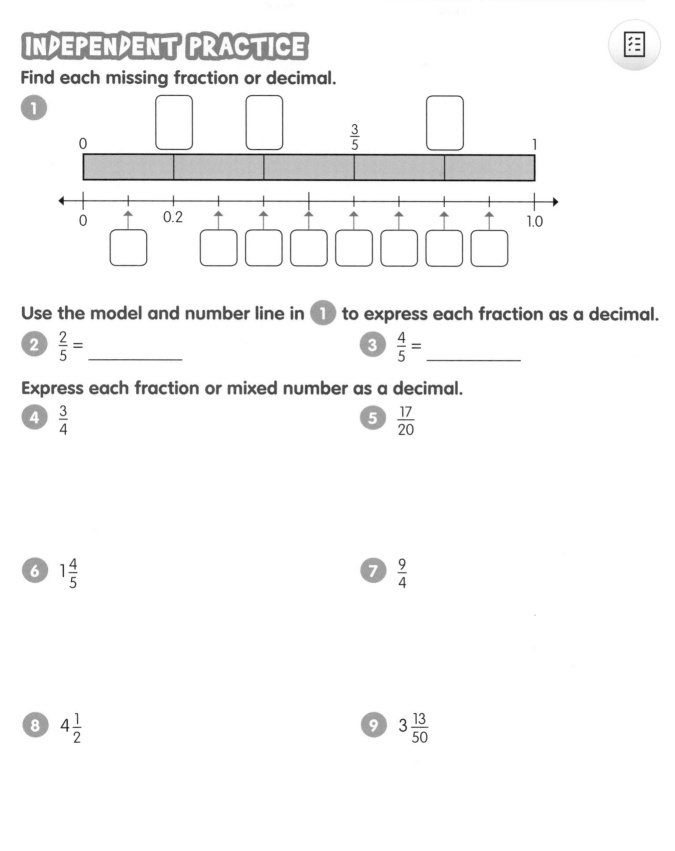

Use the model and number line in ① **to express each fraction as a decimal.**

2 $\frac{2}{5} =$ _____

3 $\frac{4}{5} =$ _____

Express each fraction or mixed number as a decimal.

4 $\frac{3}{4}$

5 $\frac{17}{20}$

6 $1\frac{4}{5}$

7 $\frac{9}{4}$

8 $4\frac{1}{2}$

9 $3\frac{13}{50}$

Express each decimal as a fraction or mixed number in simplest form.

10 0.2

11 0.75

12 0.21

13 3.6

14 5.12

15 4.35

Add. Express the answer as a decimal.

16 $\dfrac{8}{10} + \dfrac{38}{100}$

Express each decimal as a fraction.
Then, add. Express the answer as a decimal.

17 0.59 + 0.6

Mathematical Habit 3 **Construct viable arguments**

Chris and Mary compare 0.23 and 0.3.

23 is greater than 3.
So, 0.23 is greater than 0.3.

23 tenths is greater than 3 tenths.
So, 0.23 is greater than 0.3.

Do you agree? Why or why not? Explain.

Problem Solving with Heuristics

1 **Mathematical Habit 1** **Persevere in solving problems**

I am less than 8 and have only 1 decimal place. I am 8 when rounded to the nearest whole number. The digit in my tenths place is odd. The digit in my ones place is 2 less than the digit in my tenths place. What number am I?

2 **Mathematical Habit 7** **Make use of structure**

Look at the hundred square grid. How many more parts must you shade to represent 0.6?

3 **Mathematical Habit** **2** Use mathematical reasoning

Use the digits 1, 6, 2, 9, 4, and 5 to form the greatest possible decimal with 2 decimal places that makes the statement true.

3.45 > _____

4 **Mathematical Habit** **2** Use mathematical reasoning

The height of a tree is 3 meters when rounded to the nearest whole number. Which of the following could be the actual height of the tree?

| 2.39 m | 2.48 m | 3.25 m | 3.51 m |

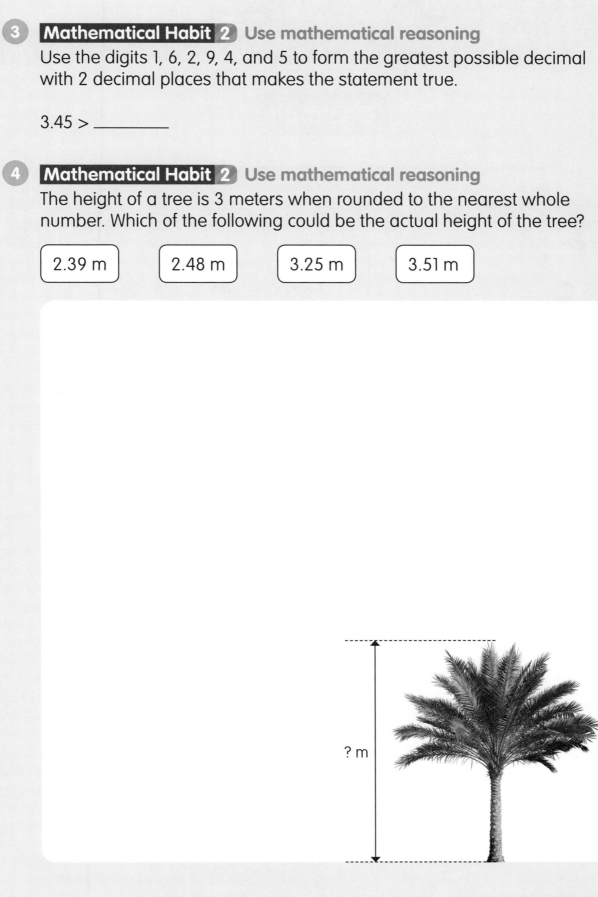

? m

CHAPTER WRAP-UP

Decimals

Understanding Tenths and Hundredths

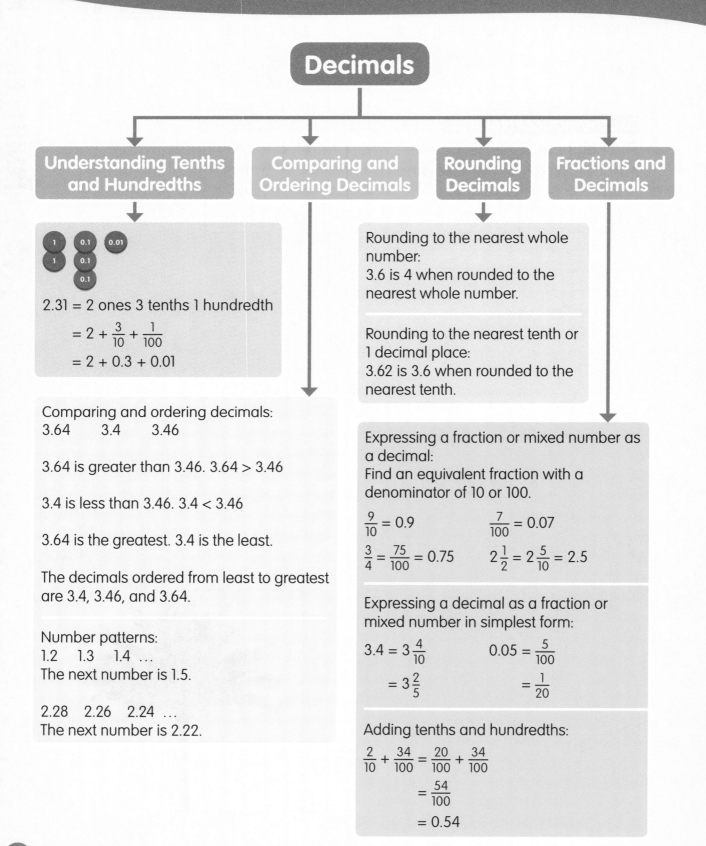

2.31 = 2 ones 3 tenths 1 hundredth

$$= 2 + \frac{3}{10} + \frac{1}{100}$$
$$= 2 + 0.3 + 0.01$$

Comparing and Ordering Decimals

Comparing and ordering decimals:
3.64   3.4   3.46

3.64 is greater than 3.46. 3.64 > 3.46

3.4 is less than 3.46. 3.4 < 3.46

3.64 is the greatest. 3.4 is the least.

The decimals ordered from least to greatest are 3.4, 3.46, and 3.64.

Number patterns:
1.2   1.3   1.4 …
The next number is 1.5.

2.28   2.26   2.24 …
The next number is 2.22.

Rounding Decimals

Rounding to the nearest whole number:
3.6 is 4 when rounded to the nearest whole number.

Rounding to the nearest tenth or 1 decimal place:
3.62 is 3.6 when rounded to the nearest tenth.

Fractions and Decimals

Expressing a fraction or mixed number as a decimal:
Find an equivalent fraction with a denominator of 10 or 100.

$$\frac{9}{10} = 0.9 \qquad\qquad \frac{7}{100} = 0.07$$

$$\frac{3}{4} = \frac{75}{100} = 0.75 \qquad 2\frac{1}{2} = 2\frac{5}{10} = 2.5$$

Expressing a decimal as a fraction or mixed number in simplest form:

$$3.4 = 3\frac{4}{10} \qquad\qquad 0.05 = \frac{5}{100}$$
$$= 3\frac{2}{5} \qquad\qquad\qquad = \frac{1}{20}$$

Adding tenths and hundredths:

$$\frac{2}{10} + \frac{34}{100} = \frac{20}{100} + \frac{34}{100}$$
$$= \frac{54}{100}$$
$$= 0.54$$

Name: _____ Date: _____

Express each of the following as a decimal.

1 $\frac{7}{10}$ = _____

2 5 tenths = _____

3 $3\frac{8}{10}$ = _____

4 $\frac{19}{100}$ = _____

5 9 hundredths = _____

6 $1\frac{53}{100}$ = _____

Express each amount in decimal form.

7 27¢ = $_____

8 499¢ = $_____

9 7 dollars 5 cents = $_____

10 25 dollars 18 cents = $_____

Fill in each blank.

11 In 23.6, the digit _____ is in the tenths place.

12 In 1.59, the digit 9 stands for _____.

Fill in each blank.

13 6.12 = 6 + _____ + 0.02

14 34.07 = 30 + 4 + _____

Compare each pair of decimals. Write <, >, or =.

15 4.1 ◯ 4.11

16 3.02 ◯ 3.2

17 0.6 ◯ 0.59

18 5.87 ◯ 5.7

Order each set of numbers from greatest to least.

19 9.08   9.8   8.09

_____ _____ _____
   greatest   least

20 0.45 $\frac{1}{2}$ 0.54

_____ _____ _____
   greatest   least

21 4.62   4.26   6.42   6.24

_____ _____ _____ _____
   greatest   least

Answer each question.

22 What is 0.1 more than 17.24? _____

23 What is 0.01 less than 6.38? _____

24 What is 0.5 more than 3.1? _____

25 What is 0.02 less than 6.74? _____

Complete each number pattern.

26 1.7   1.8   1.9   2.0   2.1   _____

27 8.65   8.62   8.59   8.56   _____   8.50

28 0.5   0.55   0.6   0.65   _____   0.75   0.8

Round each decimal to the nearest whole number.

29 9.75 _____   30 6.2 _____   31 14.9 _____

Round each decimal to the nearest tenth.

32 5.25 _____   33 1.83 _____   34 12.37 _____

Express each of the following as a decimal.

35 $\dfrac{4}{5}$

36 $\dfrac{1}{4}$

37 $3\dfrac{9}{20}$

38 $\dfrac{5}{2}$

Express each of the following as a fraction or mixed number in simplest form.

39 1.9

40 3.5

41 0.46

42 3.08

Express each decimal as a fraction.
Then, add. Express the answer as a decimal.

43 0.4 + 0.16

Assessment Prep

Answer each question.

44 Find the missing number.

$$\frac{\boxed{}}{100} = 0.49$$

45 **Part A**

Daniel has two pieces of string. String A is 3.4 meters long and String B is 2.75 meters long. Use >, <, or = to compare the two lengths. Which piece of string is longer?

Part B

Colton has a piece of string $2\frac{4}{5}$ meters long. He tells Daniel that his string is shorter than String B because 4 is less than 75.
• Explain how to correct Colton's reasoning in the space below.
• Order the three lengths from longest to shortest.

46 A piece of blue ribbon is $\frac{7}{10}$ meter long. A piece of green ribbon is $\frac{9}{100}$ meter long. What is the total length of the two pieces of ribbon?

(A) 7.9 meters

(B) 1.6 meters

(C) 0.79 meter

(D) 0.16 meter

Name: _____ Date: _____

High Jump, Long Jump

1 Cooper was training for a high jump meet. His coach recorded his best jumps each week during training.

Week	Height (m)
1	0.95
2	1.27
3	1.34
4	1.3
5	1.42

a Cooper's teammate, Luis, also had his best jumps of each week recorded. His best jumps were $\frac{4}{5}$ meter in Week 1, $1\frac{1}{4}$ meters in Week 3, and $1\frac{1}{2}$ meters in Week 5. In which of the three weeks was his best jump higher than Cooper's?

Change the fractions and mixed numbers to decimals to find out. Explain your answer.

b Luis won the high jump meet. His winning jump was higher than Cooper's best jump in Week 5, but lower than his own best jump in Week 5. What are the possible heights of Luis's winning jump? Explain your answer.

2 Rachel and Maya were training for a long jump meet. During training, Rachel jumped a distance of $3\frac{5}{10}$ meters. Maya jumped a distance of $3\frac{45}{100}$ meters. Maya thought she jumped farther than Rachel.

a Do you agree or disagree?
Explain. Use a number line or draw a model to support your answer.

b As part of her training, Rachel hopped up some steps in the sports hall. The height of each step was 0.2 meter. Skip count by 0.2 to find the total height of 6 steps.

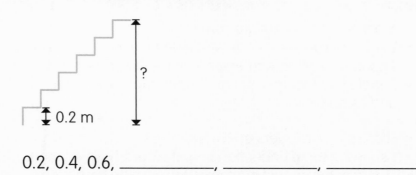

0.2, 0.4, 0.6, _____, _____, _____

Mark an **X** on the number line to show the total height of 6 steps.

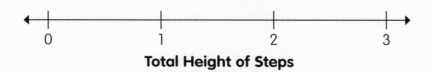

Total Height of Steps

c The table shows the distances Rachel jumped during the long jump meet.

Round	Distance (m)
1st	3.44
2nd	3.41
3rd	3.52

Order the distances from greatest to least.

_____ _____ _____

greatest   least

Rubric

Point(s)	Level	My Performance
7–8	4	• Most of my answers are correct. • I showed complete understanding of what I have learned. • I used the correct strategies to solve the problems. • I explained my answers and mathematical thinking clearly and completely.
5–6.5	3	• Some of my answers are correct. • I showed some understanding of what I have learned. • I used some correct strategies to solve the problems. • I explained my answers and mathematical thinking clearly.
3–4.5	2	• A few of my answers are correct. • I showed little understanding of what I have learned. • I used a few correct strategies to solve the problems. • I explained some of my answers and mathematical thinking clearly.
0–2.5	1	• A few of my answers are correct. • I showed little or no understanding of what I have learned. • I used a few strategies to solve the problems. • I did not explain my answers and mathematical thinking clearly.

Teacher's Comments

Glossary

B

- **benchmark fraction**

  Benchmark fractions are common fractions, such as $\frac{1}{4}$, $\frac{1}{2}$, and $\frac{3}{4}$ that can be used to compare other fractions to.

  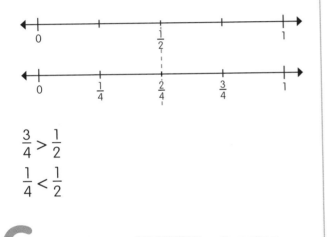

  $\frac{3}{4} > \frac{1}{2}$

  $\frac{1}{4} < \frac{1}{2}$

C

- **common denominator**

  A number that can be divided exactly by all the denominators is called a common denominator.

  6 is a common denominator of $\frac{1}{3}$ and $\frac{1}{2}$.

- **common factor**

  A factor that is shared by two or more numbers is a common factor.

  Factors of 8   1, 2, 4, 8
  Factors of 12   1, 2, 3, 4, 6, 12

  The common factors of 8 and 12 are 1, 2, and 4.

- **common multiple**

  A number that is a multiple of two or more numbers is a common multiple.

  Multiples of 4   4, 8, 12, 16, 20, 24, 28, 32, 36, 40, …

  Multiples of 5   5, 10, 15, 20, 25, 30, 35, 40, 45, 50, …

  The first two common multiples of 4 and 5 are 20 and 40.

- **common numerator**

  A number that is a multiple of the numerators of two or more fractions is called a common numerator.

  10 is a common numerator of $\frac{2}{5}$ and $\frac{5}{6}$.

- **composite number**

  A composite number has more than 2 different factors.

  12 is a composite number because it has 6 different factors: 1, 2, 3, 4, 6, and 12.

D

- **decimal**

  A decimal is a way to show amounts that are parts of a whole. A decimal is a number with a decimal point to the right of the ones place, and digits to the right of the decimal point.

  0.1 and 0.4 are decimals.

- **decimal place**

  The position of a number after a decimal point is called a decimal place.

  2.8 has one decimal place.

- **decimal point**

  A dot or symbol separating the ones and the tenths places in a decimal is called decimal point.

  0.1
  ↑
  decimal point

E

- **estimate**

  An estimate is a number close to the exact number.

  An estimate of the sum of 196 and 389 is 600.

F

- **factor**

  12 can be divided exactly by 2. So, 2 is a factor of 12.

  The factors of 12 are 1, 2, 3, 4, 6, and 12.

H

- **hundredth**

  One part out of a hundred is $\frac{1}{100}$ (one hundredth).

  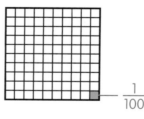

- **hundred thousand**

  10 ten thousands = 1 hundred thousand or 100,000

I

- **improper fraction**

  An improper fraction has a numerator that is equal to or greater than its denominator. It represents a fraction that is equal to or greater than 1.

  $\frac{4}{4}$ and $\frac{5}{4}$ are improper fractions.

M

- **million**

  10 hundred thousands = 1 million or 1,000,000

- **mixed number**

  A mixed number represents the sum of a whole number and a fraction.

  $2\frac{1}{2}$ is a mixed number.

- **multiple**

  A multiple of a number is the product of the number and any other whole number except zero.

  The first four multiples of 2 are 2, 4, 6, and 8.

P

- **period**

  Groups of three places are called periods.

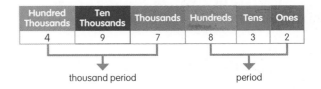

Hundred Thousands	Ten Thousands	Thousands	Hundreds	Tens	Ones
4	9	7	8	3	2

thousand period   period

- **prime number**

  A prime number has only two different factors, 1 and itself.

  5 is a prime number because its factors are 1 and 5.

R

- **remainder**

  A remainder is the number left over when a number cannot be divided evenly.

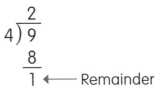

$$4\overline{)9} \quad \begin{array}{r} 2 \\ \underline{8} \\ 1 \end{array}$$ ← Remainder

S

- **simplify**

  Divide the numerator and denominator of a fraction by the same number to simplify the fraction.

  $\frac{4}{12}$ is simplified to $\frac{2}{6}$ by dividing both its numerator and denominator by 2.

  $\frac{3}{15}$ is simplified to $\frac{1}{5}$ by dividing both its numerator and denominator by 3.

- **simplest form**

  A fraction in simplest form has no common factors other than 1 in the numerator and denominator.

  $\frac{1}{4}$ is the simplest form of $\frac{5}{20}$ and $\frac{6}{24}$.

T

- **tenth**

  One part out of ten is $\frac{1}{10}$ (one tenth).

  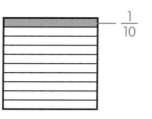

U

- **unlike fraction**

  Unlike fractions have different denominators.

  $\frac{7}{8}$ and $\frac{3}{4}$ are unlike fractions.

Index

Pages in **boldface** type show where a term is
introduced.

relating factors and multiples to, 180
share equally, 96

Dollars and cents, 364
decimals, 361–362

E

Equivalent fractions, *throughout, see for example,*
228, 231–235, 237–238, 325, 383
comparing unlike fractions, **239**–242, 251

Estimate, **52**, *see also* Estimation

Estimation, *throughout, see for example,* 62–63,
82–83, 98, 118, 154
exact answer, 55–57, 60
products, 115–117
quotient, 145–147
sums and differences, 52–53, 80
rounding, 98

F

Factors, *throughout, see for example,* **167**–171, 173,
183, 208, 210
common factors, **170**–172, 178, 212

Fraction bar, *throughout, see for example,* 222, 231,
239–240, 346, 347

Fraction circle, *throughout, see for example,* 231, 270,
288–292, 297–298, 346

Fractions, 325–326, 342
addition,
like fractions, 253–255, 326, 346
benchmark, **244**
comparing unlike fractions, 244–246
comparing, 229–230, 245–248, 250–252, 325, 327
unlike, **239**–242, 244, 246, 325
decimals, 383–386, 391–392, 396, 399
equivalent fractions, *see* Equivalent fractions
improper, *see* Improper fractions
like, *see* Like fractions
multiplication, *see* Multiplication
number lines, 226, 245–247, 249
ordering, 229–230, 247–250, 252, 325
part of a set, 227

real-world problems, 303
adding and subtracting like fractions, 303–304,
306
data in a line plot, 309–311
multiplying by a fraction, 311–312
simplest form, **232**, 235, 238, 386, 396
simplifying, **232**
subtraction
like fractions, 256–258, 326
unit fractions, 222–224, 295–296, 299, 301
unlike, *see* Unlike fractions

Frequency table, *see* Tally chart

H

Hundred thousands, **12**, 19–30, 42–42, 44–46, 80–81

Hundredths, *throughout, see for example,* **355**–360,
362–364, 366, 377, 396
adding, 387–388, 396

I

Improper fractions, **268**–274, 277, 325
with denominator of 10 and 100, 343
mixed numbers, 275–276, 278–284, 325,
328–329

L

Like fractions, 225
adding, 253–255, 326, 346
real-world problems, 303–304, 306
subtracting, 256–258
real-world problems, 303–304, 306

Line plots,
data, 309–311, 316, 330

M

Manipulative
10–sided die, 116, 146
base 10 blocks, *see* Base 10 blocks
base 10 hundred-square, *see* Base 10 hundred-
square
base 10 rod, *see* Base 10 rod

Photo Credits

1: © Gunter Nezhoda/Dreamstime.com, 24: © piotr_pabijan/Shutter Stock, 55l: © George Mdivanian/123rf.com, 55r: © nerthuz/123rf.com, 56l: © ppart/Think Stock/iStock, 56r: © Uatp1/Dreamstime.com, 57: © Katrina Brown/Dreamstime.com, 68: © scanrail/123rf.com, 69bl: © Joao Virissimo/Dreamstime.com, 69bm: © Roman Samokhin/Dreamstime.com, 69br: © creativecommonsstockphoto/Dreamstime.com, 73: © Szabolcs Stieber/Dreamstime.com, 74: © Georgii Dolgykh/123rf.com, 76: © Olivér Svéd/123rf.com, 77: Created by Fwstudio - Freepik.com, 85: © Iegor Liashenko/Dreamstime.com, 86: © scyther5/123rf.com, 88(tr to br): i) © Jason Stitt/Dreamstime.com, ii) © Ievgen Onyshchenko/123rf.com, iii) © kzenon/123rf.com, iv) © Tungphoto/Shutter Stock, 89: © Tea/Dreamstime.com, 89mm: © Roman Samokhin/Dreamstime.com, 89bm: © Joao Virissimo/Dreamstime.com, 96: © Oleksii Grygorenko/123rf.com, 99: © Miriam Doerr/Dreamstime.com, 100: © Yolanda Van Niekerk/123rf.com, 121: © MCE, 122: © MCE, 138: © MCE, 157: © Anterovium/Think Stock/iStock, 164: © Anterovium/Think Stock/iStock, 167: © MCE, 168: © MCE, 169: © MCE, 186: © piotr_pabijan/Shutter Stock, 199: © Oleksii Grygorenko/123rf.com, 201: © Rorra/Dreamstime.com, 203: © Hayati Kayhan/123rf.com, 207: Created by Fwstudio - Freepik.com, 209: © Alexander Kharchenko/123rf.com, 220t: © Oleksii Rashevskyi/123rf.com, 220b: © olegdudko/123rf.com, 220b: © Didecs/Dreamstime.com, 221: © Noneam/Dreamstime.com, 221mr: © Mrbhughes/Dreamstime.com, 221bm: © andreykuzmin/123rf.com, 221br: © heinteh/123rf.com, 236: © piotr_pabijan/Shutter Stock, 261: © movingmoment/123rf.com, 263: © MCE, 263: © vectorpocket/123rf.com, 263: © Sirichai Asawalapsakul/123rf.com, 264: © Kaiskynet/Dreamstime.com, 282: © piotr_pabijan/Shutter Stock, 297: © MCE, 300: © piotr_pabijan/Shutter Stock, 307: © Anterovium/Think Stock/iStock, 321: Created by Fwstudio - Freepik.com, 340t: © Maksym Kapusta/123rf.com, 340m: © Lebedinsk/Dreamstime.com, 340b: © Swisshippo/Dreamstime.com, 341: © Airubon/Dreamstime.com, 341t: © Maria Wachala/123rf.com, 354: © picsfive/123rf.com, 361l: © Houghton Mifflin Harcourt, 361r: © Houghton Mifflin Harcourt, 380: © piotr_pabijan/Shutter Stock, 389: © piotr_pabijan/Shutter Stock, 393: Created by Fwstudio - Freepik.com, 395: © irochka/123rf.com

NOTES

NOTES

NOTES

NOTES

NOTES

© 2020 Marshall Cavendish Education Pte Ltd

Published by Marshall Cavendish Education
Times Centre, 1 New Industrial Road, Singapore 536196
Customer Service Hotline: (65) 6213 9688
US Office Tel: (1-914) 332 8888 | Fax: (1-914) 332 8882
E-mail: cs@mceducation.com
Website: www.mceducation.com

Distributed by
Houghton Mifflin Harcourt
125 High Street
Boston, MA 02110
Tel: 617-351-5000
Website: www.hmhco.com/programs/math-in-focus

First published 2020

ISBN 978-0-358-10184-0

Printed in Singapore

3 4 5 6 7 8 9   1401   26 25 24 23 22 21
4500817280   B C D E F

The cover image shows an Angolan giraffe.
Giraffes can be found in many African countries, out on the open plains. A giraffe's long neck allows it to reach up high to feed on new leaf shoots at the top of trees. Giraffes live in herds and can run fast to get away from lions and other predators. They sleep for about four hours a day.